UNDERSTANDING CENTRAL AMERICA

UNDERSTANDING CENTRAL AMERICA

THIRD EDITION

John A. Booth

UNIVERSITY OF NORTH TEXAS

Thomas W. Walker

OHIO UNIVERSITY

Westview Press

A MEMBER OF THE PERSEUS BOOKS GROUP

Published in 1999 in the United States of America by Westview Press, 5500 Central Avenue, Boulder, Colorado 80301–2877, and in the United Kingdom by Westview Press, 12 Hid's Copse Road, Cumnor Hill, Oxford OX2 9JJ

A CIP catalog record for this book is available from the Library of Congress.
ISBN 0-8133-3070-X (paperback)

The paper used in this publication meets the requirements of the American National Standard for Permanence of Paper for Printed Library Materials Z39.48–1984.

10 9 8 7 6 5 4 3 2 1

To Patti
and
to Anne

CONTENTS

TABLES AND ILLUSTRATIONS

Tables

Figures

Photographs

Map

ACKNOWLEDGMENTS

We owe many people and institutions in the United States and Central America our sincerest thanks for their time, support, encouragement, and patience. For support that has gotten us into the field during the years this manuscript has been in preparation we wish to thank the Latin American Studies Association; the Advisory Council on Church and Society of the United Presbyterian Church, USA; the Inter-American Dialogue; the International Human Rights Law Group; the Washington Office on Latin America; Hemispheric Initiatives; Alice McGrath; the University of North Texas; the Heinz Foundation, University of Pittsburgh; and Ohio University. For collaboration in Central America we gratefully acknowledge the assistance of the Facultad Latinoamericana de Ciencias Sociales (FLACSO) and the Centro Superior Universitaria Centroamericana (CSUCA) in Costa Rica, the Asociación y Estudios Sociales (ASIES) in Guatemala, and the Confederación Nacional de Profesionales (CONAPRO) Héroes y Mártires in Nicaragua. For generously granting Thomas Walker the right to reuse some material he had originally written for a Presbyterian Church publication (incorporated into Chapters 1 through 4 and Chapter 9), we are indebted to the United Presbyterian Church, USA. Several dozen kind folks in Central America have granted us interviews and helped us collect data on their countries, without which this book would have been completely impossible to write. E. Bradford Burns, Richard E. Clinton, Jr., Sung Ho Kim, Harold Molineu, and Mitch Seligson read portions of the manuscript at different stages in its evolution and made valuable suggestions. Our thanks to Cece Hannah for her excellent typing of the first manuscript and to Steve Lohse for research assistance on the second edition. Over the years an evolving lineup of editors at Westview Press has provided us with just the right mixture of encouragement and patience as we labored on successive editions of this book. In particular, we thank Miriam Gilbert and Barbara Ellington for their assistance and guidance during work on the first two editions, and Karl Yambert and Jennifer Chen for their efforts on the third

JOHN A. BOOTH
THOMAS W. WALKER

PREFACE TO THE THIRD EDITION

This edition of *Understanding Central America* has been extensively revised from the second edition. We have taken into account the dramatic transformation of the region in terms of the formal democratization of several countries, the end of several civil wars, and rapid new economic changes wrought under the pressures of international economic neoliberalism. These processes were incomplete or in early stages when we published the second edition. Our effort to incorporate these phenomena has led us to restructure the theoretical heart of the book, expressed in Chapter 5, around the theme of regime change. Earlier editions concentrated on explaining the paradox of violent civil conflict in three Central American nations while two others remained relatively peaceful. This edition retains the explanation of the violent civil conflict of earlier editions but subsumes it under a broader theory of regime change laid out in Chapter 5. Other chapters have been revised to address the regime change theme and to provide more detailed coverage of recent events in individual countries as they bear upon the issue of democratic transformation. Hence we now have separate chapters on El Salvador and Guatemala, previously combined into one chapter. We have also greatly updated our economic analysis of the region, with an extensively revised appendix of tables of socioeconomic data and detailed attention to economic developments affecting the politics of each nation.

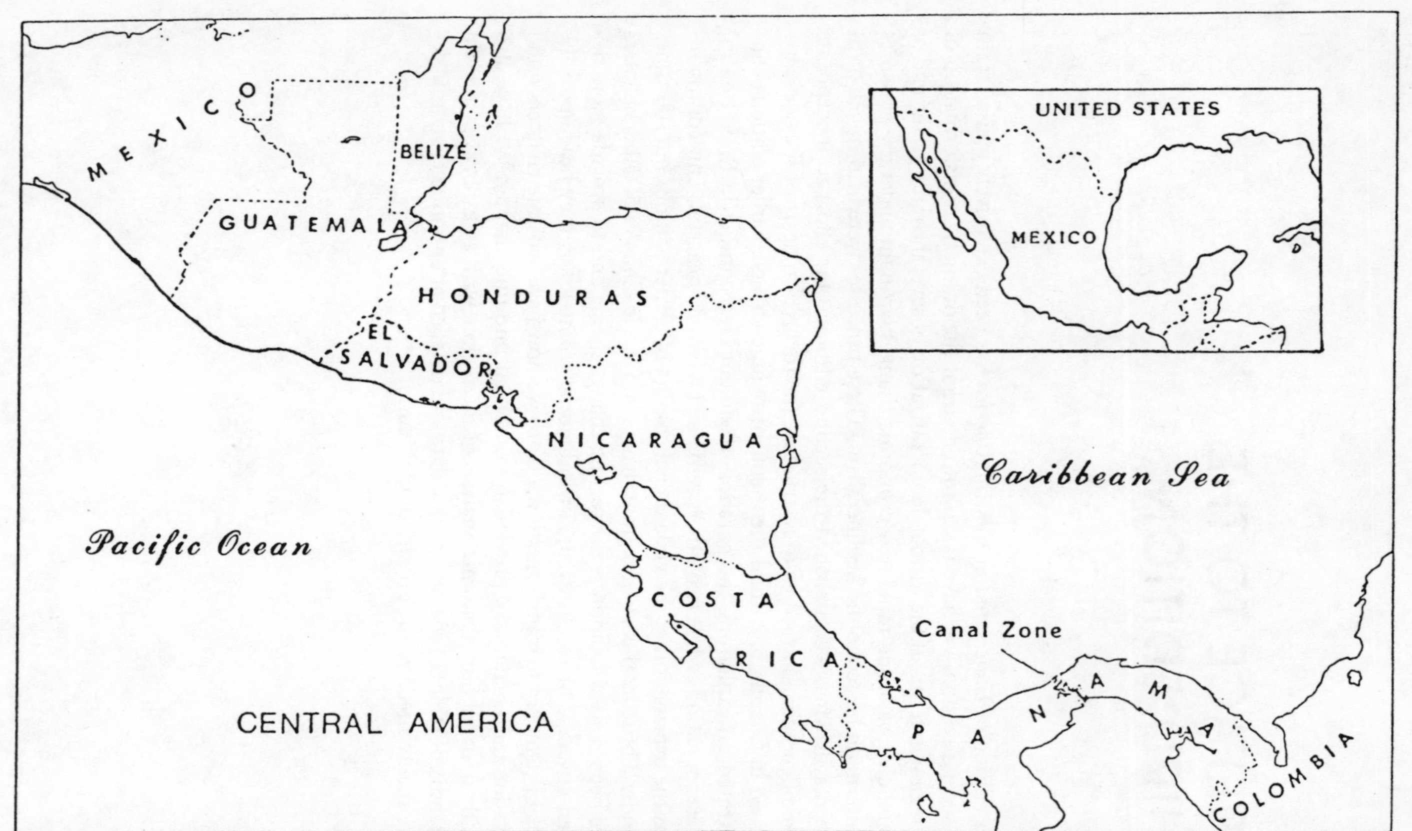

Reprinted from *U.S. Policy Toward Latin America: From Regionalism to Globalism*, Second Edition, by Harold Molineu (Boulder, Colo.: Westview Press, 1990, p. 4). Copyright Westview Press, Inc., 1990.

1

CRISIS AND TRANSFORMATION

Central America lies so close to the United States that from Miami or Houston one can fly to Managua or Guatemala City more quickly than to Chicago or Boston. The region's five countries, each profoundly shaped by proximity and trade with the United States, had a total of roughly 23 million people in 1980. In the two decades after World War II, the area seemed a placid geopolitical backwater of the United States. It was poor but friendly and making moderate economic progress despite its mostly despotic regimes. Yet suddenly in the 1960s, 1970s, and 1980s waves of state terror, revolutionary insurrection, counterrevolution, and external meddling engulfed the region, taking over 300,000 lives, turning millions into refugees, and devastating economies and infrastructures.

Previous editions of *Understanding Central America* focused on this tidal wave of violence and tried to explain why great revolutionary movements wracked three Central American countries during the 1970s and 1980s while the other two remained relatively politically stable.[1] Our answer, based on scholarly theories on the causes of revolution, was that grievances arising from regionwide economic problems and from political repression mobilized demands for reform. When Nicaragua, Guatemala, and El Salvador's regimes violently refused to accommodate these demands, their opponents and reformers gradually coalesced and radicalized into revolutionary political opposition. In Nicaragua insurrection culminated in a rebel victory and eleven years of social revolution under the Sandinistas. In El Salvador and Guatemala civil war resulted in protracted stalemate eventually followed by negotiated peace and a significant alteration of the status quo. In striking contrast, stability prevailed in Honduras and Costa Rica, whose regimes undertook modest economic and political reforms and kept repression at moderate levels. External actors, especially the United States, struggled to shape these events by providing political and material resources to the warring parties, which intensified and prolonged the conflicts.

This explanation of Central America's turmoil, however, was not the view of U.S. policymakers. In 1980 the Council for Inter-American Security's Committee of Santa Fe had published a scathing critique of U.S. Latin American policy under the Carter administration and had outlined what it hoped would be a blueprint for U.S. policy in the hemisphere for the incoming Reagan administration. The committee described U.S. policy in the late 1970s as ineffectually "hoping for the best" in the face of the dedicated, irrepressible activity of a Soviet-backed Cuba to win ultimately total hegemony over this region.[2]

> The Americas are under attack. Latin America, the traditional alliance partner of the United States, is being penetrated by Soviet Power. The Caribbean rim and basin are spotted with Soviet surrogates and ringed with socialist states.[3]

Although acknowledging domestic causes for the rise of turmoil in Central America and the Caribbean, the report heavily emphasized external communist aggression and internal leftist subversion.

The Santa Fe report went on to recommend aggressive U.S. efforts to contain and roll back the perceived rising tide of communism in the hemisphere, with particular emphasis on Central America. Policies advocated included beefing up inter-American military cooperation to isolate nations such as Nicaragua, Cuba, and Grenada; rejecting the pursuit of U.S.-style democracy; "abandon[ing] and replac[ing human rights advocacy with] a noninterventionist policy of political and ethical realism;"[4] working with the Catholic church to counter liberation theology; promoting free trade and the development of capitalist free enterprise—large and small—through aid and trade policy; fomenting nonleftist, U.S.-advised "free" labor unions; working with international lending institutions to force reductions in the role of the state in Latin American economies; and promoting education and propaganda programs to disseminate U.S. ideological values throughout the region.[5]

These policies had many sympathizers in the incoming Reagan administration. Indeed, several of the authors of the Santa Fe report soon became high-level advisers to the new president and helped shape U.S. policy toward Central America in the early 1980s. However, three years of energetic and highly public efforts to implement such policies failed to rally either the U.S. public or the U.S. Congress behind them to President Reagan's satisfaction; in 1983 Reagan appointed a highly visible presidential commission to study Central America.

In its 1984 report, President Reagan's National Bipartisan Commission on Central America (the Kissinger Commission) explained the turmoil in Central America and dramatized its gravity:

> Central America is gripped by a profound crisis. That crisis has deep roots in the region's history. . . . The crisis is the product of *both* indigenous and foreign factors. Poverty, repression, inequity all were there breeding fear and hate; stirring in a world

recession created a potent witch's brew, while outside forces have intervened to exacerbate the area's troubles and to exploit its anguish.[6]

No one familiar with Central America and its problems could disagree that both internal and external factors had shaped the region. However, there was indeed much to question about the commission's conclusions as to the nature and relative importance of such factors.

The commission looked at Central American reality in a very particular way. It sought written advice from only about one-fourth of the fifty most active U.S. scholars specializing on Central America at the time and heard oral testimony from still fewer. The commission consulted almost no scholars from Central America itself. The groups the commission visited during its one-week Central American visit were predominantly from the political center and right and generally represented dominant elites and powerful vested interests. Commission staff and expert advice were drawn from conservative think tanks, large U.S. business firms and pressure groups with Central American interests, and from the U.S. military and foreign service. At least eight of the commission's twelve members were conservatives.[7]

Given its composition and operation, it is no great surprise that the Kissinger Commission's report was a highly ideological, partisan, and analytically biased document that presented an unclear picture of Central America and stimulated a barrage of criticism.[8]

The commission was not intended to conduct an impartial and open enquiry about Central America and its problems. Rather, its purpose was to give the imprimatur of bipartisanship and its members' collective stature—and thus to ratify and legitimate—the Reagan administration's policy preferences for Central America. Based on this distorted view of Central American reality, U.S. policy toward the region, from the early 1980s until the end of the cold war, only served to exacerbate the region's problems and, in doing so, contributed mightily to the material and human costs of the conflicts.

Be that as it may, the cold war ended when the Soviet flag came down in the Kremlin for the last time on December 25, 1991, and much has changed since we originally developed our framework for understanding the region. Even in the 1980s Latin American powers, international institutions, and newly cooperating Central American governments had worked to end the region's civil wars and growing international tensions. The first fruits of these efforts were the 1987 Central American Peace Accord and a cease-fire in Nicaragua's counterrevolutionary war. Then Nicaraguans astonished almost everyone by voting their revolutionary government out of office just as the cold war was ending in 1990. Eventually, negotiated settlements also ended the bloody civil wars in El Salvador (1992) and Guatemala (1996). In both, Marxist guerrilla coalitions that had rebelled against military regimes made peace with the civilian governments that had replaced military dictatorships during the 1980s. This left all five Central American countries nominally at peace, with formerly warring factions largely tolerating each other under the watchful eye of domestic and international observers. All five Central American countries now had elected civilian governments in a liberal constitutional mode.

Given these dramatic events, our original explanation of the onset of revolution does not adequately embrace Central America's current reality. We need a broader, more encompassing view to understand Central America at the end of the twentieth century. How has the Central American isthmus moved from geopolitical crisis to emerge hugely transformed, once again relatively calm and unprecedentedly democratic? How did the crises that ensnared not only the region but neighboring Latin American nations and some of the world's great powers end and allow the region to sink once again into relative obscurity?

We have already stated why we think the turmoil of the 1970s and 1980s began. We must now answer several new questions: How are these later, and for many, largely unexpected political transformations related to the revolutionary movements? Were revolutionary turmoil and democratization distinct and unrelated, or were they parts of a larger process? Why did the wars end and fledgling liberal democracies emerge? Was the transformation from authoritarianism to liberal democracy that occurred in four of five nations inevitable, or might there have been a different outcome? Why have the outcomes in each Central American nation been so similar?

We show in Chapters 2, 3, and 4 that despite certain differences among them, Central American nations have striking commonalities of history, political and economic development, and global context. Indeed, in comparison to the cultural, economic, and geographical diversities of the world's great array of nations, Central America's small, geographically contiguous developing countries have far more in common than whatever divides them. These internal and external similarities suggest that much that affects Central America is part of a larger world dynamic. We contend that just as common forces led to Central America's rebellions, many of the same forces shaped a process of regime change that eventually led from authoritarianism toward democracy. In fact, these revolutionary movements were a key step in the process of regime change that led to the region's formal democratization.

The "Central America" upon which we focus in this report consists of five countries: Guatemala, El Salvador, Honduras, Nicaragua, and Costa Rica.[9]

Belize and Panama will not receive individual attention. Though Belize is technically Central American, that English-speaking microstate has a history that is fairly distinct from that of the other states in the region. At present this tiny republic, which only became formally independent from Great Britain in 1981, does not figure significantly in the "Central American" problem. Panama, though often lumped with the other countries of the region, is not technically Central American. Its pre-Columbian indigenous cultures were South American, and from the beginning of the national period until 1903, Panama was an integral (though poor) part of the South American republic of Colombia. "The five," however, share a common political heritage from the colonial period—in which they were administered as a unit by Spain—to the early national period, when for fifteen years (1823–1838) they formed a single state called the United Provinces of Central America. In the late nineteenth century, several ill-fated attempts at reunification once again took place, and in the 1960s the five joined to form a common market. Out of this history comes a sense of Central American national identity and, among a surprisingly large segment of the region's educated elite, an almost utopian belief that someday the larger homeland will once again be united.

Central America, as defined above, is not a big region. Indeed, its combined land mass of 431,812 square kilometers is barely larger than that of the state of California (404,975 square kilometers). Moreover, its estimated total 1998 population of around 32.1 million was about the same as California's. The country with the smallest surface area, El Salvador, is smaller even than the state of Maryland, whereas the largest, Nicaragua, is barely larger than Iowa. In population, the five varied in 1998 between a low of 3.7 million in Costa Rica (South Carolina, in comparison, had around 3.8 million) and a high of 11.6 million in Guatemala (Ohio had 11.5 million).[10]

Central America's natural resources are not particularly remarkable. However, had there been a different sort of political system than ruled most of Central America until recently, there certainly would have been enough arable land to provide adequate sustenance for the present population, while at the same time producing some primary products for export. Yet the unregulated response to international market demands by the region's agrarian elite has led to land concentration, an overemphasis on export, and inadequate production of consumer food staples. Instead of growing beans, corn, rice, plantain, and cassava for local consumption, big landholders normally concentrate on lucrative exports such as coffee, cotton, sugar, and beef. Central America also has a variety of mineral resources, though apparently not in remarkable abundance. One possible exception is Guatemala, with its nickel and its newly discovered oil reserves. Historically, Central America, or more precisely, Nicaragua, was (for a while) viewed as the logical site for a future transisthmian waterway. However, the building of the Panama Canal and the development of modern air and surface communication have made it unlikely that this potential will ever be developed.

Central America's main resource is clearly its people. Contrary to the ethnocentric stereotype often held by North Americans, Central Americans are as hardworking as most other humans on this planet. To verify that statement, one need only observe the hustle and bustle of most Central American cities at daybreak, or follow the activity of a typical Central American through the long hours of his or her daily routine. Central Americans are also remarkably resilient. The strength with which they have faced more than their share of hardship—including endemic repression, occasional civil war, foreign occupation, and frequent natural disasters, such as volcanic eruptions, earthquakes, hurricanes, and floods—is impressive to outside observers, especially those used to fairly safe natural and human environments.

This is not to say that there are not characteristics of the population of some Central American countries that pose problems. Guatemala, for instance, no matter which type of political system it adopts, will long have to struggle with the question of how to integrate the approximately half of the population that is Indian and that, by and large, does not speak Spanish. Similarly, any government in El Salvador is going to face an enormous social headache posed by the country's high density of population. Moreover, all of the countries face severe problems of poverty that affect the vast majority of their people. But such poverty is not inevitable, and, overall, the human resources of the region are a very positive factor. The dignity, determination, and remarkable humor of the Central American people must be taken as a cause for hope.

In sum, Central America is small in size and population, poor in resources, and holds a wealth of problems and troubles—for its own people as well for its neighbors and for the United States. Its small nation-states are riven by severe internal strains. They are pushed and pulled by international pressures, both economic and political, pressures that often intensify domestic strains rather than reduce them. The deepening U.S. involvement there in the 1980s and the efforts that numerous Latin American and European nations made to promote negotiated settlements to the various open and latent conflicts in the region made these strains and conflicts worthy of serious study.

U.S. interests and involvement in Central America have fluctuated widely over the past century and a half. A period of protracted U.S. inattention to Central America after the mid-1950s changed suddenly into intense U.S. concern in the late 1970s when Nicaraguans rebelled against the Somoza regime. Though they lavished attention on Central America, the Carter and Reagan administrations treated and described the region so differently as to bewilder many observers—including academic and policy experts, and especially Central Americans themselves. The Bush administration maintained an interest in Central America but gave the region much less public attention than did its predecessors, and the Clinton administration has paid the region even less.

Soviet and Eastern bloc interest and involvement in Central America have diminished to almost nothing in the 1990s, but they were once the focal point of U.S. policy in the isthmus. In the 1980s the Santa Fe document and a presidential commission had expressed grave reservations about the Soviet role in the region. Although there was ample reason even then to question the validity of what might well be described as these groups' "devil theory" of Cuban/Nicaraguan influence in Central America, the issue of external involvement must be examined. Indeed, the collapse of the Eastern bloc and the decline of communism in Europe and elsewhere require a reassessment of both past and future communist claims in Central America. There are also crises of poverty, development, and political order. In our effort to help the reader understand Central America, we will examine these crises and consider the relative importance of domestic and foreign influences on the region and how they have shaped its changing political regimes.

CENTRAL AMERICANS (photo of baby in hammock by John Booth; other photos by Steve Cagan).

2

POVERTY AND ITS CAUSES

Commonsense interpretations of the causes of the Central American turmoil often stress poverty. Poverty is, indeed, a serious problem in the region. Even the most prosperous nation, Costa Rica, has severe economic difficulties that afflict much of its populace. In Honduras, until recently the poorest of the Central American nations, the living standard of most citizens is abysmal. Most experts and even passing observers of the region recognize that poverty constitutes a crisis of great human cost that cries out for dramatic reform in social and economic systems.

Common sense betrays us, however, if we attempt to explain Central America's rebellions as simply the product of poverty. Most of the world's population lives in poverty, yet rebellion against constituted authority by the most disadvantaged is rare. Poverty alone cannot account for the revolts in Nicaragua, El Salvador, or Guatemala. Indeed, if poverty alone were sufficient to cause rebellions, Honduras should have exploded with popular fury long before Nicaragua or El Salvador. We thus encounter the paradox that among Central America's five nations, the poorest historically (Honduras) and the richest (Costa Rica) have been the most stable, while those that had the most rapid industrialization and economic growth in the 1960s and 1970s have been the most unsettled.

To affirm that poverty itself is not a direct or sufficient cause of Central America's rebellions, however, is not to say that poverty is unrelated to the turmoil. In fact, there is an important link between *becoming* impoverished and popular unrest. Large segments of Central America's poor and middle classes were becoming much worse off during the 1970s and early 1980s. It was not, then, the grinding, long-term deprivation of poverty, but this change—impoverishment, declining living conditions—that motivated much of the region's unrest. In this chapter we focus on the nature of Central American poverty—the long-term, grinding deprivation that affects large segments of the population. We describe in rather technical and abstract ways what this far-too-real poverty means for the lives of Central Americans. In Chapters 4 and 5 we will examine how impoverishment contributed to recent popular unrest and rebellion.

POVERTY

The human condition in Latin America generally lies somewhere between the extreme deprivation and despair of large areas of Africa and Asia and the relative prosperity of North America, Europe, and Japan. Within Latin America, the economic indicators of Central America as a whole fall slightly below the median for the entire region. Latin America in 1996 had a gross domestic product (GDP) per capita of $2,801, but not even relatively wealthy Costa Rica, with a GDP per capita of $2,054 approached that figure. The other four ranged from El Salvador, with a per capita GDP of $1,257, down to Nicaragua with $481.[1]

Of course, GDP per capita figures should be explained and put into context. First, for comparison, it should be noted that the United States in 1996 had a gross national product per capita of roughly $25,600. Second, we should consider that while "average" Salvadorans were attempting to make do on less than one-twentieth of that amount, they and other Central Americans were facing prices for many consumer products—food, clothing, health care—that were as high as, or higher than, those in the United States. And, finally, we should remember that the "average" indicated GDP in per capita figures is simply a statistical artifact that distorts reality. GDP per capita figures are obtained by dividing the annual total value of goods and services produced in a given country by the total population. In regions such as Central America where a small minority controls most of the resources and earns most of the income, averaging the income of the wealthy with that of the rest of the population results in per capita values that grossly overstate the real condition of most people. Indeed, the real monetary income per capita of the poorer half of the population in most of Central America probably runs between $200 and $400 per year.

The extremely low annual expendable income of the majority of Central Americans manifests itself in deplorable social conditions. Although Costa Rica from 1950 until 1980 and Nicaragua (at least for a few years after the victory of the Sandinista revolution in 1979) made strides in dealing with their most acute social problems, much remained to be done even in those countries. Moreover, in both nations economic conditions subsequently deteriorated. Thus if we consider the region as a whole, it is certainly fair to say that the typical Central American is poorly fed, poorly housed, and has little or no access to medical care, education, and cultural, or recreational opportunities.

Nutrition is a case in point. Land in the region is very inequitably distributed. Typically, the rich and the powerful, who control the best land, use it to grow export products rather than to produce staples. In a profit-driven, "free enterprise" system, this makes good sense: Export products bring greater profits than staples grown for sale internally. What this means for most Central Americans, however, is that as landownership becomes more and more concentrated in fewer hands and as fewer and fewer staples (in relation to population) are grown, the price of staples, though not as high as that of export products, rises inexorably, thus forcing the common citizen to make do on less and cheaper food. At present, Central Americans generally eat very little animal protein, deriving their essential amino acids, instead, from corn and beans. But even these foods are highly priced since domestic production is normally insufficient and has to be supplemented by costly imports.

The absolute poverty of the region is also reflected in the area of education. A substantial segment of the people has virtually no education. Official illiteracy rates for 1995 ran from a fairly respectable low of 5.3 in Costa Rica to a high of 37.5 percent in Guatemala. Honduras, El Salvador, and Nicaragua registered 27.4 percent, 22.6 percent, and 34.3 percent, respectively. (Nicaragua's 1980–1981 literacy crusade had dropped the illiteracy rate from the 1978 level of 47.4 percent to 27.7 percent in 1986. Since then, however, wars, economic crisis, and sharply curtailed education spending have dragged literacy rates down again.)[2] In addition, even the bulk of those people who are literate have only the most basic education. In elite-dominated systems geared to the export of primary products, there is little or no premium placed on educating the general citizenry. Indeed, efforts made to improve mass education are frequently viewed by local elites as dangerous. Accordingly, it is not surprising that illiteracy is so high and that even most Central Americans described as literate have only a few years of primary education.

In the area of public health, conditions are somewhat, though not much, better. Especially since World War II, with the discovery of a variety of techniques for the prevention of several communicable diseases, international health organizations have had some success in cajoling and assisting Central American regimes to reduce the frequency of certain killer diseases. This has occasioned a gradual lowering of death rates and a raising of life expectancies, which in 1994 ranged from a regional mode of around 66—64.8 years in Guatemala, 65.8 in Honduras, 66.3 in El Salvador, and 66.6 in Nicaragua—to a very respectable high of 76.2 in Costa Rica.[3] Nevertheless, though "easy" and externally imposed advances in preventive medicine have allowed Central Americans to live longer, most still face serious health problems. Local hygiene is normally poor. Most houses lack interior plumbing. Many do not even have backyard latrines. The curative medical system is grossly inadequate. Private medical care—nearly as expensive in Central America as in the United States—is simply out of the reach of the common citizen. Public facilities in most countries are so scarce as to be available only to a minority of the middle class and wealthy in the larger cities and towns. As a result, good health is largely a matter of privilege or luck.

Exacerbating the problems of poverty are high annual rates of natural increase in population. In 1996, annual population growth rates ranged from a "low" of 2.2 percent in El Salvador to 2.4 percent in Costa Rica, 2.5 percent in Nicaragua, 2.9 percent in Guatemala, and 3.0 percent in Honduras. These 1996 growth rates were lower than they had been in 1986 for Costa Rica, Honduras, and Nicaragua but had actually increased slightly in El Salvador and Guatemala.[4] The population is growing so rapidly for several reasons. First, the easy advances in medicine brought to Central America in the past four decades have significantly reduced death rates, especially among infants. Second, with the median age of the population falling into the midteens (as opposed to around thirty in the United States), a far greater share of the female population is of childbearing age. Finally, high fertility is normally related to poverty and low levels of urbanization. Unlike most of the rest of Latin America, much of Central America remains predominantly rural, despite a growing tendency toward urban growth: In 1996 Costa Rica was 50.7 percent rural, El Salvador 51.6 percent, Guatemala 58.2 percent, and Honduras 51.4 percent. In sharp contrast, Nicaragua had changed from 47 percent rural to only 25.9 percent between 1986 and 1996. Indeed, Nicaragua's 1996 rural population had actually declined 16 percent since 1980 because two decades of civil war, unstable agricultural and credit policy, and property disputes made rural life increasingly untenable. Despite its large rural component, most Central American countries' urban growth rates in the 1990s far outstripped those of the 1980s.[5] If Central America's current rates of population growth remain constant, the countries of the region will double in population every 25 years (Guatemala) to 30 years (Honduras).[6] However, the very high population growth rates of previous decades throughout Latin America have begun to tail off, and they are also slowing in three of five Central American countries. Diminishing population growth rates seem to be related to the region's rapid urbanization, which makes education more widely available to women, thus encouraging wider use of birth control devices. With its rapid urbanization, Nicaragua's population growth has fallen the most. An end to the region's wars may, however, promote a countervailing trend as fewer people emigrate, some exiles return, and fewer die from combat and related problems. As long as rapid increases in population persist, they will make meaningful efforts to reduce social inequities and uplift the human condition not only more difficult but also more urgent.

THE CAUSES OF POVERTY

Poverty in Central America is neither natural nor inevitable. It used to be argued by foreigners that Central Americans were poor because they were racially inferior. For instance, in the words of one geography text used widely in U.S. primary schools a half century ago, "except where white men have established plantations, the resources [of Central America] are poorly developed. Most of the Indians, mestizos, and negroes are poor and ignorant . . . few care to work hard. More white men are needed to start plantations and to fight tropical diseases."[7]

Of course, today we recognize that statements of that sort, which can also be found in prominent encyclopedias of the era, are racist nonsense. Likewise, it cannot be maintained that the region is lacking in sufficient resources to support its human population. El Salvador *is* overpopulated. But Central America as a whole has sufficient good land not only to engage in some export of primary products for foreign exchange but also to grow sufficient staples to feed its people. And though not exceptionally blessed in this regard, the region also has significant energy and mineral resources.

In fact, Central America's poverty is a human artifact—produced by exploitation of the many by the few. The latter, who have traditionally ruled the region for their own selfish ends, were often joined and supported in this exploitative behavior by powerful foreign interests.

What developed over time was a system that many scholars—Latin and North American alike—came to label as "dependency."[8] Though there is some disagreement on specifics, most people who write about this subject agree that dependency is a complex political, economic, and social phenomenon that serves to block the human development of the majority in certain privilege-dominated Third World countries where the economies are heavily externally oriented. In such countries, one finds that even during periods of rapid economic growth the benefit of such growth normally fails to "trickle down" in any but the most trivial way to the majority of the people. The *dependentistas* (as those who write about this subject are called) argue that the social stagnation of dependent countries is due to the combination of an income-concentrating, externally oriented, and externally conditioned form of capitalism with political systems controlled by those privileged minorities who benefit from such poorly distributed growth.

It is very important to note that in order for the dependency syndrome—with all of its negative human consequences—to exist, it is necessary for a country to have *both* an externally oriented economy *and* a socially irresponsible political elite. External economic orientation, though essential, is not enough in and of itself to cause the socially regressive dependency syndrome. The economies of Korea and Japan are both heavily externally oriented. However, the elites of those two more tightly knit societies seem to have a greater sense of social responsibility than the elites of Latin America, and, hence, externally stimulated growth has led to a general rise in standard of living. Another example of dependence without the poverty-generating dependency syndrome was provided by Cuba in the three decades from 1959 to the collapse of the Socialist bloc and the Soviet Union. Critics of the Cuban revolution are quick to point out that the island republic under its revolutionary government simply substituted dependence on the United States for dependence on the Socialist bloc. Quite so. However, what is now crucially different about post–1959 Cuba is that its revolutionary elite had the will to distribute the income from its externally dependent economy in such a way as to significantly improve general levels of health, education, housing, and nutrition. Thus it would be incorrect to argue that Cuba, whatever other problems it had, suffered from the dependency syndrome per se.

Capitalist development in dependent countries such as those of Central America is very different from that which took place in the industrialized countries. In the Western industrial nations the common citizen became crucially important to the economy as a consumer. In the United States, for instance, over 75 percent of industrial production is absorbed by domestic consumers. Therefore, even if we were to accept the argument that there is a "ruling class" in the United States, we would say that it would not be in that group's interest to exploit common citizens to the extent that they could no longer consume. For these reasons, in an internally oriented economic system like that of the United States, income redistribution devices such as the graduated income tax, social welfare programs, and a free labor movement actually serve the interest of the moneyed elite as well as that of the common citizen. However, in dependent Third World countries the tiny middle and upper classes that control the political system derive most of their income directly or indirectly from export or from the local multinational corporation-manufacture of products that the members of those classes, not the masses, consume. Accordingly, the common citizen in such a system is important not as a consumer but rather as a cheap and vulnerable source of labor.

Under this type of system, average citizens have virtually no opportunity to lift themselves up by the bootstraps because there is almost no access either to the means of production or to the riches that flow therefrom. By its very nature, the elite-run dependency system produces an inexorable concentration of both property and income. In the rural areas, stimulated by the growing lure of high profits through export, the rich and the powerful simply buy out or drive the illiterate peasant from the land. In the cities, incipient industrialization is dominated by the local elites and foreign enterprises. The latter, enjoying huge advantages in technology and brand recognition, often make the formation of locally based industry very difficult. Nevertheless, the local elites benefit in the form of contracts, services, and employment for the educated few, as well as occasional payoffs and bribes. At the same time, the advantages that accrue to a host country as a whole from the presence of outside firms are usually very limited. Such enterprises export profit directly and through the purchases of licenses, patents, and materials at inflated prices from parent companies. They tend to use capital-intensive rather than labor-intensive technology, thus causing not only a drain on foreign exchange used for the purchase of costly industrial equipment but also minimal "trickle down" in the form of wages. And finally, over 80 percent of the capital they use is raised locally, thus drying up domestic capital sources that might otherwise be available to native entrepreneurs.

This system, then, is one that favors a privileged local elite and its foreign associates while ignoring the interests of the vast majority. There are powerful economic disincentives for the privileged elites to do anything about the miserable condition of the masses. The switch to a more benign consumer-driven economic model or even a more socially responsible and controlled mixed economic system would involve a period of economic dislocation and personal sacrifice to which

many among Central America's dominant elites simply will not subject themselves without a fight.

At this point, one might reasonably ask two questions: (1) Why did the dependency system develop in Central America while a consumer-driven economy arose in North America? and (2) Why has the great bulk of the Central American people not been able to alter a system that is so contrary to their interests? Much of the answer to the first question lies in the distinct ways in which North America and Central America were colonized. North America was settled originally by European nonconformists seeking a new life and greater freedom. These people tamed the land by dint of their own labor and eventually developed into a large class of freeholders. North America did develop an aristocracy of sorts, but one that was never able completely to dominate the common citizen.

In Central America, as will be detailed later, the conquistadores sought quick riches. They superimposed their administration over that of the Indians and immediately began exacting tribute in gold and slaves. Within a matter of decades, the region had been plundered of its gold, and much of its Indian population had been decimated by slavery and contagion with Old World diseases. The Spanish system was a mercantile one that, from the very start, drained resources from the region. It was also heavily elitist with most of the physical labor being done by the subjugated masses composed of Indian *peones,* mestizos, and eventually, black slaves and mulattoes. Only in Costa Rica, which had few easily exploitable resources and not many Indians, did even a small number of Spaniards come to till the soil. Small wonder, then, that four and a half centuries later, the four northern countries of Central America were still struggling with problems of mass poverty and huge class disparities, whereas Costa Rica had developed a relatively more democratic, egalitarian, and socially just system.

This also leads us to the answer to the second question: The impoverished majority of Central Americans have not always docilely accepted their imposed lot. In fact, there have been frequent revolts when things got rapidly worse for certain groups: Indians resisted the conquistadores; peasants revolted against land concentration caused by the late-nineteenth-century Liberal reforms and the spread of coffee cultivation; peasants and workers under Nicaraguan nationalist Augusto C. Sandino rebelled against U.S. occupation from 1927 to 1933; workers led by El Salvador's indigenous communist Augustin Farabundo Marti revolted in 1932; Nicaraguans en masse successfully rebelled against the Somoza regime in 1978–1979, and mass-based insurrections took place in El Salvador and Guatemala beginning in the late 1970s.

Such struggles between popular-based movements and those in power, however, have usually been very unequal. The entrenched elite has always enjoyed an overwhelming advantage in military, economic, and propaganda resources. And the privileged elites of the region have normally been able to count on the support of foreign powers, be they the Spaniards in the colonial period or the Amer-

icans in the twentieth century. Indeed, after the Russian revolution, Central America's ruling classes learned that merely by labeling their opposition as "Bolshevik" or "Communist" they could usually win U.S. support ranging from armed intervention to economic and military aid.

All in all, however, it was not the long-term, grinding deprivation of Central Americans that led to political turmoil and rebellion in three of the region's countries in the 1970s and 1980s. It was, in fact, the relative deprivation of becoming rapidly poorer—declining living standards among large segments of the population—that sparked unrest and rebellion. Indeed, the developmental model (the economic growth plan) adopted by several Central American nations in the 1960s, based on the traditions of dependent capitalism and class exploitation described above, was itself a major cause of this growing relative deprivation.

Ironically, in the 1990s, even though the dependency syndrome had been a major contributing factor in the region's insurrections, revolution, and civil wars in the 1970s and 1980s, all five of the countries came to embrace an economic model known as *neoliberalism,* which seemed likely to accentuate the problems of dependency.

Neoliberalism in this context plays off of the term liberalism as used to describe the economic philosophy that dominated Latin America from the second half of the nineteenth century well into the twentieth century. As we will show in Chapter 3, this phenomenon (not unlike U.S. economic liberalism in the same era) promoted an unfettered market economy, a limited role for government, and expanded international trade. When that model resulted in the dependency syndrome in Latin America—with all the attendant social problems described above—regional governments engaged in a variety of types of state economic intervention and ownership to promote economic growth and greater social justice.

These state-centered development schemes, however, eventually resulted in problems such as high inflation, low productivity, and dramatic levels of foreign indebtedness. For that reason, most Latin American governments by the 1980s and 1990s embarked on programs of *structural adjustment,* which were soon dubbed neoliberalism. This new development model, pushed energetically by international lenders, the United States, and Europe, advocated certain basic changes: (1) downsizing of government by laying off public employees; (2) balancing public budgets by cutting programs and subsidies to food, transport, and public services; (3) privatization of state-owned enterprises; (4) deregulation of private enterprise; (5) devaluation of currencies to discourage imports and encourage investment; and (6) sharp reduction of tariff barriers to foreign trade. It was hoped that these measures would eliminate inflation, increase productivity, stimulate international trade (especially exports), and lay a foundation for future rapid economic growth. Although many people would be dislocated and suffer in the short run, long-term economic growth would eventually "trickle down" to everyone.

For Central Americans with a sense of history, the neoliberal fad of the late twentieth century has been worrisome. In their region, where it has been imple-

mented with near-religious fervor, this "structural reform" has tended to yield monetary and price stability and to improve growth and trade. On the other hand, as with its earlier liberal incarnation, it also has brought noticeable growth in the disparity between the wealthy minority and the impoverished majority and hurt the small middle class. Ironically, then, after having achieved real and hard-fought gains in political equality and civil rights, the Central American republics have been embarking on economic policies that are once again accentuating economic and social inequality—one of the central problems that contributed to the violence of the previous two decades. Whether the new democratic structures and institutions created as a result of those struggles will allow Central American nations to balance growth with equity—neoliberalism with socially conscious government policies—only time will tell.

3

THE COMMON HISTORY

One great truth about Central America is that whereas there are many similarities among the five countries, there are also striking differences. In large part, these similarities and differences are a product of the early history of the region from the conquest, through the colonial period, to independence, to union with Mexico, to the fifteen-year period in which the five shared a common political identity as part of the United Provinces of Central America.[1]

CONQUEST TO 1838

The conquest itself profoundly affected the nature of Central America's present-day societies. In this period, Costa Rica had an experience that immediately set it apart from the other four countries. The regions that are today Nicaragua, Honduras, El Salvador, and Guatemala were conquered in the two decades following the first Spanish penetration in 1522. As we will detail below, Spanish rule was imposed upon those Indians who were lucky enough to survive the tremendous depopulation of the region that resulted from the effects of slavery and exposure to Old World diseases. Costa Rica, however, was not settled until the 1560s because, unlike the other areas, it offered no easily exploitable resources in either gold or Indian slaves. Indeed, the hostile native inhabitants of the region were a major obstacle to European penetration. In the end, Costa Rica's Indians were neither pacified nor conquered. Instead they were for the most part either exterminated or pushed into remote areas. As a result, the population of the Central Valley of Costa Rica became heavily Iberian, and therefore, a racially distinct and exploited underclass never developed.

In the rest of Central America, however, the Spaniards were able to impose their dominion without destroying the entire population despite both passive and active resistance by the native people. Though this period meant annihilation for most of them, some Indians did survive. When the Spaniards arrived, they encountered millions of Indians in what are today the four northernmost countries of Central America. By co-opting and controlling native caciques (chiefs), the bearded foreigners proved to be very effective in extracting local riches in the form of gold and native slaves. In addition, the conquistadores unwittingly brought with them a variety of diseases to which Old World populations had become essentially immune. The Indians, having no natural immunity, perished in large numbers.

It is estimated that in western Nicaragua alone, a population of over one million natives was reduced to a few tens of thousands by the end of the conquest. It is unlikely that the Spaniards killed very many Indians outright. Careful historical research indicates that as many as half a million native Nicaraguans may have been exported as slaves to Panama and Peru. Most of these died either in passage to their destination or in slavery within a year or two thereafter. The bulk of the rest of the populace appears to have succumbed to disease.[2] Only in Guatemala did large numbers of Indians survive. Perhaps this was due to the greater difficulty the conquistadores had in completely subjugating the relatively more advanced society they encountered in that area. Perhaps, too, the cooler climates of the mountainous parts of Guatemala presented a less congenial environment for the spread of disease.

The drastic reduction in the Indian population was not the only change wrought by the conquest in the region of northern Central America. Prior to the conquest, labor-intensive agriculture typified this area. The common people grew corn, beans, peppers, and squash on land consigned to them by their caciques. Although obliged to turn over to the chief as tribute part of the crop, they were permitted to use the rest either for home consumption or for barter or sale in local markets. By the end of the conquest, however, as a result of depopulation, the bulk of former farmlands had reverted to jungle. The economy had become externally oriented, with the Spaniards controlling the region's human and natural resources to produce articles for trade among the colonies and with the mother country. The labor that produced the gold, silver, timber, and cattle products (hides, tallow, and dried beef) for export was supplied by the surviving Indians (still more numerous than their white masters). However, most of the wealth that this type of economy produced went to the white elite. The culture and process of dependent underdevelopment were now in full swing.

Many aspects of culture were also changed practically overnight as the conquistadores sought to impose their religion, language, and ways on the peoples they had conquered. Of course, nowhere was Indian culture *completely* obliterated. In Guatemala, where hispanization was least effective, the Indians retained their languages and hid many aspects of their old religion under a thin patina of Catholicism. Even in El Salvador, Honduras, Nicaragua, and Costa Rica, where the Indian populations were most decimated, some Indian traits remained. For instance, to this day, everywhere in the region, corn and beans (Indian staples) constitute the heart of local cuisine. Moreover, many place names remain Indian, as do the names of hundreds of common objects, from peppers and turkeys to grindstones. Yet, by and large, Central America was hispanicized. Spanish became the lingua franca except in rural Guatemala and certain remote regions elsewhere. A mystical, elite-supporting, pre-Reformation version of Catholicism became the nearly universal religion. Even the cities, often built on or next to the sites of pre-Columbian centers of habitation, eventually took on Spanish characteristics, with the typical Iberian arrangement of plazas, cathedrals, and public buildings.

Finally, the conquest established new class patterns. The larger pre-Columbian societies of Central America had been hierarchically ordered, with chiefs and associated elites dominating the masses. Perhaps that is why it was so easy for the Spaniards to superimpose themselves on the system. But what became most different after the conquest was a new racial configuration of class. With the exception of Costa Rica, what emerged was a highly unequal, two-class society, with people of Spanish birth or descent constituting the ruling class and everyone else comprising a downtrodden lower class. Within the lower class, there eventually evolved a subsystem of stratification as the biological union between Spaniards and Indian women produced mestizos, who though never considered equals by the Spaniards, were nonetheless of higher social status than pure Indians.

During the rest of the colonial period, from the late sixteenth century to 1821, the regions that are today the five countries of Central America (plus Chiapas in present-day Mexico) were nominally ruled by the viceroyalty of New Spain (Mexico) as the Kingdom of Guatemala. In fact, however, the viceroyalty had little control over the kingdom, which in practice was administered directly by Spain. In turn, the provinces of Central America were only loosely controlled by Guatemala. Underpopulated, geographically isolated, and economically insignificant, the tiny Costa Rican colony became a neglected backwater, helping to account for its unique evolution. Elsewhere, resentment grew between the provinces and the central administration in Guatemala as the newly emerging system of dependency inevitably caused the greatest development to take place in that administrative center. Even within individual provinces, such as Nicaragua, regional differences and rivalries developed and festered. Therefore, while Central Americans were sharing a common experience on the one hand, the seeds of division and disintegration were germinating on the other.

Besides these political factors, what is perhaps most important about this period was the continuation of economic and social patterns that had emerged during the conquest. Paradoxically, Costa Rica's relative backwardness and isolation in this period led to a more self-contained economy. A persistent labor shortage, relatively equal land distribution, and the lack of easily exploitable Indians produced a large class of free farmers with generally egalitarian values. Though such factors can easily be given too much importance, they appear to have helped Costa Rica to develop a fairly successful liberal, democratic political system by the mid twentieth century.

In contrast, in the rest of Central America, an externally oriented, elite-controlled, dependent pattern of economic activity was becoming more and more entrenched. At first, the region's human and material resources were exploited to produce cacao, silver, gold, timber, and cattle products for export. Later, this list of exports was expanded to include indigo and cochineal for the blue and red dyes needed by a growing European textile industry. As in present-day Central America, fluctuations in external demand produced periods of boom and bust in the local dependent economies. Though new groups were added to the population—black slaves and, later, the mulatto offspring of white-black unions—the social and economic gap between the white elite and the nonwhite majority remained wide. With the premium placed on export and the maximization of profits for the elites, the masses were generally allowed to consume only at a subsistence level. It is small wonder that the four republics of northern Central America are typified to this day by wide social and economic disparities and by a socially irresponsible economic elite.

Central America passed from colonial rule to formal independence with almost no violence. When Mexico broke from Spain in mid-1821, Central America also declared its independence. In January 1822, it joined the Mexican empire of Agustín de Iturbide. El Salvador resisted union with Mexico but was incorporated by force of arms. However, by mid-1823, soon after the abdication of "Agustín the First," Central America tired of its association with Mexico and declared its independence. Only the former Central American province of Chiapas chose to remain a part of the larger country to the north. From then until 1838, the region was fused—legally, at least—into a federation called the United Provinces of Central America or the Central American Republic.

At first Central Americans were very enthusiastic about the union. The idea made good sense. Clearly, Central America would be stronger politically and economically as a unit than as five tiny independent nations. Yet from the start, several factors undermined the success of the United Provinces. First, there was the long history of resentment of Guatemala by the outlying provinces. This resentment grew as Guatemala, the largest of the five states, received eighteen of the forty-one seats in the congress (according to the principle of proportional representation) and therefore dominated policymaking. Second, although the Constitution of 1824 declared the states to be "free and independent" in their internal affairs, it also contained nationalist and centralist features that tended to block such freedom. Finally, the union was also threatened by the rivalry between two emerging factions of the ruling elite that eventually coalesced into the Liberal and Conservative parties. Liberals and Conservatives clashed both within each province and across provincial boundaries; meddling in their neighbors' affairs became a common practice of Central American leaders. These factors saddled the union with constant tension and recurrent civil war. The whole experiment finally came unglued in 1838, as first Nicaragua and later the other countries split from the federation. Though there were several attempts to promote reunification later in the nineteenth century, the bitterness and national rivalries that had destroyed the United Provinces in the first place were more than sufficient to block its resurrection.

1838 TO THE PRESENT

The more than one and a half centuries since the disintegration of the Central American federation have been a time of continuing poverty and hardship for most of the region's people. The patterns of dependency and elite rule, which had taken firm root in each of the republics except Costa Rica during the colonial period, continued through the nineteenth century and into the twentieth century. Costa Rica, too, soon developed debilitating external economic dependencies. Overall, although the region as a whole did experience occasional surges of development, that development seldom benefited the majority of Central Americans. After independence, Central America's tiny, privileged elites—those who had inherited economic power and social standing—continued to use their control of government to repress popular demands. These elites perpetuated an essentially unregulated, externally oriented economic system for their own benefit. Except in Costa Rica, the continued existence of Liberal-Conservative factionalism, relatively large indigenous communities to supply forced labor, and the emergent hacienda system all helped strengthen the military's political role. Armies (at first belonging to individual caudillos) fought in the civil wars, subdued peasants who had been forceably deprived of their land, and implemented forced labor laws against these new "vagrants." This heavy military involvement in economic and political life retarded the development of civil political institutions and spawned both military rule and considerable political violence. Except for Costa Rica, Central American nations spent most of the period from 1838 until 1945 under either civilian or military dictatorships. Even Costa Rica showed little democratic promise. Although less turbulent than its neighbors, it experienced elite rule, militarism, dictatorship, and political instability well into the twentieth century.

Politics

In the nineteenth century, the basic conflict within the elite was between those people who came to call themselves "Conservatives" and those who described themselves as "Liberals." Before independence and in the first decades afterward, the Conservatives advocated authoritarian, centralized government (sometimes even monarchy), greater economic regulation, and a continuation of special privileges for the Catholic church. Liberals espoused limited representative democracy, decentralized government, free trade and reduced economic regulation, and a separation of church and state. At the same time, Conservatives tended to be more traditional rural landholders who had benefited from Crown licenses and export monopolies. Liberals were more likely to be the disgruntled large landowners who lacked Crown licenses to export their crops or urban elites concerned with commerce.

One important difference between the two groups was that whereas Conservatives generally remained wedded to more traditional economic practices, the Liberals—who by the late nineteenth century had come to dominate all the Central American nations—advocated "modernization" within an externally oriented, laissez-faire economic framework. Specifically, Liberals championed the introduction of new export products—such as coffee and bananas—and the development of government institutions and material infrastructure (highways, railroads, and ports) to facilitate growth in the export economy. Despite such early contrasts and after considerable warfare between the two factions, by the late nineteenth century ideological and policy differences between them had largely vanished. Liberals, when in power, ruled in an authoritarian manner and eventually proved willing to make accommodations with the church. Conservatives eventually came to support laissez-faire economics and the expansion of coffee production.

The Liberal and Conservative parties eventually degenerated into ideologically indistinguishable clan-based political factions. Conservatives generally ruled in the mid nineteenth century but were eventually all replaced by Liberal regimes. Liberal hegemony in Central America then lasted well into the twentieth century and, as it died, spawned an extreme right-wing form of militarism that plagued Guatemala, El Salvador, and Honduras until the 1990s. One should not confuse the Central American meaning of the term *Liberal* with the vernacular meaning of that word in the United States. Central American Liberals were exponents of classical Liberal economic policies (capitalism) and republican government. They were very "conservative" by contemporary U.S. standards. They held elitist attitudes, advocated essentially unregulated free enterprise, and generally believed the proposition that government is best which governs least. Indeed, in the U.S. political system today, modern conservatives would likely find themselves very much at home with the economic policies of nineteenth-century Central American Liberals. The modernization that liberalism brought simply tended, in most countries, to accelerate the process of concentration of wealth and income in the hands of the elite and to increase the dependency of local economies on the international economic system.

Eventually, however, Central American liberalism came under fire from more popularly oriented political movements. In Costa Rica, challenges to Liberal dominance and political reforms began in the late nineteenth century and culminated after 1948 in the abolition of the army and a variety of other changes imposed by local social democratic reformers. In El Salvador, local Liberals responded to labor and peasant discontent in the 1930s by ruling through the military, which massacred thirty thousand peasants in 1932 and occupied the presidency thereafter. By the 1970s, however, the Salvadoran military had become so powerful that it could act independently, often ignoring the wishes of its former Liberal masters.

In Guatemala in 1944, social democrats overthrew a "modernizing" dictator, Jorge Ubico, and began a mild form of democratic revolution. Although a successful CIA-sponsored counterrevolution took place in 1954, the military, not civilian Liberals, took power and ruled the country into the 1980s. In Nicaragua, U.S. armed intervention on behalf of Conservatives between 1909 and 1927 eventually led to the return of the Liberals to power in the form of the Somoza family dictatorship. The Somozas ruled Nicaragua from 1936 until a mass-based insurrection brought the social-revolutionary Sandinista National Liberation Front (Frente Sandinista de Liberación Nacional—FSLN) to power in 1979. In traditional Honduras, Liberals and Conservatives (the National party) alternately held formal office under the watchful eye of an overweening military throughout the 1980s and into the 1990s. It was only in the mid-1990s that Honduras's civilian leaders began to come to power in a real sense.

External Involvement

International pressures battered Central America after 1850. Great powers (particularly Britain and the United States) pursued economic, political, and security interests in the region. These powers were especially enticed by the possibility of constructing a transisthmian canal. Britain established the colony of British Honduras in the Guatemalan territory of Belize and the Miskito Protectorate in eastern Nicaragua to promote and protect British mining, timber, and geopolitical interests. British influence was greatest during the first half of the nineteenth century but thereafter was increasingly supplanted by that of the United States. Foreign intervention exacerbated the Central American nations' well-established penchant for interfering in each others' internal affairs and led to both international disputes within the region and overt and covert military and political intervention by outside powers.

The most flagrant case of intervention was the filibuster in Nicaragua led by Tennessean William Walker. Contracted by business partners of Cornelius Vanderbilt in an effort to wrest away control of Vanderbilt's transit route across the isthmus, Walker brought a group of mercenaries to Nicaragua in 1855. In league with out-of-power Liberals, he formed an army and toppled the Conservative government. The United States quickly recognized the fledgling Liberal government of Walker, who announced his intention to reinstitute slavery, make English the official language, and seek U.S. statehood.

Conservatives in power in the other four Central American nations agreed to send troops to oust Walker. War ensued in 1856, with Conservative forces partly financed by the British and by Vanderbilt. Walker capitulated in 1857 and fled Nicaragua under U.S. protection. He soon attempted another filibuster but was captured and executed in Honduras in 1860. The 1856–1857 struggle against

William Walker's takeover of Nicaragua, known as the National War, briefly rekindled interests in reunification of Central America, reinforced Conservative political hegemony in Nicaragua for many years, and contributed to anti-U.S. nationalism among Central Americans.[3]

By 1900 the dominant outside power in the isthmus, the United States, energetically promoted its economic and security interests. U.S. diplomats served U.S. banks by peddling loans to the region's governments. U.S. customs agents seized Central American customs houses to repay the loans, and U.S. marines intervened in domestic political problems in Honduras, Nicaragua, and Panama. When President Theodore Roosevelt could not win agreement from either Colombia or Nicaragua for a proposed canal lease agreement, he sent U.S. troops in 1903 to ensure that local and foreign insurgents could "liberate" Colombia's province of Panama and thus secured for the United States the right to build a canal through what then became the Republic of Panama. When Nicaragua's president José Santos Zelaya contemplated making a canal deal with Germany in 1909, the United States helped foment a Conservative rebellion against him and landed U.S. troops to back it up. Zelaya resigned and the new government gave the United States a canal-rights treaty that effectively guaranteed that Nicaragua would never have a canal. U.S. marines returned to Nicaragua in 1912 and remained there most of the period until 1933.

The United States flirted with Rooseveltian good neighborliness toward Central America during the 1930s. During World War II security interests led to heavy U.S. assistance to train and modernize Central America's armies. After 1945 the United States emphasized containment of communism by backing anti-Communist regimes. The United States enlisted other Central American governments to help oust the reformist civilian government of Guatemala in 1954 and to reinforce the Somoza regime after the Managua earthquake in 1972.

Fidel Castro's overthrow of the Batista regime in Cuba in 1959 reinforced the U.S. tendency to concentrate its Central American policy upon the containment of communism. During the Carter administration a novel U.S. emphasis on human rights (1977–1979) led to aid cutoffs for abusive military governments in Guatemala and El Salvador and to the ebbing of U.S. support of Nicaragua's Somoza regime. When the FSLN-led popular rebellion toppled Anastasio Somoza Debayle in 1979, however, U.S. policy in Central America shifted sharply back toward the thirty-year tradition of containment of communism. Washington lifted its military aid ban for El Salvador and involved itself deeply in trying to block the growing rebellion there.

Economic and Social Change

In the economic arena, Central America has specialized in exporting agricultural commodities since 1838. After 1850 coffee gradually became a major export throughout the region (except Honduras). During the twentieth century, other commodity export production developed (bananas, cacao, cotton, sugar, and beef), and, like coffee, each of these products was subject to great world market price swings. Cyclical recessions and depressions in the international economy hit Central America hard. Industrialization was slow, the extreme inequalities in the class systems intensified, and dependency upon imported food and manufactures grew.

Coffee production wrought major socioeconomic changes in the late nineteenth century: It concentrated landownership in the hands of major coffee growers/millers/exporters, who constituted new national economic elites that promoted and protected their interests by controlling (or sharing control of) the state.[4] Other export crops also had regional importance, but their effects on the distribution of wealth and political power were usually similar.

The agro-export elites eventually had to enlist the national armed forces to suppress popular discontent. Together they opposed socioeconomic reform so tenaciously that their rule has been labeled "reactionary despotism."[5] Baloyra described the reactionary coalitions of Central America as

> bent on the preservation of privilege [and their] monopoly of public roles and of the entrepreneurial function. . . . The dominant actors of the reactionary coalitions of Central America do not believe in suffrage, do not believe in paying taxes, and do not believe in acting through responsible institutions. Their basic ideological premise is that the government exists to protect them from other social groups in order to continue to accumulate capital without the restraints created by labor unions, competition, and government regulation.[6]

During the 1950s and 1960s Central American investors began the extensive cultivation of grains for the regional market and cotton for the international market. Except for Honduras,[7] each Central American nation by the mid-1970s had greatly reduced its smallholding and subsistence agricultural sector (small farmers) and greatly expanded migrant wage-labor forces. A large rural labor surplus developed, cityward migration by unemployable campesinos swelled, domestic food production shrank, and landownership and agricultural production became still more concentrated in fewer hands. National dependency upon imported foodstuffs rose throughout the region, as did the number of citizens directly affected by imported inflation.

Following the 1959 overthrow of Fulgencio Batista in Cuba,[8] Central American governments in 1960 formed the Central American Common Market (CACM) to spur regional economic integration, foreign investment, intraregional trade, and industrialization. One of the stated goals was to diversify and increase production so that wealth might "trickle down" to the poor and undercut the potential appeal of socialism. The CACM's goals converged in 1961 with those of the U.S. Alliance for Progress, which greatly increased public development aid to Central America and thus encouraged private investment there. During the 1960s, to varying degrees in each nation, the surge in domestic and foreign investment concentrated in the capital-intensive production of consumer goods, manufactured mainly with imported raw materials and fuel. Gross domestic products and GDPs per capita grew rapidly well into the 1970s, mainly because of a rapid increase in industrial production and productivity (see Appendix, Tables 1 and 2) and because of stable input prices.

Students of the CACM agree, however, that its industrial boom failed to absorb the rapidly growing labor supply and in some nations shifted wealth and income away from working-class groups. The number of factory and middle-class jobs grew because of industrialization until the early 1970s, but rural and urban unemployment simultaneously rose throughout the region. Moreover, the CACM's development model began to exhaust its potential for growth in the 1970s. Imported industrial raw materials suffered upwardly spiraling prices after 1967—input costs rose 150 percent from 1968 to 1976. These higher costs reduced investment rates, productivity, output growth, and the competitiveness of Central American products.[9] In Nicaragua, El Salvador, and Guatemala, the industrial sector's share of exports declined markedly (averaging roughly 6 percent overall) from the 1970–1974 to the 1975–1979 period. Balance-of-payments pressures afflicted all the Central American economies in the 1970s because of declining terms of trade (the relative costs of imports versus exports), a recession in the world economy, and higher foreign interest rates. According to Weeks, "each government in effect decided to pursue a separate strategy to weather the crisis, rather than a collective one."[10] By the end of the 1970s the CACM accord began to break down, and in the 1980s the breakdown was complete.

After World War II socioeconomic change accelerated in Central America (Appendix, Table 2). Population almost doubled between 1960 and 1980 and high growth rates persisted. The expanding commercial agricultural sector and the increasing concentration of landownership forced peasants off the land and thus swelled both agricultural labor migration and the region's urban populations. Enhanced educational programs increased school attendance, raised literacy rates, and sharply raised participation in higher education everywhere in the isthmus. Ownership of radio and television receivers and of broadcast facilities spread, and roads were improved and means of transportation developed. Such changes made communication easier and faster and brought to more and more people an awareness of their nations and their problems. Economic activity shifted away from agriculture and toward manufacturing and services. Overall economic activity (measured as GDP per capita) more than doubled between 1960 and 1980. However, this growth was unevenly distributed, and as noted, a sharp recession reduced production regionwide in the late 1970s and the 1980s.

The wrenching economic strains of the 1970s had several cascading political and economic effects on Central America, an explanation of which is the major subject of the next several chapters. First, at the macrosocial level of economic policy, Central American nations tended to try to borrow their way out of recession and political crisis and thus accumulated huge foreign debt loads while their economies eroded (Appendix, Table 1). This debt undermined economic recovery efforts, made governments more dependent on foreign lenders, and eventually forced them to undergo neoliberal structural adjustment programs in the late 1980s and 1990s. By 1996, under neoliberal policies, the region's economies were growing again and their debt problems were coming under control. Nevertheless, by the late 1990s only El Salvador and Costa Rica had recovered to or exceeded their 1980 levels of gross domestic product per capita. Tragically, Nicaragua's 1996 per capita GDP was only 48 percent of that of 1970, one of the hemisphere's historically most dramatic cases of economic collapse.

The second great consequence of the economic crisis of the 1970s was both macro- and microsocial—enormous political turmoil. At the system level, it intensified economic crisis throughout the 1980s by disrupting production and frightening away capital. At the microsocial level, rural and urban lower-class citizens' living conditions deteriorated while they witnessed the rapid enrichment of economic elites. This stimulated class conflict in the form of regionwide mobilization of protest, opposition, and demands for economic and political reform. Some governments violently repressed such mobilization, which brought about revolution in Nicaragua and lengthy civil wars in El Salvador and Guatemala. These, combined with deepening economic crisis and escalating foreign intervention in Central American affairs, set off a dramatic series of regime changes in the region's authoritarian governments starting in the late 1970s that established civilian democracies throughout the region by 1996. Only Costa Rica—the sole democracy in the region in the 1970s—escaped one or more regime transformations during this tumultuous era.

In summary, the rapid but inequitable economic growth of the 1960s and 1970s caused economic policies and class conflict that transformed Central America both politically and economically in the 1980s and 1990s. It is ironic, indeed, that the resulting political change was toward democracy and civilian rule while the economic change was a dramatic decline from which recovery is still far from certain. By and large, Central Americans today enjoy more freedom and democracy than in 1980, but most of them are also poorer.

4

INDIVIDUAL HISTORIES OF CENTRAL AMERICAN NATIONS

Although Central America's five nations have had far more in common than most other independent nations, each has had a separate history that has made it unique. Indeed, Central Americans today often dwell upon the differences among their nations. Each country competes with its neighbors in various ways ranging from trade to diplomacy to boundary disputes. Regional governments and elites often interfere in the internal affairs of neighboring countries. Citizens of each country have jokes about and nicknames for their neighbors. This chapter traces the aspects of the national sociopolitical development of each country that have contributed to the distinctive national identity of each nation.

COSTA RICA

Deviant from the patterns set in the rest of Central America during the colonial period, Costa Rica remained an exception to isthmian social, economic, and political norms thereafter. Rather isolated from the rest of Central America because of distance and rugged terrain, Costa Rica retained a much greater degree of racial and economic homogeneity than its neighbors. This is not to say that Costa Rica did not exhibit social disparities, or that it remained forever economically self-contained. Rather, the social inequities in Costa Rica were never great enough to let one class or race completely dominate others to the detriment of the majority of the populace to the extent that this occurred elsewhere in the isthmus. That is, despite its development of export agriculture, Costa Rica's economic game never became so unequal or so unfair as to allow the development of a full-blown system of dependency, with its tremendous human costs.

In the nineteenth century the roots were planted for Costa Rican democracy, despite a conspicuous absence of democratic rule for much of the era. From 1824 to 1899, one Costa Rican government in five ended by coup d'état and the country was under military rule 44 percent of the time.[1] During most of that epoch, the country was governed by moneyed rural families. Such elections as did occur were indirect, confined to a tiny, literate elite, and often rigged.

However, certain economic trends and political reforms developed that ultimately prevented a total domination of Costa Rican national politics by a landed oligarchy. The first dictator-president, Braulio Carrillo (1835–1842), for instance, increased the already fairly large number of small farmers by distributing municipal lands to the inhabitants. He also promoted the cultivation of coffee, and, in contrast to what was to happen elsewhere in Central America, he encouraged the small farmer to produce coffee beans. This contributed to the emergence of a class of smallholding yeoman farmers that kept renewing itself by expanding the agricultural frontiers.

The incipient landed elite continued to rule the country until its control was broken by the military, greatly expanded after the 1857 Central American war and led by Liberal dictator Tomás Guardia (1870–1882). Guardia immediately attacked the wealthy by confiscating some of their properties and exiling a number of their leaders. As a Liberal, Guardia also arranged with foreigners for the construction of roads and railways to move coffee to market. In the late nineteenth century, a labor shortage kept rural wages high as coffee production spread. By that time market forces in the rapidly growing coffee industry had begun to concentrate landownership and thus had pushed many smallholders off the land. But in order to secure the labor supply central to the nation's wealth, large coffee farmers had to pay decent wages and the government had to pass reformist public policies. Costa Rican peasants and workers therefore were not generally exploited or repressed as badly as elsewhere in Central America.

Despite the militarization of politics and the Guardia dictatorship, precursors of democracy developed in the second half of the nineteenth century. Elections, though indirect, elite-dominated, and often fraudulent, became important in politics by the 1840s. The growth of commerce, government, transport, immigration, and urban centers swelled the number of people available for and interested in political activity. The modernizing Liberals, both Guardia and his civilian successors, greatly expanded education spending and thus increased literacy by the turn of the century. Because the ability to read was a key criterion for eligibility to vote, increasing literacy also expanded suffrage.[2]

By 1889 an economic slowdown and the Liberals' anticlericalism generated support for an opposition Catholic Union party and its presidential candidate José J. Rodríguez. Backed by the Catholic church, Rodríguez won the vote among the electors, but the army tried to block him from taking office. Angry citizens incited by the church took to the streets and forced the army to back down. This election, sometimes incorrectly cited as the birth of Costa Rican democracy, was significant because it forced the military to respect an opposition victory and because ordinary citizens mobilized to defend an election. After Rodríguez, however, authoritarian elite rulers and election fraud returned.[3]

From 1905 to 1914, presidents Cleto González Víquez and Ricardo Jiménez Oreamuno further expanded suffrage, established direct popular election of public officials, and permitted free and open opposition campaigns for office. A brief military regime came to power in 1917 in the hard times associated with World War I. Costa Rica's last military government, it was toppled in 1919 by popular protest and an invasion by exiled elites. Civilian, constitutional rule continued thereafter, and the Costa Rican electorate expanded continuously.

The completion of the Atlantic railroad led to the development of an additional export crop, bananas. The foreign-owned banana industry, concentrated as it was in the sparsely populated Atlantic coastal lowlands, had little effect on Costa Rican politics in the early twentieth century. Later, as hard times developed, labor organizers led by Communists organized the banana plantations, and union influence and political power grew. By the 1940s, the economic slump caused by the Great Depression and World War II had caused great social dislocations. This pitted against one another factions of the political-economic elite, working classes and unions, and an emerging middle class. In the early 1940s, President Rafael Calderón Guardia, a popular medical doctor and reformist coffee aristocrat, broke with the rest of the coffee-growing political class. In a bid to dominate the government he forged an alliance with the Communist labor unions and the Catholic church and enacted and began to implement Costa Rica's first labor and social security laws.

Calderón's alliance with the Communists and, in 1948, both electoral fraud and legislative tampering with the results of the presidential election provided pretexts for a brief but violent civil war. A coalition of elite politicos angry at Calderón and middle-class elements, dominated by a junta of social democrats, rebelled against the regime. The rebels defeated the government within a few months. From that time to the present, the country's social democrats—the National Liberation party (Partido de Liberación Nacional—PLN), led for three decades by the colorful José "Pepe" Figueres Ferrer—have set the tone of Costa Rican political life. In keeping with a well-established tradition of political accommodation, the victorious National Liberation junta retained Calderón's social reforms for workers. Indeed, the junta went even further by nationalizing the banking and insurance industries. The constitution was rewritten in 1949, abolishing the army, an act that was a key to future political stability. In late 1949, the presidency was turned over to the rightful winner of the 1948 election, Otilio Ulate, who was not a part of the National Liberation movement.

When the PLN and Figueres first won the presidency in 1954, they began to expand the social legislation initiated under Calderón. Increasingly large segments of the populace received health and social security coverage. Even the conservative coalition governments that have periodically replaced the PLN in power have preserved and expanded such social welfare policies. Since 1949, scrupulously honest elections have been held at regular intervals under the auspices of a powerful and independent Supreme Electoral Tribunal. When defeated at the polls, the PLN has willingly given over control of the presidency and Legislative Assembly to an amorphous conservative opposition coalition. The PLN has won the presidency seven times and the opposition has ruled Costa Rica six times between 1949 and 1998. Opinion surveys show that Costa Rican citizens strongly support democratic civil liberties and alternation in power by the competing parties.

Despite its model constitutional democracy, all is not well in contemporary Costa Rica. On the one hand, the cost of its ambitious social welfare programs has outrun the government's ability to collect revenues. Skyrocketing oil costs and plunging export prices caused a foreign debt crisis in the early 1980s. This forced Costa Rica to devalue its currency and to adopt harsh austerity measures that sharply lowered living standards for most citizens. Although the election system remained stable throughout the recession and debt crisis, these problems have had other effects. For example, they made Costa Rican administrations very vulnerable to international pressures by the United States, which gave Costa Rica over $1 billion in economic aid during the early and mid-1980s (Appendix, Table 4). The administration of Luis Alberto Monge (1982–1986) collaborated with U.S. efforts to isolate and destabilize the Nicaraguan revolution and accepted some military assistance from the United States in an effort to strengthen the Civil Guard. These decisions aroused fears about Costa Rica's civilian democratic institutions and independence.

The administration of Oscar Arias Sánchez somewhat allayed these fears. President Arias resisted U.S. pressure to continue supporting the counterrevolution against Nicaragua. Despite criticism from Washington, Arias took the lead in promoting the Central American Peace Accord, signed in Guatemala in August 1987, for which he received the Nobel Peace Prize. The United States punished Costa Rica for these efforts by sharply cutting its economic aid for 1989–1992 (Appendix, Table 4).

Costa Rica's economy experienced fitful recovery into the mid-1990s, with GDP per capita returning to 1980 levels only by 1996 as successive governments implemented tough externally imposed neoliberal austerity measures to reduce foreign debt and debt service (Appendix, Tables 1 and 2). Rafael Angel Calderón Fournier, son of former president Calderón Guardia and a member of the Social Christian Unity party (Partido de Unidad Social Cristiana—PUSC) won the 1990 presidential election. Another famous political scion and the PLN founder's son, José María Figueres Olsen, captured the presidency in 1994 in a campaign so nasty it disheartened many Costa Ricans. The PUSC's Miguel Angel Rodríguez Echeverría won the similarly abrasive 1998 presidential contest. In 1998 voter turnout dropped to 71 percent from the usual 81 percent as several groups urged abstention to protest the campaign, economic policy, and a deterioration of the quality of Costa Rican democracy.[4]

NICARAGUA

Nicaragua is potentially one of the richest countries in Central America, with abundant arable land, considerable hydroelectric, thermal, and (possibly) fossil energy reserves, and significant timber and mineral resources. It also has access to two oceans and a lake and river system that makes it an ideal site for a transisthmian waterway. Ironically, however, Nicaraguans today are among the poorest Central Americans and Latin Americans. The reason for this paradox seems to lie in the extreme degree to which the patterns of dependency, established in the colonial period, were institutionalized and perpetuated into the twentieth century.

Nineteenth-century Nicaragua was plagued by civil wars and foreign interference. During the first several decades, the Liberal and Conservative elites, based in the cities of León and Granada, respectively, struggled with each other to control the national government. At the same time, Britain and the United States—both actively interested in building a transoceanic waterway—maneuvered against each other in an attempt to insert themselves into the power vacuum left by Spain.

At midcentury, foreign interference and the Liberal-Conservative conflict both came to a head in a war. In the late 1840s the British and Americans had almost come to blows over a British attempt to seize the mouth of the San Juan River. In the resulting Clayton-Bulwer Treaty (1850), the United States and Britain mutually renounced the right to embark on any unilateral exploitation of the region. The California gold rush of the 1850s deepened U.S. interest in Central America as a shortcut between the eastern and western coasts of North America. In 1855 one of two competing transit companies in Nicaragua and Panama became embroiled in Nicaragua's Liberal-Conservative clash. That year the Liberals, in exchange for help in the business dispute, imported a small mercenary army of North Americans commanded by adventurer William Walker to help them defeat the Conservatives. As we noted, the plan backfired when the flamboyant Tennessean seized power for himself. This left Nicaragua's Liberals so discredited by association with the "gringo" interloper that the Conservatives ruled virtually unchallenged until 1893.

In the nineteenth century, Nicaragua experienced profound social and economic changes because of the spreading coffee industry. Before 1870, intraelite turmoil and relatively low foreign economic control had permitted Nicaragua to develop an internal market and a surprisingly large free peasantry. One foreign observer stated: "Peonage such as is seen in Mexico and various parts of Spanish America does not exist in Nicaragua. . . . Any citizen whatever can set himself up on a piece of open land . . . to cultivate plantain and corn."[5] This pattern changed radically when growing international demand for coffee brought widespread cultivation of the bean to Nicaragua. Coffee production required new lands and cheap labor. Accordingly, the elite began in the 1870s to dispossess the peasant and Indian farmers in much of the northern highlands, using chicanery, self-serving legislation, and violence. No longer self-sufficient, former peasants had few options except peonage on coffee plantations. When some of the victims of the process rebelled in the War of the Comuneros of 1881, the elite-run government contained the uprising by killing thousands of the poorly armed insurgents.

The expansion of coffee production at the expense of peasant smallholding accelerated under a modernizing Liberal dictator, José Santos Zelaya (1893–1909). Zelaya also built educational and governmental infrastructure (censuses, archives, a more modern army) and defended the interests of Nicaragua and Central America against a burgeoning imperialist urge in the United States. After the United States decided to build a transisthmian canal in Panama, Zelaya began to seek a canal deal with U.S. rival naval powers Germany and Japan. To protect its canal monopoly, in 1909 the United States encouraged Zelaya's Conservative opposition to rebel against him and then landed marines to protect the rebels. In 1909, Zelaya resigned and in 1910 the Liberals relinquished power to the minority Conservative party. By 1912, however, the Conservatives had made such a mess of public affairs that a combined Liberal-Conservative rebellion occurred. That revolt was put down only after U.S. marines physically occupied Nicaragua.

From 1912 to 1933, with the exception of a short period in the mid-1920s, the United States maintained an occupation force in Nicaragua. U.S.-dominated governments in this era generally followed the dictates of Washington, even when they clearly went contrary to Nicaraguan interests. The Chamorro-Bryan Treaty of 1916, for example, gave the United States rights to build a canal in Nicaragua. The Americans had no intention of constructing such a canal; they simply wanted to block possible competition for the U.S.-built waterway just completed in Panama. In 1928, another puppet government under U.S. pressure gave Colombia several important Nicaraguan islands, including San Andrés, in order to assuage Colombian resentment of the U.S. role in taking Panama from Colombia in 1903.

And finally, during the latter part of this period, the Nicaraguan government gave in to U.S. pressure to create a modern constabulary—a combined army and police force. A movement to resist U.S. occupation of Nicaragua sprang up in 1927, led by the charismatic local guerrilla-patriot Augusto C. Sandino. U.S. marines could not put down Sandino's resistance, so an embrionic Nicaraguan National Guard (Guardia Nacional) was significantly enlarged to assist in the struggle. The war was a standoff, and the United States eventually withdrew its troops at the turn of the year 1932–1933. The National Guard then became the vehicle by which its first Nicaraguan commander, Anastasio Somoza García, created and consolidated the Somoza family dictatorship, which was to brutalize and oppress Nicaragua for over four decades.

As the first Nicaraguan commander of the National Guard, Anastasio Somoza García had Sandino assassinated in 1934 and used the guard to seize political power in 1936. Thereafter, three Somozas held power from 1936 until 1979. So-

AUGUSTO CÉSAR SANDINO (in checked shirt) (photo courtesy of *Barricada*).

moza García was either president or the power behind puppets until his assassination in 1956. His son, Luis Somoza Debayle, ruled directly or through puppets until 1967. Luis's younger brother, Anastasio Somoza Debayle, was "elected" to the presidency in 1967 and held power from then until 1979. Throughout this period, there were two primary pillars of support for the Somoza dynasty: the United States and the Nicaraguan National Guard. The guard, always under the command of one of the Somozas, was purposely isolated from the people and allowed to become thoroughly corrupt—a means of ensuring its loyalty to the Somozas. It became a sort of Mafia in uniform. The guard ran prostitution, gambling, and protection rackets and took bribes and extorted kickbacks for a variety of activities, both legal and illegal.

U.S. support for the Somozas was secured in two ways: personal ingratiation and political subservience. The Somozas were masters at cultivating Americans. Each was educated in the United States, spoke fluent vernacular English, and knew how to be a "good old boy" among ethnocentric, often homesick North American diplomats and visitors. On the political plane, the Somozas always supported U.S. policy, be it anti-Axis during World War II or anti-Communist thereafter. They allowed Nicaragua to serve as staging grounds for the CIA-organized exile invasions of Guatemala (1954) and Cuba (1961), contributed a small force to participate in the U.S. occupation of the Dominican Republic in 1965, and offered to send Nicaraguan troops to fight in both Korea and Vietnam.

As a result, U.S. support for the Somozas was usually strong and highly visible. Especially after the beginning of the Alliance for Progress in 1961, the United States gave Nicaragua many millions of dollars in aid for social and economic projects (despite ample evidence that the Somozas and their accomplices were stealing much of the aid). U.S. ambassadors were normally unabashedly pro-Somoza. What is more, during the 1960s and 1970s, the dictatorship received U.S. military support far out of proportion to such aid given to other Central American countries (Appendix, Table 4). In fact, by the time the Somozas were finally overthrown, their National Guard was the most heavily U.S.-trained military establishment in Latin America.

The Somoza system accelerated the income-concentrating processes of dependency. In the 1950s, large numbers of peasants were pushed off their Pacific lowlands farms when, in response to increased international demand and prices, the rich and powerful took over these areas to cultivate cotton. Income concentration also took place in cities as the Alliance for Progress and the new Central American Common Market stimulated commercial and industrial growth. Most of the benefit of this growth accrued to Nicaraguan investors in joint ventures with foreign multinational corporations. The bulk of the Nicaraguan economy came to be concentrated in the hands of three huge financial groups, each centered around a local bank with links to corresponding foreign banks. The heart of one of these groups was the Somoza family, which is commonly estimated to have increased its fortune from around $50 million in the 1950s to well over $500 million by 1979. Meanwhile, the situation for the common citizen had become simply intolerable.

Gross social inequity, coupled with the inability of the last of the Somozas to make even cosmetic reforms, led ultimately to an insurrectionary overthrow of the family dynasty in 1979. This dramatic upheaval and regime transformation ushered in two decades of change.

For eleven years the revolutionary Sandinista National Liberation Front (Frente Sandinista de Liberación Nacional—FSLN) experimented with social and economic reforms on behalf of the poor majority while creating an electoral system and constitution that laid the foundations for democratic government and rule of law. Nevertheless, economic destabilization and collapse (Appendix, Tables 1 and 2), promoted by a combination of revolutionary public policy and the hostile actions of U.S. administrations, led ultimately to the 1990 electoral defeat of the Sandinistas and their replacement by the government of U.S.-supported Violeta Barrios de Chamorro.[6]

Although very conservative in social and economic matters, Chamorro showed surprising independence from Washington in her pursuit of political reconciliation to heal animosities exacerbated by a decade of revolution and U.S.-promoted civil war during the Sandinista period. However, Chamorro's successor, Arnoldo Alemán (elected in 1996), also an economic conservative, shared none of her peacemaking inclinations. Thus, by the late 1990s, the fragile democracy created in the 1980s was being tested by both a rapidly deteriorating social situation and the politically polarizing behavior of the country's new regime. Although the Chamorro and Alemán governments stabilized the economy, controlled inflation, and reduced foreign debt, GDP per capita remained the lowest in the isthmus and well below Nicaragua's 1960 GDP per capita level (Appendix, Tables 1–3, 5).

In October 1998, Hurricane Mitch dealt Nicaragua another of its seemingly endless natural and human calamities. Dozens of inches of rain fell in just a few days when the storm stalled over Nicaragua. Catastrophic flash flooding and mudslides devastated much of the country and killed over two thousand people. International assistance quickly flowed in to help with the short-term damage, but the long-term harm promised to be enormous. The rain and floods washed away crops and livestock, destroyed roads and dozens of vital bridges, and left tens of thousands of survivors homeless. The enormous loss of infrastructure, farms, business, and investment will undoubtedly set back the country's feeble economy and reverse the modest growth that had begun during the Chamorro administration.

EL SALVADOR

To casual visitors in recent decades, El Salvador's most striking characteristic has been its overpopulation. Indeed, foreigners sometimes argue that the tiny country is essentially inviable, lacking the resources to support its teeming population. That argument, however, is fallacious. Other densely populated countries (Holland, Japan, China) manage to feed their people. In fact, the real problem in El Salvador is an extreme maldistribution of resources brought about, as in the rest of northern Central America, by centuries of external dependence and elite control.[7]

During most of its first century after independence in 1823, El Salvador was controlled by a Liberal elite. Occasionally, Conservative rulers were imposed by Guatemalan intervention, but these were exceptions. Like their counterparts elsewhere in the region, Salvadoran Liberals were staunch advocates of free enterprise and economic modernization through expanding agricultural exports and building up the economic and service infrastructure. The mestizo and Indian masses were regarded somewhat ambivalently as both obstacles to progress and as labor resources to be used as the elite saw fit.

El Salvador entered the national period with most of its economy built around the production, extraction, and export of the dye indigo. However, by the mid nineteenth century, cheaper European chemical dyes sharply cut international demand for the deep blue colorant, forcing El Salvador's privileged elite to turn to coffee production as a substitute. The best land for coffee was the higher, volcanic terrain previously disdained by the large landowners. The mountain slopes, however, were occupied by mestizo and Indian communal farmers whose ancestors had been displaced from the valley floors by the Spanish. The would-be coffee growers thus used their control of the government to gain access to good coffee land by legislating communal landholdings out of existence.

In 1856, the state decreed that individual communes must plant at least two-thirds of their lands in coffee or be confiscated. Lacking the considerable capital necessary to buy and plant coffee trees and wait several years for a crop, many communes were wiped out. Those communes that survived the 1856 legislation received the coup de grace by two laws in the early 1880s. These laws simply declared communal holdings to be illegal and established "vagrancy" rules that effectively forced the now landless peasants to work on the coffee plantations. Salvadoran peasants, of course, were angered by this legalized theft of their land and forced labor schemes. Unsuccessful popular uprisings punctuated the final third of the nineteenth century, but the promoters of coffee prevailed. In the end, the privileged classes brought El Salvador into the twentieth century with one of the most unequal patterns of land distribution in all of Latin America. A coffee elite, henceforth known as the "fourteen families," controlled a lion's share of the country's resources.

Although the seizure of the best lands in the temperate highlands was essentially complete by the end of the nineteenth century, the expansion of coffee continued elsewhere well into the twentieth century. In 1929, for instance, the socially conscious editor of *La Patria* wrote: "The conquest of territory by the coffee industry is alarming. It . . . is now descending into the valleys displacing maize, rice and beans. It is extended like the conquistador, spreading hunger and misery, reducing former proprietors to the worst conditions—woe to those who sell!"[8]

By the 1930s, the situation reached a political breaking point. The Great Depression had lowered the demand and price for Salvadoran exports. Predictably, the coffee elite attempted to cushion itself from the impact of price declines by cutting the already miserable wages of the plantation workers. On top of this, popular hopes for justice were greatly fueled by an aberrant period of democratic reform in 1930–1931 and then dashed by the rise of yet another reactionary dictatorship, led by General Maximiliano Hernández Martínez. The result of all this turmoil and economic travail was an ill-coordinated peasant uprising in January 1932, to which the government security forces and landowners responded with the massacre of over 30,000 peasants (only a small minority of whom were actual insurgents). The original organizer of these uprisings, a charismatic Marxist intellectual, Augustín Farabundo Martí, was captured before the revolt and both shot and beheaded in its wake. His memory, like that of Sandino in Nicaragua, would continue to have an impact on his country decades later.

The six and a half decades that have elapsed since the rise of General Hernández Martínez in 1931 and the 1932 massacre (known to this day as the "Slaughter"—*la Matanza*) forms an epoch in Salvadoran history. Whereas previously the Liberal elite had normally ruled through civilian dictators drawn from among themselves, they henceforth entrusted direct control of the government to an uninterrupted series of military regimes. Hernández Martínez ruled dictatorially, both protecting the interests of the coffee elite and initiating modernizing and developmental projects that some of the elite opposed. Post-World War II reformist pressures from labor, middle-class elements, and within the military brought the end of the Hernández Martínez regime in 1944. In 1948 the armed forces restructured its system of rule by establishing a military-dominated political party, the Revolutionary Party of Democratic Unification (Partido Revolucionario de Unificación Democrática—PRUD). Despite its name, the party did not promote revolution, democracy, or unity—it was the military's device for maintaining political control, "an impressive machine of patronage and electoral mobilization."[9] In 1960 the PRUD was replaced by its own clone, the National Conciliation party (Partido de Conciliación Nacional—PCN).

After 1948 the Salvadoran armed forces—with the support of much of the national bourgeoisie, which it defended—ruled essentially on behalf of themselves, becoming increasingly powerful and corrupt. Rule by the military developed a cycle of "change" that kept everything very much the same. First, responding to popular unrest and national problems, a group of progressive young military officers who pledged to break with the past and institute needed reforms overthrew an increasingly repressive regime. Next, the most conservative elements of the army, influenced by members of the oligarchy, reasserted themselves and let the reforms lapse. This produced civil unrest which, in turn, led to increased repression,[10] disaffection by another military faction, and a new reformist coup.

One such cycle produced the PRUD between 1944 and 1948. Another cycle culminated in the PRUD's restructuring itself into the PCN in 1961. On January 25, 1961, just after John F. Kennedy was inaugurated in the United States, a conservative coup that had been encouraged by the Eisenhower administration took place in El Salvador. Although Kennedy quickly recognized the new government, he apparently also pressured the interim junta to begin implementing mild democratic and social reforms. Accordingly, the mid-1960s became a time of reformist rhetoric and growing popular hope for change. During this period the opposition Christian Democratic party (Partido Demócrata Cristiano—PDC) was born. The PDC's very popular leader, José Napoleón Duarte, espoused gradual reformism of the sort supported by the U.S.-created Alliance for Progress and the Central American Common Market. Duarte twice won the mayoralty of San Salvador on the PDC ticket.[11]

This reformism inevitably faded. The moneyed elite was alarmed by the mild reforms proposed under the Alliance for Progress and began to press conservative elements in the military to crack down. Indeed, El Salvador's establishment press had labeled President Kennedy a "Communist" for his insistence on agrarian reform. When the PDC's Duarte apparently won the 1972 election, the regime reacted by throwing out the results and installing rightist Col. Arturo Armando Molina in the presidency. After an unsuccessful barracks revolt on Duarte's behalf, the army arrested and tortured the defrauded candidate, then sent him into exile.

A new reform-repression cycle lasted from 1972 through 1979, spanning the presidencies of two more PCN-imposed military rulers, Molina (1972–1977) and

Carlos Humberto Romero (1976–1979). By the late 1960s, the Alliance for Progress and the mild reformism it had espoused had gone the way of the passenger pigeon. Industrial growth had proceeded at a rapid pace, but no "trickling down" of wealth was taking place. Indeed, real wages and living standards for the Salvadoran working classes were deteriorating rapidly and thus spawning unrest (Appendix, Tables 5 and 6). U.S. assistance to El Salvador in the 1960s and 1970s heavily emphasized military aid (Appendix, Table 4). The fact that the Molina and Romero presidencies came to power through vote fraud and became steadily more violently repressive did not alter Nixon and Ford administration policies toward El Salvador. Seeking to contain a feared expansion of Soviet influence, the United States placed paramount importance on maintaining stability and blocking growing pressures for social revolution.

As we shall show in Chapter 7, the accelerating deterioration of economic conditions among the Salvadoran working classes in the 1970s stimulated popular unrest. The period from the 1972 election fraud until 1979 was marked by explosive popular mobilization. Student organizations, labor and peasant unions, and a variety of opposition parties ranging from the Christian Democrats to the small Communist party increased their efforts to politicize the people to defend their interests. Leftist rebel groups appeared for the first time since 1932.

One key element in the political ferment in El Salvador during the 1970s was activist Roman Catholic priests, nuns, and laypersons who had become committed to real social change.[12] This movement, sometimes identified as inspired by "liberation theology," arose as a response to calls by the Second Vatican Council and the Second General Conference of Latin American Bishops of 1968 to make a "preferential option for the poor" and to work for social justice. It organized hundreds of Christian base communities (*comunidades eclesiales de base*—CEBs) to discuss and implement the "social gospel." In addition, between 1970 and 1976, it trained over fifteen thousand catechists and lay "delegates of the Word," who carried a similarly activist message to the rural poor. Logically, these activities heightened grass-roots awareness of the unjust nature of the Salvadoran political and economic system and spurred protests, peasant organization, and other forms of pressure for change.

By mid-1977, the year in which human rights advocate Jimmy Carter became president of the United States, El Salvador had reached an explosive state. The Church was clearly under attack by both the military and the privileged elite. In 1976, presidential candidate Romero had threatened to expel or kill all Jesuits. Soon after Romero assumed the presidency, two priests were killed, ten were exiled, and others were arrested, beaten, or tortured. The Carter administration criticized the Romero regime's human rights record and threatened to cut off military aid. The Salvadoran government, however, astounded Washington by rejecting both the criticism and further military assistance. Unchecked by external or internal brakes and confronted with rising opposition, the Romero government unleashed a wave of terror that was taking over a thousand lives per month by 1979.

PRIMERO DE MAYO (May Day) DEMONSTRATION IN EL SALVADOR, 1988. People with signs representing grass-roots organizations; government response (photos by Steve Cagan).

El Salvador descended into civil war between 1979 and 1981. A supposedly reformist coup d'état on October 15, 1979, brought to power a junta and cabinet that included the military, business interests, and the Social Democratic and Christian Democratic parties. Fearful of "another Nicaragua" in Central America, the Carter administration reversed field and renewed military assistance to the Salvadoran junta and armed forces. Because the junta did not control human rights abuses, most political moderates withdrew from the government. Several moderate and leftist parties formed the Revolutionary Democratic Front (Frente Democrático Revolucionario—FDR). Five Marxist guerrilla groups united to form the Farabundo Martí National Liberation Front (Frente Farabundo Martí de Liberación Nacional—FMLN) which received the backing of the FDR.

From 1979 to 1992, El Salvador underwent a civil war that claimed over 75,000 lives. Despite the war, massive U.S. aid kept the Salvadoran economy in better shape than those of its neighbors (Appendix, Tables 1, 2, and 4). Although elections brought civilian presidents to office (José Napoleon Duarte in 1984 and Alfredo Cristiani in 1988), the system was far from democratic since it functioned under a reign of state-sponsored terror and wholesale violation of human rights carried out by the U.S.-backed Salvadoran military and associated "death squads."

In the early 1990s, however, with the cold war at an end, the United States—which had previously insisted on a military solution—reversed course and backed a United Nations and regionwide effort at negotiated peace. The comprehensive peace agreement, signed in early 1992, formally included most of the basic reforms for which the FMLN had been fighting for more than a decade: reforms affecting military and security forces and judicial, electoral, and other governmental institutions.

Although few aspects of the peace agreement were implemented to the letter, El Salvador's civilian, constitutional government after 1992 was considerably more democratic and respectful of human rights than military governments had been when the civil war was starting (1979–1981). The military and police were purged and reduced in size, and cleaner elections were held. Even though the establishment's presidential candidate, ARENA's Armando Calderón Sol, won the still imperfect election of 1994, the former guerrillas established themselves as the second largest congressional party both that year and again in 1997, and won the mayoral race in the capital city, San Salvador, in the latter election. A significant process of political transition had begun, aided by rapid economic growth.

GUATEMALA

Although its large, unintegrated Indian population sets Guatemala apart from the other countries of modern Central America, it shares many historical legacies with its neighbors, especially with nineteenth-century Nicaragua and El Salvador. An early period of Liberal-Conservative conflict was followed, later in the century, by a consolidation of Liberal control. The Liberals implemented their "reforms," which produced profound socioeconomic realignments and shaped many contemporary social and political problems.

The Liberals, who took control of Guatemala in 1871, dominated the nation, with minor exceptions, until the mid-1940s. They began major reforms under dictator-president Justo Rufino Bárrios (1873–1885). Bárrios pushed hard to modernize his country by building roads, railways, a national army, and a more competent national bureaucracy, by promoting the new crop, coffee, and by encouraging foreign investment. He opened Church and Indian communal lands to "modern" cultivation by large landowners (latifundists). By 1900 coffee accounted for 85 percent of Guatemala's exports, and as landownership concentrated increasingly in their hands, latifundist coffee growers dominated Guatemalan economics and politics. Once they were forced from their land, the Indians were then coerced into being laborers on the coffee plantations through the same sort of debt-peonage systems and "vagrancy" laws seen elsewhere in northern Central America in this period.

In the late nineteenth century, the construction of a rail link to the Atlantic coast gave rise to the banana industry. Soon after the turn of the century, the U.S.-based United Fruit Company (UFCO), at first mainly a shipper/exporter, had squeezed out Guatemalan banana growers and eventually came to own many key public utilities and vast tracts of land. The Liberal development program continued in the twentieth century. In politics, Manuel Estrada Cabrera's brutal dictatorship (1898–1920) inspired Nobel laureate Miguel Angel Asturias's chilling novel of state terror, *El Señor Presidente.* Big coffee plantations, a large number foreign owned, continued to expand inexorably at the expense of many subsistence smallholdings.

When the world economy collapsed in 1929, Guatemala's exports plummeted and worker unrest grew rapidly. The nation's tiny labor movement and incipient Communist party became targets for repression by President Jorge Ubico, who in 1931 assumed dictatorial control of the political system. He violently suppressed the labor movement, Communists, and other political activists, while strongly centralizing power in the national government. Ubico continued to promote the development of government and economic infrastructure (banks, railways, highways, telephones, the telegraph, and electrical utilities). Although originally an admirer of certain Fascists such as Mussolini and Franco, Ubico took the opportunity provided by World War II to confiscate over $150 million in German-owned properties, mainly coffee plantations. He "modernized" vagrancy laws so that the government could oblige Indians to work a certain number of days for the state. This effectively converted the government into Guatemala's major labor contractor.

Labor unrest, middle-class pressures for democratization and reform, and a loss of U.S. support caused Ubico to resign in 1944. Student- and labor-backed military reformers called elections for later that year. Educator and former exile,

Juan José Arévalo Bermejo, who described himself vaguely as a "spiritual socialist," won the presidency. During his five-year term, Arévalo began numerous reforms, instituting social security, a labor code, professionalization of the armed forces, rural education, public health promotion, and the formation of cooperatives. Arévalo vigorously encouraged union and peasant organization and open elections. Arévalo's economic policies, which have been described as an "explicit attempt to create a modern capitalist society,"[13] did not address the root of the country's social problems—the extreme maldistribution of land.

In 1950 Guatemalans elected a young army officer, Jacobo Arbenz Guzmán, to succeed Arévalo. Arbenz sought to deepen the revolution's social reforms despite growing conservative and U.S. opposition. He legalized the Communist party, called the Guatemalan Labor party (Partido Guatemalteco del Trabajo—PGT), in 1951, which became very active in organizing labor and in promoting agrarian reform. A 1952 Agrarian Reform Law began the confiscation and redistribution of farmland to 100,000 peasants. Over 500 peasant unions and 300 peasant leagues formed under the Arbenz government.[14]

Arbenz's reforms and the rapid organization of peasants and workers threatened the rural labor supply system and shifted economic power toward workers and peasants and away from latifundists and employers. The threatened interests took action when Arbenz nationalized land belonging to United Fruit and offered compensation to the company at its previously declared tax value. Several highly placed Eisenhower administration officials had direct ties with UFCO. The nationalization, the presence of a few Communists in the government, and an attempt by Arbenz to purchase light arms from Czechoslovakia caused the United States to label the Arbenz government as Communist.

Beginning about 1953 the United States set out to destabilize Guatemala's Arbenz administration with a program of financial sanctions, diplomatic pressure in the Organization of American States, and Central Intelligence Agency (CIA) disinformation and covert actions. This culminated in a CIA-backed conspiracy with a disloyal rightist army faction. In June 1954 the tiny, CIA-supported National Liberation Army, led by Col. Carlos Castillo Armas, invaded Guatemala. The armed forces refused to defend the government and Arbenz had to resign.[15]

As the head of the National Liberation Movement (Movimiento de Liberación Nacional—MLN), Colonel Castillo Armas assumed the presidency, backed by the United States and the hierarchy of the Catholic church. With ferocious anti-Communist propaganda, the counterrevolution dismantled the labor and peasant movements, killing and jailing thousands in the process, repressed political parties, revoked the Agrarian Reform Law, and returned confiscated lands to their former owners. As working- and middle-class and prorevolutionary organizations were suppressed, "there began a continuing . . . promotion of upper-sector interests."[16] Military and business sectors made sharp gains in political influence within the government. Foreign policy became closely identified with the United

States, and U.S. and multinational aid programs promoted economic growth and financed extensive infrastructure development.

The MLN developed into a substantial political party during the late 1950s, drawing together coffee plantation owners, municipal politicians and bureaucrats, owners of midsized farms, and certain military elements united in anticommunism and in their hostility toward the reforms of the 1944–1954 revolution. Castillo was assassinated in 1957 and confusion followed. Amid accusations of fraud and in an atmosphere of increasingly bitter recriminations between the armed forces and the MLN, the army annulled the 1957 plebiscite, which the MLN had won, and imposed Gen. Miguel Ydígoras Fuentes as president. The Ydígoras government promoted Guatemala's participation in the Central American Common Market, permitted CIA-backed anti-Castro Cuban exile forces to train in Guatemala, and continued police terror against supporters of the revolution and labor and peasant leaders.

Continued violence plus the growing corruption of the Ydígoras government prompted an abortive coup by reformist army officers in 1960. Escaped remnants of the plotters formed the nucleus of the first of several rebel groups. The leaders of the Revolutionary Armed Forces (Fuerzas Armadas Revolucionarias—FAR) and the 13th of November Revolutionary Movement (Movimiento Revolucionario del 13 de Noviembre—MR-13) eventually adopted a Marxist-Leninist ideology and guerrilla war strategy patterned after that of Fidel Castro in Cuba. U.S. military aid to the Guatemalan armed forces increased rapidly, but despite such assistance, early military operations against the guerrillas proved ineffective. Dissatisfaction within military ranks culminated in Col. Enrique Peralta Azurdia's overthrow of Ydígoras in 1963; counterinsurgency operations thereafter expanded rapidly.

In 1965 the military decided to return the government nominally to civilians, and the 1966 election campaign was generally free and open.[17] The Revolutionary party (Partido Revolucionario—PR) candidate, Julio César Méndez Montenegro, who denounced the twelve-year counterrevolution, won the presidency. After Méndez took office, however, military counterinsurgency accelerated while the armed forces' hold on the political system actually deepened—despite the presence of a civilian president in the National Palace. The army's 1968 Zacapa campaign took an estimated ten thousand civilian lives and dealt the guerrillas a severe blow, in the process earning its head, Col. Carlos Arana Osorio, the sobriquet of "the Butcher of Zacapa."

After a decade of reform/revolution and another of counterrevolution, Guatemalan society had become sharply polarized between reformist and conservative segments. For some, the 1966 election signified the breakdown of the counterrevolution and, therefore, a call to radical action. Several right-wing "death squads" formed and commenced acts of terror against persons vaguely associated with the Left and with reformist politics. Regular national security forces (army and police), peasant irregulars armed by the government in areas of insurgency, and right-wing terrorist groups permitted (and encouraged) by the regime conducted the Right's terror campaign. Drastic, often indiscriminate actions by the police and proregime terrorists targeted mainly the government's political opposition, but many victims were completely apolitical. As a result, the reform-oriented opposition was effectively intimidated, demobilized, and disarticulated.

In these circumstances, the presidential elections held in 1970—though the ballots were counted honestly by the Méndez government—resulted in victory for Col. Carlos Arana Osorio, the nominee of both the MLN and the military's own Institutional Democratic party (Partido Institucional Democrático—PID). With U.S. aid at its all-time high during his administration, Arana definitively consolidated the military's political power and deepened its corruption. An aggressive economic modernization program created huge public sector enterprises and projects (some under army control) to increase the financial autonomy of the armed forces and the amounts of graft available to top officers. Terror against unions, political parties, and suspected critics of the regime escalated anew.

Despite the nomination of military officers as presidential candidates by each of the parties, Arana, by a fraudulent count of the 1974 election, imposed Gen. Eugenio Kjell Laugerud García as his successor.[18] Laugerud's government briefly moderated repression, encouraged cooperatives and union resurgence, and pushed a major development project for the potentially oil-rich northeastern Petén, where many high-ranking officers acquired large tracts of land.

The disastrous earthquake of February 4, 1976, took some 25,000 lives, mainly in the western highlands, and sparked new political and economic unrest by unions, university students, and the urban poor. The FAR resurfaced and two new, Indian-based guerrilla organizations, the Guerrilla Army of the Poor (Ejército Guerrillero de los Pobres—EGP) and the Organization of the People in Arms (Organización del Pueblo en Armas—ORPA) also appeared. All grew rapidly and began overt military activity in the late 1970s. When President Laugerud stepped up repression, the Carter administration's State Department criticized Guatemala's human rights record. Guatemala responded in 1977 by refusing to accept further U.S. military assistance. Economic assistance to Guatemala, however, continued during the Carter administration.

In the political turmoil of the 1978 election, all parties again nominated military officers as presidential candidates. Gen. Romeo Lucas García (nominated by the military's PID and the PR) won the election on an apparently fraudulent count.[19] The Lucas García government brutally crushed Guatemala City protests against increased bus fares in late 1978. As opposition parties grew in 1978–1979, security force death squads assassinated dozens of national and local leaders of the Democratic Socialist party (Partido Socialista Demócrata—PSD), Christian Democratic party (Partido Demócrata Cristiano—DC), and the reformist United Front of the Revolution (Frente Unido de la Revolución—FUR). Hundreds of union leaders, university faculty, and student leaders also disappeared or were assassinated during the Lucas government.

In the countryside, peasant organizations led by the Peasant Unity Committee (Comité de Unidad Campesina—CUC) stepped up organizing. The CUC staged a major strike against sugar planters in 1980. In 1978 and 1979 the regrouped FAR and ORPA began military activity in the western highlands; they apparently enjoyed considerable popular support. As a part of its stepped up counterinsurgency efforts, the army implemented draconian measures—including massacres of Indian villagers—to discourage support for the guerrillas. Despite such massive human rights violations, Guatemala continued to receive new economic assistance from the United States that totaled over $60 million from 1979 through 1981.[20]

The relative prosperity of Guatemala had strengthened the military regime in the late 1970s, but the regional recession, with sharp declines in production (Appendix, Table 1), finally arrived in Guatemala in 1981 and 1982. The recession quickly ruined the army's image as an economic manager and alienated the once supportive business community. When President Lucas fraudulently manipulated the results of the 1982 presidential election to benefit his defense minister, Gen. Aníbal Angel Guevara, discontent arose within the army itself. A group of young officers who desired certain reforms (reduced military corruption and withdrawal from direct participation in rule) overthrew Lucas just after the election. They asked a retired general and former DC presidential nominee, Efraín Ríos Montt, to head the government and to take steps to restore the presidency to civilians.

The highly eccentric Ríos Montt—a fundamentalist Protestant—soon proved overly fond of his new job. He took steps to consolidate power fully and gave signs of intending to stay. Ríos Montt had promised a return to civilian rule, but he proposed reforms to the electoral system that would have actually strengthened army control of the elections and weakened the political parties. Although Ríos Montt's rule brought some reduction of urban death squad activity, the army sharply escalated its rural counterinsurgency activities. The unprecedented levels of violence and social dislocation wreaked by the army devastated entire indigenous communities and cultural groups.[21]

Complaints from the parties, external legitimacy problems stemming from the de facto nature and brutality of the regime, and unease about Ríos Montt's increasingly assertive promotion of his sect and religious ideas proliferated. The same reformist element within the army that had put Ríos Montt in power in early 1982 ousted him in an August 1983 coup led by the defense minister, Gen. Oscar Humberto Mejía Víctores. Upon assuming the presidency, Mejía accommodated many of the parties' objections about the election laws, conducted a relatively clean election of delegates to a constituent assembly in 1984—albeit within a climate of extreme political repression. The constituent assembly rewrote the Guatemalan Constitution so as to increase the autonomy of the armed forces and to pave the way for the November 1985 national election. The army's brutal counterinsurgency campaign, political assassinations, disappearances, and overall violence remained largely unchanged under Mejía.

In late 1985 Guatemala conducted a clean national election after a campaign distinguished by the candidates' universal fear of advocating—indeed, even of mentioning publicly—socioeconomic reforms or human rights improvements. Christian Democrat Vinicio Cerezo Arévalo won the presidency in a runoff, and his party captured a majority of the congress.[22]

Guatemala's new civilian regime, with the enthusiastic backing of the United States, then embarked upon what many observers believed was a last chance to avoid a general uprising or bloody civil conflict as in Nicaragua or El Salvador. Not even Cerezo himself seemed very optimistic about his prospects for remaking the Guatemalan political system. When asked about his chance to win effective ruling power away from the military, promote human rights and social reform, and solve looming economic problems, Cerezo reportedly quipped, "I am a politician, not a magician!" He and the Guatemalan Congress faced daunting problems. The economic recession of the early 1980s continued (Appendix, Tables 1, 2, and 6), a high level of human rights abuse continued, and the guerrilla conflict persisted despite the army's counterinsurgency war. Throughout the second half of his five-year term, Cerezo's administration was roundly criticized—even within his own party—for corruption and for failure to make progress on socioeconomic reforms, economic recovery, or human rights. Cerezo's greatest success came mainly in external affairs, where his endorsement of and work for the Central American Peace Accord contributed significantly to its signing in Guatemala in August 1987.[23]

By the late 1980s both the weak civilian administration and the guerrilla groups, united under the Guatemalan National Revolutionary Union (Unión Revolucionaria Nacional Guatemalteca—URNG), decided that the best alternative to protracted civil war and military stalemate lay in a negotiated settlement. However, as long as the cold war persisted, little progress was made toward that goal.

The 1990s, however, brought three new civilian governments with gradually increasing autonomy from the military: The first was that of conservative Jorge Serrano Elías, which lasted from 1990 until his unsuccessful 1993 attempt to grab dictatorial powers through a "soft" coup.[24] After Serrano was removed from office for violating the constitution, former human rights ombudsman Ramiro de León Carpio served out Serrano's term through 1995. Third was the government of pragmatic conservative Alvaro Arzú, elected in 1995. A series of rapid and vital changes in Guatemala's international environment affected all three of these civilian governments: the end of the cold war, a more favorable U.S. attitude toward peace negotiations, and the end of the Nicaraguan revolution in 1990 and of the Salvadoran insurrection in 1992. This permitted the Serrano, de León, and Arzú governments to talk directly with the URNG guerrillas. Momentum in the negotiations built rapidly under Arzú, who step by step achieved the agreements that culminated in a comprehensive peace accord in December 1996.

As in El Salvador earlier in the decade, the Guatemalan peace agreement, though not implemented to the letter, appeared to represent a transition to a system that would be much less violent and more respectful of basic human rights. Guatemala's economy, badly eroded during the 1980s, began growing again in the 1990s (Appendix, Tables 1 and 2). The long civil war's end, modest external debt, and a package of fiscal reforms suggested that Guatemala's economic recovery could accelerate in the late 1990s.[25]

HONDURAS

Honduras is an unusual and paradoxical country. By a geological quirk, its soil lacks the rich volcanic material prevalent throughout the region's other countries. Geographically isolated, with broken terrain, and very poor transportation facilities, Honduras did not develop a significant export economy in the nineteenth century and remained mainly a subsistence economy. The common people of Honduras were even poorer than their Nicaraguan, Salvadoran, or Guatemalan counterparts. Honduran history, however, reveals little mass rebellion or guerrilla warfare. Until very recently, the country was a calm eddy in Central America's troubled waters.

The reasons for this social and political stability in the face of mass poverty are several. Honduras never really developed so coherent or powerfully privileged an elite class as did its three neighbors, Nicaragua, El Salvador, and Guatemala. Of course, there have always been some rich Hondurans, but their wealth remained regionally based. Unlike the rest of Central America, coffee became a significant export crop for Honduras only after World War II.

When commercial banana production was introduced at the turn of the century, foreigners, not Hondurans, were responsible. The banana industry developed along the sparsely populated northern coast and displaced few peasant or Indian communal holdings. Indeed, though land was generally poor in quality, it was nearly always plentiful in Honduras; thus, poor peasants could usually find free or cheap land to farm. Virtually no land shortage developed until the mid twentieth century, when foreign market demands and urban population growth led wealthier Hondurans to begin a process of concentrating landownership.

These economic development patterns had other ramifications.[26] First, since there was no need to quell an angry, dispossessed, and exploited rural working class, the Honduran army remained rather weak well into the twentieth century. Second, the banana industry contributed to labor relations unlike those seen in neighboring nations. Because banana companies were foreign owned, Honduran governments were not very keen on keeping banana workers' wages down. Indeed, rising wages meant more basic consumption and thus helped Honduran entrepreneurs. Moreover, because banana production was less labor intensive than, for instance, coffee production, the companies could pay higher wages without becoming less competitive. Strikes were frequent, but Honduran governments felt less inclined to use force to suppress workers and the companies were more willing to make wage concessions than often proved true in other countries or in the production of other crops. Thus, although labor unions were not formally legalized until 1954, they had existed informally and operated fairly freely for many decades. Over the long haul, Honduras developed a much larger (and politically more potent) organized work force than other Central American countries.

In another contrast with neighboring nations, the Liberal/Conservative debate began much later in Honduras. In the nineteenth century, the country was dominated by a succession of nonideological caudillos who simply succeeded each other by force of arms. Party development began in earnest when a Liberal, Marco Aurelio Soto, was president (1876–1883). True to the Liberal vision of the era, he began efforts to modernize the nation, build a service infrastructure and state apparatus, and to attract foreign investors. By the end of the century the Honduran Liberal party (Partido Liberal de Honduras—PLH) was formed. Liberals dominated the political scene until the 1930s. Their conservative counterpart—the National party—was born in 1923, but was able to take power only when the PLH split in the 1932 election. National party caudillo Tiburcio Carías Andino was elected in 1932 and held the presidency until 1949—giving Honduras its longest period of political stability.

Following Carías's retirement, Liberal-National conflict over control of power intensified. The Liberal party's electoral strength recovered with the rapid expansion of labor union movement in the early 1950s. National party efforts to keep the Liberals out of power prompted the army in 1956 to seize power in order to end the dispute; there followed a year of military rule. When the military relinquished power, PLH candidate Ramón Villeda Morales swept the 1957 election. Villeda's government signed the Central American Common Market accords and passed several modernizing social policies, including social security, labor, and agrarian reform laws. Despite such symbols of progress, Honduras remained the poorest country in Central America.

From the mid twentieth century onward, Honduras developed problems and patterns more typical of the rest of Central America. As noted earlier, land hunger first became a real problem during this period. This was due in part to appropriation of peasant-occupied lands by larger landholders as the latter sought to take advantage of increased internal and external commodity markets. Another important cause was a sudden rise in population growth rates due to improved public health conditions and practices developed during World War II. The rapid increase in demand for land in the 1950s and 1960s led to greater tension between classes and increasing peasant mobilization.

An additional growing similarity between Honduras and other Central American nations came from the militarization of its political system. With the advent of the cold war, labor unrest in the banana plantations was commonly blamed on "Communist agitators." As part of its general regional strategy to contain communism, the United States "concluded several agreements to train and equip the loosely organized armed forces of Honduras, and since the early 1950s, over one thousand personnel [had, as of 1979] taken courses in U.S. facilities."[27] Although from the 1950s through the 1970s there was virtually no guerrilla opposition to the Honduran government, much of the U.S. military training of the era dealt with counterinsurgency and put a strong emphasis on "national security." In 1973–1980 U.S. aid to Honduras rose sharply compared to earlier periods, especially military assistance (Appendix, Table 4).

Not surprisingly, the increasing factionalism and conflict within and between the Liberal and National parties left a power and leadership vacuum. This vacuum, plus the growth of the military's strength, contributed to an expansion of the armed forces' involvement in politics. Whereas civilian caudillos had run the country for the first half of the twentieth century, the armed forces since the 1956 coup have ruled directly or have powerfully influenced civilian rulers from just offstage.

Honduran military rule, however, until the 1980s was rather more benign than in neighboring states. The military acted more as an arbiter between other political groups than as an agent of a ruling class. Labor, peasant, and political party organizations were generally tolerated. Catholic priests and nuns were allowed to carry the "social gospel" to the poor and to build grass-roots organizations. And especially after the birth of the Alliance for Progress and Central American Common Market, there was much talk of basic socioeconomic reforms, some directly promoted by military governments.

In 1963 Air Force Col. Oswaldo López Arellano overthrew Villeda Morales and assumed power in coalition with National party figures. The regime repressed labor and peasant activism and began to enlarge and strengthen the armed forces. The regime's conservative economic policies, certain disadvantageous trade relations built into the Central American Common Market, and the 1969 war with El Salvador led to growing public unrest as López's presidency ended. The failure of the successor National-Liberal coalition to deal with growing national turmoil prompted López Arellano, now a wealthy general, to seize power once again. This time, with the support of labor and peasant sectors and other progressive elements, he implemented several populist programs, including a modest agrarian reform.

Military participation in rule changed character in the late 1970s. Embarrassed by a bribery scandal, López transferred power in 1975 to Col. Juan Alberto Melgar Castro, the first of two hard-line military dictators who abandoned López's populist reforms and curtailed civilian participation in national administration. Melgar was overthrown in 1978 by Col. Policarpio Paz García. Despite the rapid changes in regimes, the military strove to promote national economic development and turned away from social programs. Although the Melgar and Paz regimes largely ignored questions of social justice, they remained relatively respectful of basic human rights and permitted certain civil and political liberties. There were no death squads, no systematized tortures, and no rash of disappearances. The press remained relatively free and boisterously critical of the military regimes.

Despite their developmentalist goals, the armed forces proved quite inept as rulers and economic managers. By the late 1970s corruption scandals, deepening economic difficulties, the fall of the Somoza regime in Nicaragua, and growing pressures from spurned civilian politicians created powerful incentives for the military to abandon power. Although the Carter administration never severed military assistance to Honduras, it brought pressure on General Paz to relinquish power. Under such internal and external pressures, the military called elections in 1980 for a constituent assembly that would rewrite the constitution; in November 1981, presidential elections were held.

Liberal Roberto Suazo Córdova won a clear majority and took over the formal reins of power in January 1982. Col. Gustavo Alvarez Martínez became head of the armed forces. Prospects for a true democracy were soon clouded, both by the performance of Suazo and Alvarez, and by policies of the new Reagan administration. Washington put heavy pressure on Honduras to lend itself to U.S. efforts to overthrow the Sandinista government of Nicaragua and to curtail the activities of Salvadoran guerrillas inside Honduran territory. A U.S. military spokesman neatly summarized the U.S. appraisal of the situation: "Honduras is the keystone to our policy down there."[28] Suazo and Alvarez accepted the presence of U.S. troops on continuous "maneuvers," the construction and expansion of military bases and facilities in Honduras, and even U.S. training of Salvadoran troops. Sanctuary and overt cooperation were provided to the contra army that the United States was developing to attack Nicaragua's Sandinista government. Honduras thus became the active ally of the U.S. military strategy for Nicaragua and El Salvador,[29] leading some wags to claim the country had become an aircraft carrier—the USS *Honduras.* In exchange for all this, Honduras received hundreds of millions of dollars in U.S. assistance—especially military aid (Appendix, Table 4).

This military assistance program rapidly expanded the size and power of the armed forces and permitted Alvarez to overshadow and intimidate the civilian president and congress. Relations with Nicaragua deteriorated badly. By 1984 the U.S.-financed contra forces in Honduras had begun to rival in number the Honduran military and had severely disrupted public order along the Nicaraguan border. In 1983 Honduras already had death squads, whose membership included public security force and Nicaraguan exile elements; political disappearances and murders became increasingly commonplace. As repression grew and domestic political tensions rose, several leftist guerrilla groups appeared and began operations—a novelty in Honduras. Though very weak and extremely fragmented, the Honduran guerrilla movement continued to grow as the decade proceeded.

In 1984 senior armed forces officers ousted Alvarez from his command because he had deepened Honduras's role in the U.S.-Nicaragua imbroglio. Another sore spot was Alvarez's insensitivity to the military's tradition of corporate decision-making and his decision to permit the training of Salvadoran soldiers—until then hated enemies—at a new U.S. training facility at Puerto Castillo. In 1984 and 1985 Suazo's increasingly high-handed maneuvering to retain the presidency provoked a grave constitutional crisis. In an astounding twist of events the armed forces called labor and peasant groups, already angered by the poor state of the economy and falling wages (Appendix, Tables 1 and 6), into the street to confront the regime and thus force Suazo to permit elections to go forward. The stratagem worked: A Suazo antagonist, the PLH's José Azcona Hoyos, won the 1985 presidential election.[30]

Azcona's tenuous civilian government survived, propped up—in one of the region's great ironies—by organized labor, the military, and the U.S. government.[31] In 1990 the Liberals lost the national elections to a National party ticket headed by Rafael Callejas. Although the cold war was over and the United States was now promoting democratic reform rather than human rights–abusive counterterror, President Callejas stubbornly refused to reform the military. Indeed, the human rights situation actually deteriorated under his presidency.

With the 1994 inauguration of human rights lawyer Carlos Roberto Reina of the Liberal party, Honduras would gradually fall into line with the rest of post–cold war Central America in improving human rights and military reform. The inordinate powers of the military and the police—legacies of military rule in the 1970s and enhanced during the 1980s—were curbed, and respect for human rights improved. As the data in the Appendix (Tables 1, 2, and 6) reveal, Honduras's overall economic performance also improved in the late 1990s, but wages continued to erode in this chronically and persistently poor nation.

Within a few months of the inauguration of Reina's successor, Carlos Roberto Flores Facussé, a natural catastrophe dealt Honduras a devastating economic and social setback. Hurricane Mitch stalled over Honduras in October 1998 and dumped several feet of rain onto the country's deforested mountains and many unplanned, ill-drained communities. Calamitous flooding and mudslides resulted. They demolished entire towns and neighborhoods in the capital, ripped out roads and bridges, and left some five thousand dead and hundreds of thousands homeless. International aid flooded in, but the long-term economic damage from the hurricane would be enormous as crops were lost, critical service infrastructure disrupted, and thousands of businesses and agencies damaged.

5

REVOLUTION, REGIME CHANGE, AND DEMOCRATIZATION: A THEORY

Central America's political regimes have changed enormously and repeatedly in the late twentieth century. It took the United States two wars and two centuries of evolution to move from authoritarian rule by Britain to constitutional democracy with voting rights for the whole populace. In contrast, in less than two decades Honduras, Nicaragua, El Salvador, and Guatemala all traversed a similar political distance from authoritarianism to civilian democracy—although by different paths. This places into dramatic relief the significance of what transpired in the region. In less than the decade since we developed our original framework for understanding the region in the first edition of this book, so much has changed that it has redefined what we must account for.

Our original goal and theory sought to explain the somewhat perplexing occurrence of revolutionary insurrections in three Central American countries in the 1970s and 1980s, while two neighboring countries escaped such violent turmoil.[1] Since then, the efforts and cooperation of Latin American powers, international institutions, and Central American governments ended the lengthy civil wars in Nicaragua (1990), El Salvador (1992), and Guatemala (1996), and the 1990 election in Nicaragua terminated the Sandinista revolution. Elections during the 1980s replaced the military regimes of Honduras, El Salvador, and Guatemala with civilian governments.

Four of the region's five nations thus underwent dramatic, multiple regime changes from the military authoritarian status quo of the 1970s to civilian democracy by the 1990s. How can one explain such extensive and far-reaching political transformation? One way is to set forth a theory that might draw together and explain these diverse phenomena: political stability, guerrilla insurgency, military reformism, personalistic authoritarianism, socialist revolution, and civilian-led liberal democracy. Because propounding such a wide-ranging theory seems likely to be a daunting chore for even so small a part of the world as Central America, it may be helpful first to organize the material that must be explained. We begin by taking inventory of the Central American regimes from 1970 onward in order to identify the scope of the change.

AN OVERVIEW OF REGIME CHANGE IN CENTRAL AMERICA

We define *regimes* as coherent systems of rule over mass publics established among a coalition of a nation's dominant political actors. The coherence of the system of rule refers to the existence of a persistent and identifiable set of political rules by which access to power and decisionmaking occur.[2] Regimes are thus distinct from the separate governments or administrations that operate under the same general rules. For instance, Costa Rica has had a single civilian democratic regime since the 1950s, consisting of a series of constitutionally elected presidential administrations. Likewise, Guatemala in the 1970s had a military authoritarian regime, subdivided into governments headed by various president-generals.

One regime may be differentiated from another when it changes both the fundamental rules of politics and the makeup of its coalition (a regime shift). We propose six basic regime types that roughly cover the Central American experience between 1970 and 1998: *military authoritarian,* dominated by a corporate military establishment in coalition with a narrow range of civilian sectors; *personalistic military,* the only case of which was Nicaragua, dominated by the Somoza family and military in coalition with segments of the Liberal and Conservative parties and key financial sectors; *reformist military,* dominated by reformist military elements and intent upon a liberalizing or democratizing political transition; *civilian transitional,* with elected civilian rulers backed by a strong military and mainly incorporating center and rightist parties; *revolutionary,* the only example of which was Nicaragua's Sandinista-led center-left coalition; and *civilian democratic,* with elected civilian constitutional governments, broad coalitions, and political competition open to parties from left to right.

Table 5.1 displays Central America's regimes since 1970 according to this scheme. In the span of three decades only Costa Rica remained politically stable, that is, did not change regimes. Among the other four countries we count eleven regime shifts (changes between categories). Nicaragua's 1978–1979 insurrection led to a revolution in which elections were established, eventually permitting the electoral defeat of the revolutionary government in 1990. Honduras's military regime, anxiously eyeing neighboring Nicaragua's revolutionary turmoil at the end of the 1970s, moved quickly to transitional civilian democratic rule. Full civilian democracy came only in 1996. El Salvador and Guatemala traversed three

TABLE 5.1 Central American Regime Types, 1970–1998

Costa Rica	*El Salvador*	*Guatemala*	*Honduras*	*Nicaragua*
CD[a]	MA	MA	MA	PM
	RM (1979)	RM (1982)	RM (1980)	Rev (1979)
	CT (1984)	CT (1985)	CT (1982)	CD (1990)
	CD (1992)	CD (1996)	CD (1996)	

NOTE: Explanation of regime type notation: CD = civilian democratic, CT = civilial transitional, MA = military authoritarian, PM = personalistic military, RM = reformist military, and Rev = revolutionary. See text for fuller explanation of types. Date of inception of new regimes is in parentheses.

[a]Uninterrupted from 1949 to the present.

similar stages after military authoritarian rule: In each a military-led reformist regime engineered a transitional civilian regime during civil wars; the settlement of each war eventually ushered in a much more inclusive civilian democratic government.

How and why did these regime shifts occur? We should consider both what caused the changes and what the mechanisms or processes of change were. First, what were the causes? Based upon the histories laid out in previous chapters, several complex and interacting factors are the most likely candidates: Rapid economic growth followed by severe reversals generated widespread mass and special interest mobilization and demands for political and economic reform. Grave economic problems and mass unrest also undermined authoritarian coalitions. Governments' violent resistance to and repression of those demanding reform drove opposition unification, radicalization, and revolutionary insurrection. Military fears of a revolution like Nicaragua's led armed forces to initiate political reforms and eventually to the establishment of transitional civilian regimes with democratized rules. Once wars began, the incapacity of the military to defeat armed insurgents after years of combat and attrition eventually led both sides to accept negotiated regime changes. Although largely absent in the early 1970s, external pressures to adopt elections in place of military rule gained intensity in the 1980s. Various external actors increasingly viewed civilian democracy—or at least elections—as the key to settling civil wars. Particularly important in this process, and a step that affected at least three Central American regime changes, was the end of the cold war between the United States and the Soviet Union at the end of the 1980s. This epochal event sharply altered their and others' behaviors in Central America.

If these were the likely causes, what were the particular processes or instruments of Central American regime shifts? How did the changes occur? Military coups d'état ushered in reformist military episodes in El Salvador, Guatemala, and Honduras. A widely based mass insurrection initiated the revolutionary regime in Nicaragua. Hoping to manage change and thus protect their interests, transitional military regimes voluntarily began holding fairer elections that eventually returned civilians to power in Honduras, El Salvador, and Guatemala. The Nicaraguan revolutionary government also established an election system that elected the Sandinistas once. However, after a period of sharp economic decline propelled by the U.S.-sponsored contra war, Nicaraguans voted the Sandinistas out of office in 1990. Negotiated settlements of three civil wars admitted previously excluded actors into the political arena.

Given these multiple and complex regime changes, our original explanation of the onset of revolutionary movements—instrumental in only three of eleven cases—does not adequately embrace the Central American experience at the end of the twentieth century. We require a broader, more encompassing view to understand how Central America has moved from authoritarian stasis through geopolitical crisis to emerge transformed and surprisingly democratic. We must explain how the seven regime transitions not directly driven by revolutionary insurgency relate to the broader political and economic forces. Were the revolutionary turmoil and democratizing steps distinct and unrelated processes, or were they both products of a larger common process? Finally, why were the outcomes in each Central American nation so similar despite the quite divergent paths of regime change in the region?

As we have shown in previous chapters, despite certain differences among them, Central American nations have marked commonalities of history, global context, and political and economic development. These similarities strongly suggest that much that affects Central America is part of a larger world dynamic. We contend that just as common forces led to Central America's rebellions, many of the same forces shaped the overall process of regime change that eventually led from authoritarianism toward democracy. In fact, the revolutionary movements were key steps in the process of regime change that led to the region's formal democratization.

A THEORY OF REGIME CHANGE IN CENTRAL AMERICA

An explanatory argument integrating Central America's insurrections and democratization can be developed within a framework of regime change theory. To begin, we will very briefly review the political science literatures on regime change, revolution, and democratization. We will then show the considerable extent to which the three overlap and inform each other. These common features make it possible to derive a more general theory to explain the recent remarkable transformation of Central American politics.

Students of regime change have focused on the causes, processes, and outcomes of regime change. Barrington Moore explored how the characteristics of several established regimes and the interaction of their various actors led to the particular characteristics of new regimes.[3] Guillermo O'Donnell examined the role of military–middle-class coalitions as bureaucratic authoritarianism replaced civilian governments in Argentina and Brazil.[4] The contributors to Juan Linz et al.'s *The Breakdown of Democratic Regimes* examined the nature of democratic regimes and both the causes of and processes involved in the collapse of such regimes when they are replaced by authoritarian rule. Some decades later, O'Donnell et al.'s *The Transitions from Authoritarian Rule* performed a similar exercise for authoritarian governments of southern Europe and Latin America.[5] Mark Gasiorowski has employed quantitative analysis to account for factors that contribute to regime change.[6]

In sum, from the regime change literature we know that regimes are systems of rule over mass publics established among a coalition of a nation's dominant political actors. Regime coalition members benefit from inclusion in the regime. Social and economic change can generate and mobilize new political actors who may seek inclusion into the ruling coalition and its benefits and who may or may not be admitted by those within the regime. Contented, indifferent, unorganized, or effectively repressed populations do not seek inclusion in the regime, nor do they violently rebel. Strong, flexible regimes with satisfied allies rarely collapse or wage war against their populations.

In a classic work, Charles Anderson explains that Latin American regimes have corporatistic tendencies, one implication of which is that new actors are admitted to the regime coalition only when they prove themselves capable, if excluded, of destabilizing the existing regime. Regime transformations in the region are thus often highly conflictive because excluded forces have to fight for inclusion.[7] This view accounts for the well-documented case of Costa Rica's last regime shift. The narrowly based coffee-grower-dominated quasi-democracy of the 1930s was disrupted by emergent working- and middle-class actors. The latter forged a new regime after winning a brief but violent civil war in 1948.[8]

A second relevant theoretical literature is that on political violence and revolution, part of which, perforce, also examines regime change. We have extensively reviewed this literature in earlier editions, so we will merely highlight key portions here.[9] First, for a rebellion to occur there must be a fundamental basis of conflict that defines groups or categories of affected persons that provide "recruiting grounds for organizations."[10] What bases of conflict are most likely to lead citizens to widespread rebellion, a phenomenon that John Walton usefully designates the *national revolt*?[11] Walton, Theda Skocpol, Jeffrey Paige, Mancur Olson, and many others generally agree that rapid economic change and evolving class relations typically drive the mobilization required for a violent challenge to a regime.[12] For agrarian societies, inclusion into the world capitalist economy through heavy reliance upon export agriculture may harm huge sectors of the peasantry, urban poor, and middle sectors, providing large numbers of aggrieved citizens.

Once motivated, groups must organize and focus their struggle for change upon some target, most likely the state or the regime. Rod Aya and Charles Tilly have shown that effective organization for opposition requires the mobilization of resources and emphasize the key role of the state in shaping rebellion. The state or the ruling coalition are typically the targets of national revolts, but the state also reciprocally affects the rebellion as it both represses rebels and promotes change.[13] Walton, Skocpol, Jack Goldstone, and Ted Gurr concur that once a contest over sovereignty begins, political factors such as organization and resource mobilization by both sides eventually determine the outcome.[14] Goldstone and James DeFronzo particularly emphasize the contribution to successful revolutionary movements of both external actors and interelite competition, elite alienation, and factors that may weaken the state's capacity to act.[15] Perhaps the most satisfactory explanation is that offered by Timothy Wickham-Crowley.[16] Rejecting single-factor theories, he argues that Latin American history in recent decades demonstrates that successful insurrection requires a combination of four factors: the right social conditions in the countryside; an intelligent and flexible guerrilla movement; a despicable target regime ("mafiacracy"); and the right international conditions.

The third literature we must examine is the rapidly growing body of scholarship on democratization. What domestic forces lead to democratization, the process of moving from an authoritarian to a democratic regime? The four main explanations focus on political culture, political processes, social structures and forces (both domestic and external), and leaders and elites. The cultural approach argues that the ideal of political democracy can evolve within a society or spread among nations by cultural diffusion among elite and mass political actors.[17] Elite and mass preference for democracy promote its adoption and help sustain a democratic regime. In contrast, process approaches examine the mechanics of and paths toward democratic transition.[18] In these emphases they resemble and somewhat overlap the regime change literature.

Structural theories emphasize how shifts in the distribution of critical material and organizational resources among political actors can lead to democracy.[19] Democratic regimes emerge when the distribution of political and economic resources and the mobilization of actors permit formerly excluded actors to disrupt the extant authoritarian coalition. Another structural approach involves the imposition of democracy by external actors.[20] The fourth approach examines the roles of leaders.[21] Key societal elites must engineer specific democratic arrangements (elite settlements) and agree to operate by them. The broader the coalition of political forces involved, the more stable and consolidated a democratic regime will be.

While different in emphasis, these three literatures have much in common. All three concern the process of regime change or efforts to promote it, although the democratization literature emphasizes transition in one particular direction. Elements of all three envision a polity as having numerous actors, whose makeup and roles can evolve. They jointly treat political regimes as coalitions of key actors that survive through successful mobilization of resources in and around the state or governmental apparatus. All three recognize that regimes can enter into crisis, whether through challenge from without or deterioration from within or the erosion of state capacity. All three have causal explanations for change, although there are divergent emphases and outright disagreements both within and between fields over the importance of such factors as psychology, political culture, leaders and elites, masses, and social structures. However, the more sophisticated treatments in the revolution/violence and democratization literatures tend to treat causality as both complex and multiple.

Finally, in each of these fields and from a substantial literature on foreign policy, there is a recognition that international constraints can shape regime change.[22]

Foreign governments can act as players in domestic politics, strengthening a prevailing regime by supporting it or weakening it through opposition or withheld support. External actors can supply resources to domestic actors, altering their capacity to act and relative strength. Key external actors can pressure domestic actors to adopt certain policies or regime types, employing as inducements such vital resources as money, trade, arms, and political cooperation. The international context can also constrain a nation's regime type by demonstration effect—having mostly democratic neighbors makes it easier to adopt or retain a democratic regime.

From these elements we advance the following outline of a theory of regime change: Political systems are, for our purposes, nation-states with defined populations and territorial boundaries. Political systems exist within an international context consisting of various types of actors, including nation states, formal and informal alliances among nations, the world political economy, international organizations, political and ideological groupings. Political regimes are coherent systems of rule over mass publics established among a coalition of the nation's dominant political actors. Political actors within nations include individuals but, more importantly, encompass organized groups, factions, ideological groupings, parties, interest sectors, or institutions, each pursuing objectives within the political system and each with resources to bring to bear. Actors may or may not constitute part of the regime coalition, the group of actors who dominate and benefit most from the state, its resources, and its policymaking capacity.

Political regimes persist based upon two factors. They must constantly satisfy an endogenous objective of managing the state and economy so as to benefit coalition members enough to retain their loyalty. They must also continuously satisfy an exogenous objective consisting of keeping actual and potential outside-the-regime actors (both domestic and external) content or indifferent or, if neither of these, keeping them disorganized, immobilized, or otherwise effectively managed or repressed. Many factors have the potential to disrupt or destabilize a regime. International or domestic economic forces may disrupt the political economy of a regime (harm a nation's established economic system or the security of regime coalition's members or other actors). Such forces may include rapid economic growth followed by a sharp downturn, or a sharp recessive episode by itself. Powerful external actors (a major regional power or hegemon, for instance) may withdraw active support and resources from a regime or may shift from tacit support to active opposition to it, thus creating a permissive external environment for actors that might challenge a regime. Ideologies or different real-world polities may suggest alternative political and economic rules (republicanism instead of monarchy, socialism instead of capitalism, or civilian democracy instead of military authoritarianism) to key actors within or outside the regime coalition.

A regime experiences a crisis when such forces (1) undermine the loyalty and cooperation of some or all of the coalition members, (2) undermine the resource base and capacity of the regime to respond to challenges or opponents, or (3) mobilize external actors against the regime. Regime crises can take various forms based upon the severity of the challenge and distribution of resources among actors. Regime coalition members may renegotiate the regime's political rules and benefits and deny significant adjustments to outside actors. Regimes may make policy changes to mollify aggrieved outside actors. Regimes may initiate cooptative incorporation of new coalition members to quell a disruptive challenge to the regime; this will typically involve some reform of extant political rules and payoffs. (We consider this combination of alterations—change in the coalition membership plus an adjustment of the rules—to constitute the minimum adjustments necessary to be classified as a regime change.) Outside-the-regime actors may initiate a violent challenge to the regime's sovereignty via a coup d'état, insurrection, or even an external invasion. Inside-the-regime actors may also employ a coup to displace incumbents or, more interestingly, to initiate a new regime.

The development and outcome of the regime crisis will depend upon the ability of the regime and its challengers to mobilize and deploy their respective resources. The closer the regime and its challengers are to parity of material, political and human resources, and the stronger both are, the longer and more violently they will struggle over power. The dominant actor (such as the military) in a weak to moderately strong regime confronted with a weak but potentially growing opposition might initiate a regime change (cooptative reform and the inclusion of new actors) in order to minimize expected damage to its interests. Other things held equal, a strong, flexible, resource-rich regime will be most likely to reform and/or successfully repress or continue to exclude its opponents and to survive. A weak regime confronting a strong opposition coalition may be overthrown and replaced by a radically different, revolutionary regime that will subsequently exclude some or all of the old regime's coalition. A protracted regime crisis, especially a lengthy civil war, eventually increases the likelihood of a negotiated settlement and major regime transformation with new political rules, redistributed benefits, and the inclusion into the political game of both the challengers and key old-regime actors.

The consolidation of any new regime will derive from the eventual resolution of forces among the various political actors, which may, in turn, depend heavily upon the role of external actors. A single regime shift may not bring enough change to permit political stability. Military reformism, for instance, although intended to pacify a polity by including certain new actors and by enacting policy reforms, may utterly fail to satisfy violent opponents with antagonistic ideologies.

Despite establishing a new coalition, new rules, and new policies, a revolutionary regime may quickly attract direct or indirect external opposition. To the extent that important actors (internal or external) remain unsatisfied or unsuccessfully repressed, the consolidation of a new regime will fail. Protracted instability for a newly constituted regime, we believe, increases the likelihood of its failure and further regime shifts.

EXPLAINING REGIME CHANGE IN CENTRAL AMERICA

From the common elements of the theories examined above we offer the following propositions to account for the origin and development of regime change in Central America since the 1970s. The argument emphasizes the world economic and geopolitical and ideological context and its evolution, the regimes present in the 1970s and the causes of the crises that undermined them, regimes' and actors' responses to crisis, and the interplay of resources and external forces that shaped the ultimate outcome.

The Evolving Context

The U.S. View. The geopolitics of the cold war predominated on the world scene in the 1970s and set the context for Central American geopolitics. U.S. policy was preoccupied with the threat of the Soviet Union and its perceived desire to expand its influence within the Western Hemisphere. The United States thus tended to regard most of the region's political and economic reformists and the opponents of Central America's friendly, anticommunist, authoritarian regimes as unacceptable potential allies of pro-Soviet/pro-Cuban communism. Civilian democracy, though an ideological preference of the United States, remained secondary to security concerns in this tense world environment. U.S. promotion of civilian democracy was therefore seen as too risky because it might encourage leftists.

Central America's authoritarian regimes thus usually enjoyed the political, military, and economic support of the United States. Indeed, U.S. military personnel training Latin American officers during the cold war used special manuals that explicitly advocated the use of illegal detention, torture, and murder (state-sponsored terror) against a wide spectrum of groups opposed to pro-U.S. regimes.[23] This behavior created a profound contradiction between the proclaimed values of the United States and the reality of U.S. policy in the region. It also caused Central Americans in the center and on the left to be highly skeptical of the virtues of formal electoral "democracy" as practiced against a backdrop of unprecedented levels of state terror under pro-U.S. regimes.

Actually, U.S. thinking regarding the ideological geopolitics of Central America took several twists and turns from the late 1970s through the early 1990s. In the latter half of the 1970s, Congress and the Carter administration viewed the inhumane anticommunist authoritarian regimes of Nicaragua, Guatemala, and El Salvador as unacceptable. This policy change encouraged Central America's reformists and revolutionaries and briefly created a favorable international environment for regime change. After the Sandinistas' victory in 1979, however, U.S. human rights policy in Central America was "put on the back burner,"[24] and Washington once again began advising Central American regimes to clamp down on "subversives." When that posture ran up against congressional opposition in the first few years of the Reagan administration, U.S. diplomats once again began stressing democracy, insisting on formal elections in pro-U.S. countries, albeit against a background of state terror. This policy was continued under George Bush until the end of the cold war, when Washington's second-order preference for civilian democracy could come to the fore, thus allowing support for the peace process and the emergence of cleaner, more inclusive elections in El Salvador and Guatemala.

Central American Viewpoints. Prior to the late 1970s, many leftists in Central America had shared Fidel Castro's profound distrust of U.S.-sponsored electoral democracy. (Most moderate reformers likely preferred real electoral democracy but were repressed by U.S.-sponsored regimes.) However, from the time of their victory in 1979, many Sandinistas viewed electoral democracy as an organizational arrangement for the polity that was compatible with the economic/participatory democracy it sought to construct. The FSLN also viewed electoral democracy as a strategem that might enhance the acceptability of their revolution to the openly hostile United States and their Central American neighbors. Thus in 1984 they put in place a well-designed electoral system for selecting the government.

Whatever they may have initially envisioned as the ideal type of post-victory government, the insurgents in El Salvador (by 1982) and Guatemala (by 1986) had decided not to fight for an all-out victory but rather for a negotiated settlement that would include demilitarization and the installation of a system of civilian rule in which they would be able to take part. Much later, the armed forces of each nation—exhausted by the long civil wars—decided that they could accept electoral rules of the game with the leftists included in exchange for peace and institutional survival.

The Views of Other Actors. European nations, other Latin American nations, and such international organizations as the United Nations and Organization of American States once largely deferred to U.S. influence in the region. However, during the 1980s they became increasingly fearful that the isthmian civil wars and U.S. intervention could escalate further. These external actors therefore embraced and promoted electoral democracy as the mechanism for promoting their interest in the pacification of Central America.

The Catholic church in the isthmus was influenced by liberation theology in the 1960s and 1970s, a phenomenon that encouraged social mobilization, which, in turn, led in some cases to insurrection. By the 1980s, however, the institutional Church had come to downplay liberation theology while emphasizing democratization and improved human rights as a means toward achieving social justice.

In summary, the geopolitical and ideological contexts within which Central America's regimes and actors operated evolved substantially from the early 1970s through the mid-1990s. (1) The powerfully influential United States initially blocked electoral democracy in Central America for security reasons but eventually embraced it for instrumental reasons and an evolving perception of its security vis-à-vis the region. (2) Although many on both the right and left wing in Central America initially opposed electoral democracy, tactical and ideological needs deriving from geopolitics and protracted civil wars ultimately led most to accept and pursue the model. (3) Other external actors, especially European and Latin American powers and international organizations, moved from effective indifference toward electoral democracy in Central America to embracing it for their own security interests.

The 1970s Regimes

In the early 1970s only Costa Rica among the region's nations had a broadly inclusive, constitutional, civilian-led democratic regime. This regime had evolved from that country's 1948 civil war and 1948–1949 revolution.

The other four nations had military-dominated authoritarian regimes: Nicaragua had a personalistic military regime dominated by the Somoza clan and a narrow coalition made up of key business interests and parts of the two major parties. Guatemala and El Salvador had corporately run military authoritarian regimes, allied with some business and large-scale agricultural interests and with the collaboration of weak political parties. Honduras had a military authoritarian regime that incorporated one of the two strong traditional political parties and tolerated a very strong but anticommunist labor sector.

Causes of Regime Crises

A wave of economic problems afflicted all five Central American countries in the late 1970s and early 1980s. Rapidly escalating oil prices and resultant inflation, the deterioration of the Central American Common Market (in the mid- and late 1970s), and natural or economic catastrophes (e.g., the 1972 Managua earthquake, 1978–1979 Common Market trade disruptions) greatly reduced real income and employment among working-class and some white-collar sectors.

The grievances caused by increasing inequalities, declining real income, economic/natural catastrophes, and the political dissatisfactions of would-be competing elites led in the mid- and late 1970s to various events: the development of opposition parties; the rapid growth of agrarian, labor, neighborhood, and community self-help organization; and reformist demands upon the state and protests of public policy. Regime coalitions experienced some defections, and the economic resources of all five regimes eroded.

Regime Responses to Crisis

In both the short and long term, Central American regimes responded quite differently to unrest, mobilization, and demands for change. In the short term, the divergences were most striking. Where regimes responded to demands with ameliorative policies to ease poverty and permit the recovery of real wages, with political reform, and with low or modest levels of force or repression, protests failed to escalate further or subsided. Costa Rica's regime did not shift. Honduras's military authoritarian regime voluntarily returned power to civilians. In contrast, where regimes responded in the short run by rejecting ameliorative policies and—with U.S. assistance—sharply escalating repression by public security forces, protests and opposition organization and resource mobilization increased, rebellions occurred, and regime crises ensued (Nicaragua, El Salvador, and Guatemala).

In the longer run, the regimes that responded with violent repression and refusal to ameliorate the effects of economic crisis thus found themselves facing violent, broadly based insurrections. They struggled to mobilize the economic and political resources to resist the revolts, including seeking external assistance, especially from the United States. They also eventually undertook fundamental regime change itself (liberalizing and democratizing their rules and broadening their coalitions) and various other policy reforms in the struggle to manage, repress, divide, and isolate their violent challengers.

Outcomes

The outcome of Central America's regime crises depended upon the relative success of each regime in mobilizing and maintaining domestic and external material support and organization. Failure to stabilize the situation (to placate or repress enough outside-the-regime actors) led to regime shifts.

Nicaragua. Somoza lost direct U.S. and regional support and vital economic resources, permitting the Sandinistas to oust him and establish the revolutionary regime with a center-left coalition and revolutionary rules. The excluded Somocista Liberals and an increasing number of other disaffected economic and political forces formed various outside-the-regime forces, including the U.S.-backed contra rebels. The revolutionary regime's response to its regime crisis and the counterrevolutionary war included nearly continuous economic and political reform, including the adoption of democratic electoral rules in 1984. Soviet support waned after 1987, and the Iran-contra scandal suggested that U.S. support for the contras might also erode. The 1987 Peace Accord eventually facilitated a cease-fire and then a negotiated end to the war. In the 1990 election Nicaragua's voters, disillusioned by a collapsing economy and the contra war, replaced the FSLN government and ended the revolution. This ushered in a new nonrevolutionary civilian regime, with both the left and elements of the right participating. In 1996 Liberal Nationalists returned to the arena and won the election, possibly consolidating a postrevolutionary regime.

Honduras. Faced with domestic turmoil and the Nicaraguan revolution next door, the Honduran military regime made a quick, preemptive transition to civilian democracy. The traditional Liberal and National parties dominated the fairly inclusive regime. The armed forces, however, flush with massive political, economic, and military resources earned by cooperating with U.S. efforts to defeat the revolutionary left in Nicaragua and El Salvador, retained great power and influence. This delayed transition to civilian democracy until after the military's power was eventually trimmed by reforms in the mid-1990s.

El Salvador and Guatemala. A coup d'état in El Salvador in 1979 and another in Guatemala in 1982 instituted reformist military regimes. These governments repressed moderates and centrists who remained outside the regime coalitions while they attempted but failed to defeat leftist rebel coalitions. The failure of this strategy, plus pressure from the United States (a major resource supplier to the Salvadoran regime), led to the adoption of civilian transitional governments that, although weak, governed with broader coalitions and liberalized rules. This behavior won over some of the political center in each country, depriving the rebel coalitions of important allies and resources and contributing to the stagnation of both civil wars. The Central American Peace Accord of 1987 provided a mechanism for eventual negotiations between the parties to the stalemated civil conflicts. Military exhaustion, U.S. exasperation with the Central American quagmires, and the end of the cold war led to shifts in all actors' positions. The United States, other outside actors, national militaries, the civilian reformist regimes, and the rebels all eventually embraced more inclusive civilian democracy and some economic reforms, position changes that helped settle both wars.

DISCUSSION

Since the 1970s Central American polities have undergone dramatic transformations: Rapid, inequitable economic development drove mass mobilization and protest that shattered several seemingly stable, U.S.-backed authoritarian regimes, which variously gave rise to military-led reformism, violent insurrection, and revolution. From such disparate initial outcomes, however, a new and coherent pattern emerged by the 1990s—all of Central America's governments became civilian electoral democracies. The following chapters trace in much greater detail the transformation of Central America's regimes country by country.

6

REVOLUTION, COUNTERREVOLUTION, AND DEMOCRATIC TRANSITION IN NICARAGUA

Although much of Central America passed from dictatorship and violent conflict in the 1970s and 1980s to relative tranquillity and democratic forms in the 1990s, Nicaragua alone made this transition through a successful insurrection and more than a decade of revolutionary government. This unique case, with its possibly unique implications for the future, therefore deserves careful examination. In this chapter we will look closely at both the revolution—its origins, nature, and legacy—and the process of democratic transition that began in the 1980s and continued into the postrevolutionary period of the 1990s.

ROOTS OF CLASS CONFLICT

Under the direction of the Somozas and the stimulus of the Central American Common Market and Alliance for Progress, Nicaragua underwent rapid industrialization and expansion of commercial export agriculture during the 1960s and early 1970s. Overall economic growth statistics were impressive; per capita gross domestic product rose an average of almost 3.9 percent for the decade 1962–1971, and an average of 2.3 percent between 1972 and 1976 (see Appendix, Table 1). One gauge of the extent and speed of social change during the CACM boom is that between 1960 and 1970, real GDP per capita in Nicaragua rose by 54 percent—by far the greatest increase in the region. This jump in overall production was accompanied by other kinds of social change: Between 1960 and 1980 Nicaragua had Central America's biggest surge in urban population and manufacturing output and its biggest drop in the agricultural work force (see Appendix, Tables 2 and 3).

Income

Despite such impressive growth, policies of the government prevented the benefits from this new economic activity from finding their way into the pockets of poorer Nicaraguans. Unions were generally repressed, wages—normally set by the regime—were kept low, and consumer prices rose rapidly. The data in Tables 5 through 8 (Appendix) reveal what happened to the income and living conditions of working-class Nicaraguans during this period of very rapid economic growth. Consumer prices in Nicaragua rose at a moderate average of about 3.6 percent per year between 1963 and 1972 (see Appendix, Table 5). But then the 1973 Organization of Petroleum Exporting Countries (OPEC) oil embargo and subsequent rapid escalation of oil prices set off a severe wave of inflation—from 1973 through 1977, consumer price increases averaged 10.7 percent per year.

Inflation might not have been a problem for ordinary Nicaraguans had their earnings kept pace with prices. But the wages earned by working-class people did not keep up with soaring consumer prices. An index of real working-class wages (wages corrected for consumer price increases) in manufacturing, transportation, and construction for the period from 1963 through 1979 is presented in Table 6.[1] Real working-class wages rose in Nicaragua from 1963 until about 1967. But by 1970 real wages had peaked and gone into a decade-long slide that by 1979 had eaten away over one-third of their 1967 purchasing power. Therefore, during the 1970s, employed, wage-earning Nicaraguans suffered a palpable drop in their ability to feed and shelter their families.

There are other indications that income was shifting away from working-class Nicaraguans in the 1970s. One such measure is the share of national income paid out as employee compensation (Appendix, Table 7). A decrease in the value of the index of employee compensation indicates a relative shift of income away from salaried and wage-earning workers and toward investors and entrepreneurs. During the 1960s, Nicaraguan employees' share of national income increased, but then it took a sharp drop in 1974 and 1975. Although it is somewhat risky to estimate changes beyond the 1975 end of our data, the working-class wage trends reported for Nicaragua in the later 1970s (Appendix, Table 6) strongly suggest that the employee share of the income pie most likely shrank still further.

Although unfortunately we lack an earlier bench mark for comparison, we can state that income inequality between rich and poor Nicaraguans had become very great by 1977, when the wealthiest fifth of the people earned 59.9 percent of the national income, while the poorer half were left with only 15.0 percent.[2] The devastating December 24, 1972, earthquake probably triggered this shift in income away from wage earners when it put tens of thousands of white- and blue-collar workers out of work.

Nicaragua's middle class, which experienced a decade of improving living standards during the 1960s, suffered a sharp reversal as of 1973. Middle-class employment opportunities shrank markedly in the mid-1970s as many small businesses and commercial jobs were destroyed by the Managua earthquake. Nine thousand manufacturing jobs disappeared from 1972 to 1973 (about 13 percent of the total), as did fifteen thousand service sector jobs (over 7 percent of the total). Many new jobs appeared in the poorer-paid and lower-prestige construction sector, which nearly doubled in size by 1974, and in the informal sector.[3] Those who remained employed found their salaries subjected to a stiff surtax to finance reconstruction (much of the proceeds of the surtax were being stolen by corrupt officials). The work week was also increased by as much as 25 percent, but with no increase in salary.[4]

Employment

Not only did real wages and income distribution shift, to the detriment of working-class groups during the CACM boom, but also employment opportunities in Nicaragua failed to keep up with the rapid growth of the work force. Moreover, underemployment—an inability to find full-time work or acceptance of agricultural wage labor because of insufficient farmland for family subsistence farming—was generally believed to affect from one to five times as much of the economically active population as did unemployment. Data on unemployment from 1970 through the early 1980s appear in Table 8 (Appendix).[5] Overall, Nicaraguan unemployment rates rose steadily from less than 4 percent in 1970 to 13 percent in 1978—more than tripling, despite rapid economic growth. Among groups hit very hard by unemployment were workers left jobless by the earth-quake, and peasants forced off the land by the rapid expansion of agricultural production for export.

Wealth

During the 1960s and 1970s, Nicaragua's three major capitalist factions, which centered around the Banco de América, the Banco Nicaragüense, and the Somoza family interests, began to converge.[6] Once separated from each other by regional, clan, and political party differences, these great investor factions increasingly prospered and intertwined their investments under the CACM industrialization boom and the stimulative economic policies of the Somoza regime. Following the Managua earthquake, however, the Somoza faction became aggressively greedy and began to undermine the relative positions and profits of the other investor groups. At the same time, growing political and labor unrest caused many Nicaraguan capitalists to doubt whether the regime could continue to promote beneficial growth. Anastasio Somoza Debayle's once-growing support among the upper classes began to erode in the mid-1970s and thus prevented the development of a unified bourgeoisie.

In agriculture, concentration of land ownership increased from the 1950s through the 1970s, especially in the fertile and populous Pacific zone. High cotton prices permitted speculating largeholders to squeeze subsistence cultivators off the land and into an already oversupplied wage labor market.[7] "The process of agricultural development was a concentrator of both land and income."[8] By 1977, the 1.4 percent of farms larger than 350 hectares[9] contained 41.2 percent of the cultivated land, but roughly 60,000 campesinos had no land at all. Small farms (less than 4.0 hectares) made up 36.8 percent of Nicaragua's farms but occupied only 1.7 percent of the cultivated land. In the 1950s

> the State favored policies oriented to preferentially support those agroindustries [belonging to the Somozas' and their cohorts]. This situation intensified in the following decade and [included] not only financial, trade, and credit policies . . . but also the use of the public budget and institutions to supply them with labor, machinery, electricity, administrators, transport, etc.[10]

In sum, both relative and absolute measures of income and wealth reveal that during the 1970s poor and middle-class Nicaraguans lost some of their share of overall national income and wealth, and suffered a sharp drop in their real earning power. Such a loss in both relative economic standing and effective income doubtless gave many Nicaraguans strong economic grievances.

POPULAR MOBILIZATION

The decline of working-class wages in the late 1960s and early 1970s was followed by the revitalization of the nation's long suppressed industrial labor movement,[11] which stepped up organization, work stoppages, and strikes in pursuit of wage gains in 1973–1975.[12] A decline of middle-class living standards due to inflation and to the effects of the Managua earthquake also spawned considerable growth of union membership and organization and a surge of strikes by public sector white-collar workers, such as teachers and health personnel. Catholic social workers, missionaries, and priests began organizing unions among Pacific-zone peasant wage laborers in the 1960s. As a tool for teaching the gospel, Catholic social promoters also organized hundreds of small Christian Base Communities (CEBs) among urban and rural poor people. These CEBs taught catechism and encouraged community self-help activism.[13] Peasant unions increasingly pressed for wage gains, and CEBs, for better urban services and housing. CEBs among the urban poor multiplied rapidly after the Managua quake, as did similar Protestant-organized self-help groups. The peasant union movement gained great momentum after 1975.[14]

As the economy deteriorated, especially after 1974, Nicaraguan private sector pressure organizations grew and became more boldly critical of the government. Such private sector groups increased their calls for political and economic reform. For example, the Democratic Liberation Union (Unión Democrática de Liberación—UDEL), dominated by business leaders, appeared in 1974. UDEL not only called for reform but also attempted to promote some "trickle-down" development of cooperative business enterprises to benefit poorer Nicaraguans.

New opposition political parties (particularly, the Social Christian) became increasingly active in Nicaragua in the 1960s and 1970s,[15] and new anti-Somoza factions of the old Conservative and Liberal parties developed during the 1970s. Elements from the Conservative party united with the Social Christian party and the anti-Somoza Independent Liberal party in the National Opposition Union (Unión Nacional Opositora—UNO) to contest the 1967 national election. Student opposition to the regime grew rapidly during the 1970s. The Sandinista National Liberation Front (Frente Sandinista de Liberación Nacional—FSLN), the only surviving rebel group of some twenty guerrilla bands that had appeared between 1959 and 1962, greatly expanded its links to and support from university student groups during the 1970s.[16]

GOVERNMENT REPRESSION AND ITS EFFECT ON OPPOSITION

President Anastasio Somoza Debayle declared a state of siege and began a program of demobilization in late December 1974 after an embarrassing FSLN hostage-taking incident. During the resultant three-year reign of terror in rural areas (especially in the department of Zelaya), the National Guard murdered several thousand (mostly innocent) people suspected as subversives or possible FSLN sympathizers. Among the victims were many Catholic lay catechists, CEB members, and countless peasants in zones where the FSLN supposedly operated.[17] During a brief lifting of the state of siege because of Carter administration pressure, public protests against the regime rose rapidly. The government reacted by redoubling repression by the National Guard, especially in urban areas. The guard openly targeted youths from the early teens up because they were suspected of pro-Sandinista sympathies. The military and police dragged hundreds from their homes and the streets and murdered them. From 1977 on, the National Guard conducted an ever-intensifying war against the people of Nicaragua. Such repression eventually drove thousands, especially young people, to join the FSLN.

Following the January 1978 assassination of Pedro Joaquín Chamorro, bourgeois elements redoubled their activity in opposition to the Somoza regime. Key business interests such as the Superior Council of Private Initiative (Consejo Superior de la Iniciativa Privada—COSIP) joined with unions and moderate parties to support general strikes, and to form the Broad Opposition Front (Frente Amplio Opositor—FAO). Strongly backed by the United States and Nicaragua's Catholic hierarchy, the FAO strove unsuccessfully to negotiate an end to the Somoza regime before the FSLN could overthrow it militarily.[18]

Popular uprisings occurred all over urban Nicaragua between August and October 1978. On August 23, 1978, a small Sandinista unit seized the National Palace, taking more than two thousand hostages, including most members of the Chamber of Deputies. They negotiated the release of sixty Sandinistas from prison, a ransom, and safe passage out of the country. Days later, opposition leaders called a successful general strike. In September, thousands of people spontaneously attacked National Guard posts and drove the regime's troops out of several communities. These community revolts in Masaya, Rivas, Jinotega, Matagalpa, Estelí, and several parts of Managua typically occurred without significant advanced coordination by the FSLN. But the National Guard brutally crushed each uprising, one by one. The guard would concentrate its forces around each rebel town, cut off its utilities, and then shell and bomb it for several days before sending troops in to recapture it. These wars against the rebellious towns inflicted catastrophic losses of civilian life and massive damage to property and public services.

The FSLN, split for several years over tactics, realized that popular outrage had doomed the regime and rendered its tactical debate sterile. The three Sandinista factions quickly reunified in 1979 under the Joint National Directorate (Dirección Nacional Conjunta—DNC) and began to build a network of wealthy and influential supporters that included a dozen prominent citizens, known as the Group of Twelve (Grupo de los Doce). When the FAO-regime negotiations collapsed in early 1979, moderate and even conservative anti-Somocistas turned to the Sandinistas as the last option to defeat the regime. In 1979 the FSLN forged the United People's Movement (Movimiento Pueblo Unido—MPU) and National Patriotic Front (Frente Patriótico Nacional—FPN) coalitions, confederations of regime opponents made up of virtually all opposition forces in Nicaragua. The MPU and FPN, under the military leadership of the FSLN, were committed to the defeat of the Somoza regime. In May 1979 an FSLN-led provisional government was formed in San José, Costa Rica, to formally embody the opposition's revolutionary claim to sovereignty.

By opening its military ranks to all regime opponents and by forging broad alliances, the FSLN availed itself of extensive financial, organizational, and human resources within Nicaragua for the final offensive against the regime. Its military ranks flourished, ballooning from less than 500 troops under arms in mid-1978 to between 2,500 and 5,000 by June 1979. Other key resources mobilized by the revolutionary coalition in 1979 included effective control over several parts of northern Nicaragua, sanctuary for bases and political operations in Costa Rica, diplomatic support from France and various Latin American regimes in the Organization of American States (OAS), and some external financial and arms support. FSLN agents purchased Belgian automatic rifles from private arms dealers in the United States and took delivery at a base camp in Honduras. Cuba, Venezuela, Panama, and Costa Rica cooperated in delivering a shipment of Western-made arms via Costa Rica for the final offensive of June 1979. Whenever FSLN forces entered a community in combat, many local residents would spontaneously fight alongside them or assist them in other ways, thus vastly enhancing the guerrillas' numerical strength and capabilities. This massive and direct popular combat participation inestimably strengthened the insurgents.

OUTCOME OF THE CHALLENGE TO SOVEREIGNTY

The FSLN and opposition coalition's unity, material resource base, popular support, military capacity, and external support all grew rapidly in late 1978 and 1979. The FSLN-MPU/FPN coalition's revolutionary government in exile in 1979 took advantage of enthusiastic support from Costa Rica, where it enjoyed political sanctuary and popular sympathy and where the FSLN had secure bases. Within Nicaragua, FSLN troops enjoyed massive voluntary popular support and assistance in combat against the National Guard.

The decline of the Somoza regime's strength in 1978 and 1979 presents a clear contrast to the opposition's growth. Nicaragua's population had risen in spontaneous revolt against Anastasio Somoza Debayle's government in dozens of incidents in late 1978. By late 1978 the regime had lost the support of virtually all social classes and interest sectors, save portions of Somoza's Liberal Nationalist party (Partido Liberal Nacionalista—PLN) and the National Guard. PLN and regime supporters—many very corrupt and anxious to escape with as much of their wealth as possible—began to abandon Nicaragua in late 1978 and early 1979. Neighboring Honduras and Costa Rica were soon flooded with Mercedes Benz autos driven out by Somoza cohorts and their families. The flow of desertions from Somoza's closest collaborators became a flood after National Guard troops casually murdered ABC reporter Bill Stewart before the network's own cameras on June 20, 1979. The tyrant's associates sensed that that horrible television footage had stripped away their last pretense of legitimacy outside Nicaragua.

The Carter administration had announced its opposition to Somoza's continued rule, a key loss of a traditional external prop for the regime. The United States cut off new aid to Nicaragua in the 1979 budget and prevented pending deliveries by some of Somoza's arms suppliers. Although the U.S. government wanted Somoza out of office, it also tried very hard but ineffectually to prevent the Sandinistas from winning power. Elsewhere in the hemisphere, the Organization of American States and numerous Latin American regimes had openly sided with the opposition by 1979. The cornered National Guard fought tenaciously against the Sandinistas and Nicaraguan people, but was progressively encircled and pushed back toward Managua during the seven-week final offensive. Having looted the

THE TRIUMPH. FSLN troops in a liberated military vehicle arriving at Somoza's bunker in Managua, July 1979 (photo by Thomas Walker).

national treasury of dollars for himself and his associates, Somoza ultimately gave up and left Nicaragua for Miami on July 17, 1979. When the guard collapsed two days later, the Sandinista-led rebel coalition took power. These dramatic events mark the first great regime change we examine in Central America, Nicaragua's passage from personalistic military rule to revolution. This regime change started not only a long process of transformation and violent resistance in Nicaragua but set in motion much change elsewhere in the isthmus (Chapters 7–9).

THE REVOLUTION

The revolutionary government faced an incredible array of problems. The war had killed 50,000 people—almost 2 percent of the populace. (An equivalent loss to the United States would be 4.5 million, or well over seventy-five times the U.S. death toll in the entire Vietnam War.) There was also an estimated $1.5 billion in property loss, all-important export and domestic staple food crops had gone unplanted, and the new government had inherited $1.6 billion in international debts from the old regime. To its great chagrin, the new government realized that it would have to assume and pay Somoza's debt in order to remain creditworthy in international financial circles. There were also serious longstanding problems of public health, housing, education, and nutrition, all of which had been exacerbated by the war.

The revolutionary coalition led by the Sandinistas sought to destroy the Somoza regime and its economic power base, to replace the old regime's brutality and inequality of treatment of Nicaraguans with a fairer, more humane, and less corrupt system, and to reactivate the war-damaged economy. The Sandinistas themselves wanted to move the economy toward socialism in order to improve the lot of the lower classes, to build a participatory democracy under their own leadership, and to integrate all Nicaraguans into the national social and political system. Others in the coalition disagreed about much of the Sandinistas' revolutionary program and hoped to wrest power from the FSLN or at least share power with it. Such profound differences over the ends of the revolution quickly established the lines of political conflict in revolutionary Nicaragua and shattered the anti-Somocista alliance.

U.S.-Nicaraguan Relations and the Contra War

The Sandinistas' main long-term concern was a fear that the United States might try to reverse the course of the Nicaraguan revolution, as it had done in the cases of other reformist or revolutionary Latin American governments (Guatemala in 1954, Cuba in 1961, the Dominican Republic in 1965, and Chile in 1973). Although the Carter administration had criticized and opposed Somoza, it had also worked tenaciously to keep the Sandinistas from power. For example, the United States had supported the FAO-Somoza negotiations of 1978, approved a $66 million International Monetary Fund loan to the Somoza regime in early 1979, and attempted to persuade the OAS to send "peacekeeping" troops to Nicaragua in June 1979. At the time of the FSLN victory, the CIA had sent DC-8 jets disguised with Red Cross markings to Managua to evacuate Somoza's officer corps to Miami.[19] Even before the Sandinistas came to power, President Carter had authorized the CIA to fund certain segments of the press and labor movement.[20]

The Carter administration offered the new regime a nervous hand of friendship in the form of diplomatic recognition, emergency relief aid and the release of suspended loans from prior years' aid packages in 1979, and a new $75 million loan commitment in 1980. In 1979–1980 the Sandinistas had fairly good working relations with U.S. Ambassador Lawrence Pezzullo but felt increasingly apprehensive about U.S. links to the several thousand national guardsmen who had escaped to Honduras and the United States. In fact, first the Argentine military and then the CIA quickly became involved in organizing the ex-Somocista forces, which were beginning to conduct terrorist activities in Nicaragua from their refuge in Honduras.[21] The behavior of the incoming Reagan administration simply confirmed the Sandinistas' worst fears. During his campaign, candidate Reagan had promised to try to reverse the Nicaraguan revolution, and his advisers had talked of "destabilizing" the Sandinista government. The 1980 Republican platform had "abhor[red] the Marxist-Sandinist takeover" in Nicaragua and called for cutting off all aid. As soon as Reagan took office in 1981, he claimed (with very little evidence) that Nicaragua was the main source of arms for the rebel movement in El Salvador. President Reagan immediately cut off the balance of the $75 million loan, as well as wheat purchase credits approved by President Carter.

The United States then began a policy of steadily escalating harassment, pressure, and aggression against Nicaragua. One aspect of that policy was indirect military pressure via massive aid to build up the Honduran military, continuous "maneuvers" in Honduras of from one thousand to several thousand U.S. troops, and intensive aerial, seaborne, and covert espionage of Nicaragua. Another aspect was constant U.S. efforts to isolate Nicaragua diplomatically from its neighbors in Central America. These pressures, sweetened with large amounts of U.S. aid, persuaded both Honduras and Costa Rica to provide sanctuary to anti-Sandinista rebels. The United States also succeeded in blocking progress toward an agreement among Central American nations negotiated by the Contadora nations (Mexico, Panama, Colombia, and Venezuela). The United States successfully pressured multilateral lending and development agencies to cut off credit to Nicaragua, and on May 7, 1985, the United States embargoed trade with Nicaragua. Reagan administration spokespersons and the Department of State conducted a publicity campaign—as energetic as it was inaccurate—to discredit and defame the revolutionary government of Nicaragua and to exalt those of the Sandinistas' enemies who might prove most malleable for U.S. purposes.

The centerpiece of the Reagan administration's strategy for Nicaragua was a military and political effort to topple the Sandinista regime. In 1981 Reagan gave the CIA $19.8 million to support and augment an exile army of anti-Sandinista counterrevolutionaries. (Their original sponsors and organizers—Argentine Army Intelligence Battalion 601—were also central actors in Argentina's infamous "Dirty War.") The Nicaraguan counterrevolutionaries, whose nucleus consisted of former National Guard officers and soldiers and political allies of the former dictator, became known as the "contras." By 1982 attacks across the Honduran border were occurring almost daily. Contra forces regularly sabotaged bridges and other economic targets and had taken almost a thousand civilian and military lives within Nicaragua by the end of that year.

By the following year five major groups made up the contra forces; the most important among them were the Honduras-based Nicaraguan Democratic Force (Fuerzas Democráticas Nicaragüenses—FDN) and the Costa Rica-based Revolutionary Democratic Alliance (Alianza Revolucionaria Democrática—ARDE) and two Miskito Indian groups. In 1983 the contras began extensive guerrilla operations within Nicaragua, especially in the rugged terrain of the northeast and southeast. The CIA added to the destruction caused by the contras by blowing up Nicaraguan oil storage tanks and pipelines and mining harbors on both coasts. The CIA also supported the contras with intelligence, funding, and training (including a comic-book-style manual on sabotage for contra foot soldiers and a more sophisticated training book for contra leaders, *Psychological Operations in Guerrilla Warfare,* which recommended political assassinations of pro-Sandinista civilians and the deliberate creation of martyrs from among anti-Sandinista ranks).[22]

By 1985 the contras had amassed some 15,000 persons under arms but had achieved no significant successes against the Nicaraguan military. They had, however, established a clear record of economic sabotage, atrocities against civilians, and had taken some 13,000 lives. In the mid-1980s, the U.S. Congress was proving to be an increasingly unreliable funding source for the contra war and had placed legal restrictions on U.S. efforts to topple the Sandinistas. As a consequence, the Reagan administration made increasing efforts to fund and assist the contras covertly. These efforts included operations (some of them only marginally legal and some flatly illegal) by the National Security Council's Col. Oliver North and by other executive branch agencies. They resulted in huge monetary "contributions" by private domestic actors, friendly foreign governments, and allegedly, even the infamous Medellín cocaine cartel—which, according to sworn testimony at the Noriega trial by one of its former bosses, Carlos Lehder, chipped in $10 million on one occasion alone.[23]

When the Iran-Contra scandal broke in October 1986, placing further U.S. funding to the contras in doubt, the Reagan administration pressed the contras to intensify their offensive within Nicaragua. Supported by a legal CIA-run military supply operation in 1987, this offensive brought the war to its destructive peak and eventually raised the death toll for the entire war to just under 31,000. Despite the great increase in combat operations within Nicaragua, the contras' military successes remained very limited. After the Central American Peace Accord was signed in August 1987, the contras eventually entered negotiations with the Sandinista government (1988), and the war began to wind down.

A contra political directorate had been organized by the United States in the early 1980s to present a more palatable public front that might facilitate continued funding by Congress. However, this unified front proved quite unstable and broke apart more than once. In its last form, the contra directorate was called the Nicaraguan Resistance (Resistencia Nicaragüense—RN) and was feuding internally even as it negotiated with the Sandinistas. Although there had been considerable contra exfiltration to Honduras and most contra units had virtually disbanded by early 1989, the new Bush administration called for continued U.S. aid to help hold them together. Direct U.S. aid to the contras by 1989 had totaled over $400 million. In the long run, they would not be formally disarmed and disbanded until mid-1990, months after the Sandinistas were forced from office through the externally manipulated election of February 1990.

The Revolutionary Government

What kind of government was it to which the Reagan administration reacted so antagonistically? The FSLN consolidated its political dominance over the new government by early 1980, while maintaining other coalition members on the

THE CONTRA WAR. Peasant children in a feeding program at a war refugee agricultural self-defense resettlement camp (photo by Steve Cagan). Infrastructural damage: A food storage facility destroyed by the contras (photo by Thomas Walker). Repatriated contras who had laid down their arms in 1985 in accordance with the Nicaraguan government's amnesty program declared late in 1983 (photo by Steven Cagan).

junta, in the cabinet, and in the Council of State (Consejo de Estado). Though it was clear that the FSLN's nine-man DNC held ultimate veto power over the nature of the government and its programs, the Sandinistas created a pluralist system in which representatives of the upper-class minority were encouraged to participate. Upper-class, business, and various political party interests, while present in the coalition, were not allowed to dominate policy and therefore became increasingly antagonistic toward the FSLN. The regime maintained a dialogue with major business interests through their principal representative, the Superior Council of Private Enterprise (Consejo Superior de la Empresa Privada—COSEP),[24] and with a coalition of parties that had taken on the role of opposition to the regime.

The Sandinistas sought to build their own brand of democracy, one that emphasized popular participation in formulating and implementing public policy and the distribution of services and programs to the great mass of poor Nicaraguans. At first scornful of national elections because the dictatorial old regime had always manipulated them, the revolutionary government announced its intention in mid-1980 to postpone national elections until 1985. Immediately after the rebel victory, however, local elections took place all over Nicaragua. The Sandinistas also encouraged the widespread formation of grassroots organizations of women, workers, peasants, youth, children, and neighborhoods. Through these organizations hundreds of thousands of Nicaraguans debated and voted on issues, worked collectively to solve local problems, took part in carrying out national health and literacy campaigns, petitioned their government, and met with officials, elected officers, and representatives to governmental bodies and national organizations. The formation of labor unions was also encouraged, and organized labor grew rapidly. Labor's demands for higher wages, however, soon ran afoul of government needs for economic austerity and the FSLN desire for dominance within the movement.

The Sandinistas argued from the first that the new system must tolerate diversity of political opinion, not only because they had come to power as part of a coalition, but also because they were trying to maintain a mixed economy that required the cooperation of the privileged classes and because the international climate required political pluralism for the survival of the revolution. When the junta added new pro-Sandinista groups to the Council of State in 1980, several other party groups cried foul and began to coalesce into an open opposition to the government. The climate for political opposition within the revolution remained open, but not completely free. Other parties suffered from constraints on their press coverage and public activities under the State of Emergency decreed in response to the contra war in 1982, and proregime crowds (*turbas*) sometimes harassed critics of the regime, especially between 1982 and 1984.

The Council of State debated and passed election and party laws that had been heavily influenced by the opposition. The government set national elections for president and National Assembly (to replace the junta and Council of State) in

November 1984. Most restrictions on parties and the press were lifted for the campaign; free and uncensored access to government radio and television was provided; and a vigorous campaign ensued among seven parties. International observers and the press[25] overwhelmingly agreed that the election occurred without fraud or intimidation by the FSLN, though it was marred by the decision of one conservative coalition not to participate and by the effort of another party's presidential candidate to drop out late in the campaign. U.S. pressure—part of the U.S. campaign to discredit the revolution in the United States and abroad—played a major role in dissuading these groups from taking part in the election. Daniel Ortega Saavedra, DNC member and coordinator of the junta, was elected president, with 63 percent of the total vote. Opposition parties divided about one-third of the National Assembly.

The National Assembly, elected in 1984 and inaugurated in 1985, was actually a constituent assembly. Its most immediate task was to write a new constitution for the republic. Contrary to the criticisms of the Reagan administration and its backers, the process through which Nicaragua went in order to produce its 1987 constitution was remarkably open and democratic. The constitution was written in very simple, direct language and provided a good framework for the rule of law, protection of human rights, checks and balances, and fair, competitive elections to be held at regular six-year intervals.[26] The new election system, constitution, and government structures formalized and institutionalized the revolutionary regime. It left the Sandinistas in power, but presiding over a regime that had much in common with other electoral democracies—the government accepted constitutional restraints and could be replaced in an election. Ironically, though Nicaraguan opposition figures in the 1980s were routinely quoted in the U.S. media condemning the allegedly totalitarian and undemocratic character of the constitution, most such criticism disappeared when the Sandinistas were voted out of power in 1990.

In all, despite the external attack and obstruction by their U.S.-backed enemies, the Sandinistas were quite successful in beginning their revolution.[27] They shaped a new governmental system, reactivated and reshaped much of the war-ravaged economy, and implemented numerous social programs. Health services were dramatically expanded both in curative and preventative medicine, and national vaccination and health education campaigns significantly lowered rates of polio, malaria, and infant mortality. A massive literacy crusade raised literacy rates from slightly under 50 percent to about 87 percent. Agrarian reform programs promoted increased national self-sufficiency in food production, formed thousands of cooperative agricultural enterprises, and distributed hundreds of thousands of acres of farmland to individuals and cooperatives.

The growth of the contra war, however, forced the government to reorganize itself in order to defend the revolution—which, ironically, also meant the postponement of many of its central social and economic programs. By 1987 over half of the national budget went for military expenditures and the armed forces had been expanded to 60,000 regulars and over 100,000 militia. (Pentagon experts normally recommend a ratio of about 10 government troops to contain 1 guerrilla or irregular troop.) Evidence of the shift in government priorities soon became tangible for Nicaraguans. Social reforms, medical, health, and educational programs and public service development all suffered noticeably from the heavy military spending burden. Medical care deteriorated, garbage pickup and water service in Managua were curtailed, schools began to go without supplies and repairs, buses and taxis rusted for lack of parts and repairs. From 1979 through 1983 we noticed in our periodic visits to Nicaragua that the regime had made evident material progress in recovery from the 1972 earthquake and the 1977–1979 war. From 1984 on, each visit showed new signs of physical decay and reversals of earlier progress.

Human Rights

The human rights performance of the revolutionary government, though not perfect, was unusually good for a revolutionary regime and vastly superior to that of Somoza and the other governments of northern Central America.[28] The government moved swiftly to prevent its own supporters and forces from perpetrating human rights abuses in the chaotic days after seizing power. It established a new Sandinista Police and Sandinista Popular Army and worked to curtail abuse of authority by their officials. It humanely treated thousands of captured National Guard troops and officials, who were investigated, tried for their crimes, and sentenced. International human rights agencies have criticized the unfair procedures of the Special Tribunals, which tried the 6,300 former guardsmen, but these special courts dismissed charges against or acquitted 22 percent of the prisoners. Despite the heinous crimes of which some prisoners were convicted, none were executed. By 1985 more than half of those sentenced had completed their sentences, received a pardon, or had been released on appeal.[29]

Despite the correct suspicion that the opposition newspaper was receiving CIA funding to publish antigovernment propaganda,[30] the regime allowed *La Prensa* to operate for almost three years without precensorship. During that period, however, the government closed the bitterly critical paper several times, for two to three days on each occasion, for publishing false information in violation of the press law. Under the mounting pressure of the contra war, the revolutionary government in 1982 decreed a State of Emergency that suspended most civil guarantees and implemented prior press censorship. All media, including FSLN's own *Barricada* and the proregime *El Nuevo Diario,* as well as independent radio news programs, underwent prior censorship of news content thereafter. Censorship eased substantially and many other civil rights were restored in 1984 before the national election, but an expansion of the war in 1985–1986 led to reinstitution of many restrictions in that period. The government closed *La Prensa* indefinitely in June 1986 for supporting U.S. aid to the contras,[31] but permitted it to reopen without precensorship after the Central American Peace Accord was signed.

Two other areas of human rights proved most problematic for the revolutionary government. In 1982 the growing contra war prompted relocation of eight thousand Miskito Indians from their homes in the war zone along the Río Coco to inland camps. Poorly handled by the regime, the relocation angered many Miskitos, caused thousands to flee, and led many to join two anti-Sandinista guerrilla groups. "The external conflict created a context in which Miskito demands for self-determination were seen by the Sandinistas as separatist and related to U.S. efforts to overthrow the government by arming indigenous insurgents and by attempting to turn world opinion against the Sandinistas through false accusations of 'genocide.'"[32]

With such perceptions, military and judicial authorities in the Atlantic zone did abuse Miskito rights, further worsening tensions in the area.[33] (We must insist here that all credible observers concur that the Reagan administration's often repeated charge of a "genocide" of the Miskito was false.[34]) By late 1983 the government realized the gravity of its errors. It began autonomy talks with Atlantic Coast indigenous peoples, aimed at increasing local self-determination, and in 1985 it permitted the Miskito to return to their homes. Tensions subsided and Miskito support for the contras had all but disappeared by late 1986; a very progressive autonomy law was passed in 1987.

The practice of religion remained generally free in Nicaragua under the revolution, but the government became increasingly intolerant of those who expressed antiregime political goals through religious practice or groups. The government admitted many foreign missionaries of various sects and permitted churches to take part in the literacy crusade of 1980–1981. Many Catholics and numerous Protestant congregations, having provided much of the logistical support to the FSLN during the insurrection, ardently supported the new government and its policies. The hierarchy of the Catholic church, however, strongly and increasingly opposed Sandinista rule, and Church-regime conflict became overt by 1982. Certain Protestant sects' missionaries were denied entry to Nicaragua, and pro-FSLN groups on one occasion occupied properties of one sect before being evicted by the police.[35]

Relations between the government and Catholic church eroded rapidly during and after the trip of Pope John Paul II to Nicaragua in 1983. Each side apparently acted deliberately to provoke the other during the planning and execution of the visit. Archbishop Miguel Obando y Bravo became the leading figure of the internal opposition to the Sandinistas by 1984. From that time through the end of the Sandinista period, Obando (elevated to cardinal in 1985) and the Nicaraguan Council of Bishops were constant in their sharp criticism of government policy. The Iran-Contra hearings in the United States in 1987 revealed that Cardinal Obando had even received laundered financial support from the CIA. For its part, the Sandinista government punctuated its escalating criticism of the Church's po-

RELIGION AND REVOLUTION IN NICARAGUA. Lay "Delegates of the Word" being trained by a prorevolutionary priest to teach the social gospel (photo by Thomas Walker). Junta Coordinator Daniel Ortega (under the second "A" in "Nicaragua") and other government officials participating in the open session of the 1981 Central American Congress of the Student Christian Movement (photo and copyright by Tommie Sue Montgomery, 1981).

litical role with efforts at dialogue.[36] The Sandinistas expressed their displeasure by periodically closing Catholic Radio and by deporting a dozen foreign-born priests active in opposition politics. Finally, in 1986, when Bishop Pablo Antonio Vega and Father Bismarck Carballo (a spokesman for the Archdiocese of Managua) endorsed the $100 million aid package for the contras being considered by the U.S. Congress, they were exiled.[37] Following the signing of the Central American Peace Accord in August 1987, however, these and other priests were permitted to return to Nicaragua.

In summary, assailed by increasing domestic criticism, worsening economic woes, and the continued contra war, the revolutionary government's human rights performance began to deteriorate in 1982. Things improved noticeably around the 1984 election, but the government suffered clear reversals and further decline after 1985. By 1986, Nicaragua's eroded human rights performance received more criticism by human rights organizations. Repression of government critics and opponents remained much less violent than in Guatemala and El Salvador but had clearly become more pronounced than before. International human rights observers cited the Nicaraguan government for intimidation, harassment, and illegal detention of opponents, independent union leaders, and human rights workers, as well as for press censorship, curtailment of labor union activity, and poor prison conditions. The human rights climate improved again in late 1987 and early 1988 but eroded somewhat in mid-1988 when domestic opposition elements staged a series of demonstrations. By late 1988, however, the human rights climate improved again as the government offered concessions to the opposition and announced national elections for early 1990.[38]

The Economy

Economic policy reflected moderation and pragmatism and varied greatly from models followed by other Marxist-led governments. The revolutionary government renegotiated the terms of the international debt it inherited from the Somoza regime. It also sought and obtained hundreds of millions of dollars in grants and "soft" loans from various governments and international organizations—mainly in the West. And though it confiscated the properties of the Somozas and their cohorts, it preserved and sought to encourage a private sector that accounted for between 50 and 60 percent of GDP. Within two years, the economy had recovered much of its prewar level of production. Agrarian reform did not take a radical form with heavy emphasis on state farming, but rather was responsive to peasant demands for individual or cooperative smallholdings.[39] Although it made many errors of execution of agrarian policy, the government adopted credit and pricing policies that encouraged key sectors of private export agriculture—the largest farmers—to keep producing. U.S. pressures to curtail Western credit to and trade with Nicaragua led ultimately to increasing reliance on the Eastern bloc for credit (Appendix, Table 9), other aid, and trade in the mid-1980s.

Despite such progress, Nicaraguan capitalists felt quite insecure under the revolutionary government and were generally reluctant to invest. Among factors contributing to their sense of insecurity were the business sector's lack of control over the political system and the Sandinista leadership's Marxist philosophy. Another was the substantial change in the rules of the economic game that came about when the revolutionary government nationalized the import-export sector, a key source of profits and of control over the business environment. Moreover, the industrial sector suffered from a general decline of the Central American Common Market due to the exhaustion of the growth potential of the CACM's import-substitution development model, from a general worldwide economic recession, and from the U.S. credit and trade embargoes.[40]

The Sandinista government quickly adopted several policies to benefit the majority of poor Nicaraguans—wage increases, food price subsidies, and expanded public services in health, welfare, and education—but such policies were undermined by new exigencies. As economic austerity needs became more pressing, the newly expanded labor movement was legally prohibited from striking. (In fact, despite this prohibition, many strikes took place and were generally tolerated.) Because taxes could not cover the array of services being attempted, the government borrowed heavily abroad. As the contra war forced the government to spend more and more on the military, security and social welfare spending could no longer be financed simultaneously out of existing tax and foreign credit revenues. In order to maintain continued critically needed foreign credit and with the external debt at over $5 billion by 1986, the revolutionary government had to enact further severe austerity measures to curtail imports (sharp currency devaluations, reduction of food subsidies and social program spending) in 1985 and 1986.

Because of the war, some government economic mismanagement, austerity measures, and declining public and private investment, consumer prices soared (Appendix, Table 5), shortages of many products grew rapidly between 1985 and 1989, and popular living standards and services deteriorated. "Urban wages in 1988 had fallen, according to some statistics, to only 10 percent of 1980 levels."[41] Interestingly, a major cause of the rapid acceleration of the economic crisis in 1986–1988 was apparently the sharp reduction in Soviet bloc economic assistance registered in 1986–1987 (see Appendix, Table 9). As the economy went increasingly out of control, inflation reached 1,200 percent in 1987 and a mind-boggling 33,602 percent in the following year. Only by enacting ever harsher austerity programs in late 1988 and early 1989 was the embattled government able to bring inflation for 1989 down to 1,690 percent.[42] In doing so, however, it drastically reduced social services and benefits for the common citizen and threw thousands of government employees out of work.

THE CONSERVATIVE RESTORATION

The 1990 Election

We noted earlier that in 1984, when the revolution was still quite successful and the Sandinistas were still popular, the U.S. approach to Nicaragua's election had been to urge an opposition boycott and to paint the whole procedure as a "Soviet-style farce." By the late 1980s, however, internal conditions in Nicaragua had changed so radically that U.S. strategy toward the next regularly scheduled elections—those of 1990—could be altered significantly. Washington policymakers knew that in any democratic system, when economic conditions get bad, voters tend to vote incumbents out of office. By 1989—the time of the run-up to the election—the U.S.-orchestrated "low-intensity war" and related policies of economic strangulation had brought a level of economic hardship to Nicaragua that would be almost incomprehensible to most U.S. citizens. U.S. policymakers were also aware that the Nicaraguan people were tired of the continuing toll in lives the war was taking. The 30,865 Nicaraguans on both sides who had died by the end of 1989[43] represented almost 1 percent of the country's population—equivalent proportionately to 2.25 million American citizens if the United States were to suffer a similar loss.

Accordingly, the U.S. strategy for Nicaragua's 1990 election consisted of two tracks. The first involved denunciations of the electoral laws, procedures, and conditions as apparent insurance should—as many polls suggested they might—the Nicaraguan people defy conventional wisdom and reelect the FSLN. The groundwork would thus have been laid to denounce the Sandinista victory as a fraud. The second track, however, involved working to ensure an opposition victory. As part of this track, Washington used millions of covert and promised overt dollars[44] to weld a united opposition (the National Opposition Union—UNO) out of fourteen disparate and squabbling microparties[45] and then to promote the electoral success of its candidates—in particular, Violeta Barrios de Chamorro for president. In the words of one State Department official at the time, the United States "micromanaged the opposition."[46] Another part of the second track was to apply massive external pressure on the Nicaraguan electorate. The contra war was escalated sharply from the time of voter registration in October 1989 onward.[47] President Bush described President Ortega as "an animal . . . a bull in a china shop."[48] Violeta Chamorro was received and embraced at the White House, and there were promises that both the war and the economic embargo would end should she win.

Under these circumstances, although both authors of this book had believed the opinion polls that predicted a Sandinista victory, it should not have been surprising—particularly to political scientists—that UNO scored a clearcut victory on February 25, 1990. Chamorro won about 55 percent of the valid presidential votes compared to Daniel Ortega's 41 percent. Of 92 seats in the National Assembly, UNO captured fifty-one, the FSLN won thirty-nine, and two independent parties took one apiece. Thus on April 25, 1990, Daniel Ortega placed the sash of presidential office on the shoulders of Chamorro, and an era of national self-assertion and moderate revolutionary change in Nicaragua came to an end.

A Unique Type of Transition

Characteristically, official Washington, much of the U.S. media, and many anti-Sandinista leaders in Nicaragua jubilantly hailed the inauguration of Violeta de Chamorro as a watershed passage for Nicaragua from what they often labeled a Marxist totalitarian dictatorship to Western-style democracy. That description, however, wildly distorts and rounds off the edges of reality. Nicaragua's transition had begun over a decade earlier and had yet to be fully consolidated as this edition was being written.

In a much more nuanced and accurate interpretation, Philip Williams argues that after the overthrow of Somoza in 1979, the revolutionary government had introduced two types of democracy in succession—"popular revolutionary democracy," typified by the mushrooming activity of grassroots organizations in the early 1980s, and more traditional electoral and constitutional democracy from 1984 onward. He concludes that "the unique legacy of ten years of revolution makes the consolidation of electoral democracy alone much more problematic in Nicaragua than in other Latin American cases."[49] Unlike the cases of Chile, Argentina, and Brazil, where formal democracy had returned immediately after long periods of violently demobilizing dictatorships, in Nicaragua post-Sandinista governments would have to contend with widespread grassroots participation by ordinary Nicaraguans who became politically active in the 1980s. Nicaraguan politics would be "messier" but in some senses arguably more democratic than elsewhere.

Williams was correct, but the legacy of the 1980s proved to be even more complicated than he expected. The U.S.-sponsored contra war and associated virulent propaganda and violence and repression by both sides had also left Nicaragua deeply polarized. This polarization and hatred would make the consolidation of democracy in post-1990 Nicaragua very difficult despite (indeed, in part because of) the mobilization of ordinary Nicaraguans into politics.

The Chamorro Years, 1990–1997

The Chamorro years are difficult to evaluate.[50] On the one hand, the new administration's economic and social policies caused considerable harm to the poor majority. There was no growth in per capita GDP from 1990 through 1996, the worst economic performance in Central America, and real wages remained at a tiny fraction of their levels in prior decades (Appendix, Tables 1, 2, and 6). Indeed, according to the United Nations Development Program's Human Develop-

THE END OF AN ERA. Revolutionary President Daniel Ortega places the sash of office on the shoulders of his U.S.-approved successor, Violeta Barrios de Chamorro, on April 25, 1990 (photo courtesy of *Barricada*).

ment Index (which is based on per capita income and social indicators such as education levels and life expectancy), Nicaragua's rank among nations had dropped from 85th in the world when Chamorro took office to 117th by the time she left.[51] On the other hand, her administration succeeded in taming runaway inflation and, after several years, restarted modest economic growth (Appendix, Tables 1 and 2). Most laudable, however, was President Chamorro's effort to make peace and bind up the political wounds of the Nicaraguan family. She believed that reconciliation was essential for successful governance in the short run and democratic consolidation in the future.

FORMAL PEACE IN NICARAGUA. At El Almendro in remote central Nicaragua, President Chamorro receives an AK47 rifle from a contra combatant in a ceremony on June 9, 1990, marking the end of the war (photo by Peter Northall, courtesy of the Regional Coordinating Body for Economic and Social Research [CRIES], Managua). At approximately the same time, near Yalí in northern Nicaragua, troops of the United Nations observer group in Central America give certificates of demobilization to thousands of contras and destroy the weapons they choose to turn in (photos by Juan Bautista Castagnino, head of Human Rights and Guarantees for the Organization of American States observer team in Nicaragua).

Economic and Social Policy. It would be unfair to say that the Chamorro administration introduced economic neoliberalism to Nicaragua. In fact, the Sandinistas had implemented harsh "structural reforms" in the late 1980s in response to the hyperinflation caused mainly by spending on the contra war. But the new administration embraced neoliberalism with enthusiasm and intensified its implementation. Government properties were privatized, government expenditures were cut, budgets were balanced, and tariff barriers were lowered.

Although these policies curbed inflation and eventually resulted in slight economic growth, they inevitably pummeled the poor majority. The downsizing of government, cutbacks in social services, privatization of state enterprises, credit policy that favored export agriculture over peasant production of domestic foodstuffs combined to exacerbate the misery of ordinary Nicaraguans. Unemployment, underemployment, drug addiction, crime rates, homelessness (especially among children), and domestic violence all soared.

Moreover, the nature of social programs changed rapidly. Public education was most drastically affected as ideologically conservative administrators quickly replaced textbooks that stressed national and prorevolutionary values with U.S.-approved and financed generic texts, many years out of date. As in the Somoza period, in those texts that dealt with Nicaraguan history, entire segments of reality were either downplayed or ignored (such as Sandino, the revolution, and its leaders). When asked about this one-sided presentation of history, one education ministry official commented simply, "History is written by the winners."[52]

Further aggravating the social picture, the demobilization of the contras and the bulk of the national armed forces threw tens of thousands of young men—with little training or experience in anything except violence—into the streets. Although the Chamorro administration promised ex-combatants land and resettlement benefits in the peace agreements of 1990, it ultimately fell far short of fully meeting these obligations. Sporadically, throughout the 1990s, rearmed contras ("recontras"), ex-Sandinista military ("recompas"), and mixed units of both ("revueltos") engaged in renewed guerrilla activity or banditry in rural areas.[53] Although organized armed conflict tended to decline after the mid-1990s, there were still cases of it even as this was being written in 1998.[54]

Politics and Government. Given that between its insurrection against Somoza (1978–1979) and the contra war (1981–1990) Nicaragua had lost almost 3 percent of its population (for comparison, the United States suffered about 2 percent dead on both sides during its civil war), it is not surprising that the period of the Chamorro administration was marked with intense political invective and conflict that sometimes turned violent. Indeed, what is really surprising is the fact that during this period considerable progress was made toward national reconciliation and democratic consolidation.

Grassroots organizations—representing the poor majority of Nicaraguans—played a significant role in the politics of this period. The Rural Worker's Association (ATC), the National Union of Farmers and Ranchers (UNAG), and mixed contra/compa groups of ex-combatants were involved in the negotiations regarding the privatization of state farms, successfully insisting that some of the land be deeded to former workers and ex-combatants. The National Workers' Front (Frente Nacional de Trabajadores—FNT) did the same in the privatization of urban state-owned properties. At other times, when the government was unresponsive, these and other groups marched, demonstrated, and went out on strikes to force government respect for their interests.

Meanwhile, the Chamorro administration steadfastly eschewed pressures from the United States (until 1993) and right-wing members of UNO to engage in a vengeful "de-Sandinization" program. Instead, she wisely allowed Sandinista General Humberto Ortega to remain as head of the military. Thus assured that there would not be an anti-Sandinista bloodbath, the FSLN accepted the rapid demobilization of the army from over 80,000 to less than 15,000 (and by 1998 to 12,000). In addition, the Chamorro government, the FSLN leadership, and a wide spectrum of politicians engaged in frequent bargaining, negotiation, and pact making. This ultimately resulted in a majority consensus in the National Assembly, which made possible the promulgation of a new Military Code (1994), some revisions of the 1987 Constitution (1995), and the passage of a "Property Stability Law 209" (1996) that set a framework for dealing with property disputes arising out of the revolutionary period. Clean elections held on the Atlantic Coast in 1994 also seemed to bode well for a successful consolidation of democracy.

However, many problems arose. Most of the ideologically diverse parties in the UNO coalition were soon alienated by President Chamorro's attempts at pact making, especially her gestures of reconciliation toward the Sandinistas. Many ex-UNO party leaders had won positions as mayors in Nicaragua's largest cities. Nurtured by U.S.A.I.D. funding destined exclusively for municipalities that had voted the Sandinistas out, these individuals engaged in public works and neopopulist politics, which won them wide popular support. Under their leadership, the old Liberal party—the majority party of Nicaragua until it became corrupted by the Somozas—resuscitated as various splinter Liberal parties fused under the banner of the Liberal Alliance (Alianza Liberal—AL). The Liberals did well in the Atlantic Coast elections of 1994, and they would win the national elections of 1996. A nasty dispute over constitutional reforms to strengthen the National Assembly, expand the Supreme Court, and prevent presidential self-succession paralyzed the government for much of 1994 and 1995.[55]

The 1996 Election. For the authors of this book, both of whom had been official observers at the elections of 1984, 1990, and 1996, the 1996 vote left much to be desired. In the politically polarized atmosphere of Nicaragua at the time, the right wing had insisted on a series of last-minute changes in the electoral law and in the personnel of the Supreme Electoral Council. The procedural modifications were hard to operationalize on such short notice, especially with the insufficient funding provided, and personnel changes introduced many inexperienced and partisan people into the system. Each step of the election suffered anomalies: registration, the campaign, preparation and delivery of materials, organization and operation of polling places, voting, vote reporting, and vote tabulation.

The worst problems occurred when mishandling of vote counts and materials at numerous precincts snarled the counting process after the polls closed. The Supreme Electoral Council (Consejo Supremo Electoral—CSE) found so many irregularities that it took over a month to announce official results. Ultimately the CSE had to throw out the votes from hundreds of precincts. Perhaps significantly, the bulk of them occurred in the three departments—Managua, Jinotega, and Matagalpa—whose electoral councils were under newly appointed Liberal presidents.

Against this background, the Liberal Alliance was triumphant, and by a margin that made the discarded presidential votes immaterial. AL presidential candidate Arnoldo Alemán beat perennial FSLN candidate Daniel Ortega by 51 as opposed to 38 percent of the vote. In the National Assembly, the Liberals took 42 seats as opposed to 36 for the FSLN and 15 divided among nine minor parties. Both Ortega and the presidential candidate who placed third denounced the Liberal victory as illegitimate. Later, however, the FSLN accepted the outcome of the election.[56]

Although this disorderly spectacle could not have significantly affected the final outcome of the presidential race, it could hardly have had a positive impact on the civic attitude of ordinary Nicaraguans. An impressive 86 percent of the electorate appears to have voted.[57] Yet, for those citizens who became "nonvoters" as a result of local tally annulments and others who heard the denouncements and saw images of widespread confusion and possible corruption via the media, the sense of voter efficacy must have been significantly diminished.[58]

The Beginning of the Alemán Administration

Arnoldo Alemán, the fifty-year-old lawyer/farmer who was inaugurated president in January 1997, had been a Liberal since the Somoza era. During the revolutionary period he developed a burning hatred for the Sandinistas, who in 1979 nationalized the banking conglomerate for which he worked and in 1989 seized his agricultural properties and put him under house arrest while his wife was dying of brain cancer. Elected to the Managua city council in 1990, he maneuvered to have himself chosen mayor by the council. As mayor, he governed as a neopopulist using U.S. aid funds to carry out highly visible public works for which he took full credit, employing the politically faithful, mixing with and proclaiming his concern for the poor, and identifying the Sandinistas as the cause of most of the country's problems. With financial and moral support from the Cuban and Nicaraguan exile communities in Miami, he and other Liberal mayors worked to create the Liberal Alliance out of various Liberal microparties that had survived the fall of Somoza.

Ironically, the Liberal victory of 1996 was also facilitated by the earlier behavior of some Sandinista leaders who badly undermined the party's image. As lame ducks in 1990, the FSLN government passed unseemly laws transferring much state property to top Sandinistas (dubbed "la piñata"). Out of power in 1994, the old guard discredited itself further by clinging to party leadership when challenged during a reform effort in 1994. A schism resulted; the breakaway Sandinista Renovation Movement (Movimiento de Renovación Sandinista—MRS) in 1995 tore much of the intellectual heart and talented leadership out of the FSLN just as the united and well-financed Liberals were gearing up for the 1996 election. Observers agreed that the 1995 schism stripped the FSLN of much of its resources, talent, and organizational capacity and that Daniel Ortega had become the party's virtual *caudillo.*[59]

Since this edition was written barely a year and a half into the Alemán administration, it seemed unfair to predict that government's ultimate impact on the process of democratic consolidation in Nicaragua. It was clear, however, that this beginning was not auspicious. Harboring an intense hatred of the Sandinistas and having not played a central role in the bargaining and consensus building that went into the National Assembly's rewriting of the "rules of the game" in the mid-1990s, Alemán and his Liberal plurality in the legislature immediately called into question the legitimacy of the 1994 Military Code, the 1995 amendments to the 1987 Constitution, and the 1996 Property Stability Law 202. The AL and some allied parties maneuvered to deprive the FSLN of their rightful number of seats on the executive body of the National Assembly.

These moves resulted in a prolonged period of chaos featuring general strikes, demonstrations, angry invective, renewed armed insurgency, FSLN boycotts of the National Assembly, constitutional challenges, sporadic attempts at public dialogue, and behind-the-scene bargaining between the leaders of the two major political forces. On the positive side, grassroots organizations representing peasants and urban workers were again active in defending their interests—especially as they related to the property issue.

Eventually, both international and domestic pressure for a compromise became irresistible. In the fall of 1997, private negotiations between legal teams for the FSLN and the government resolved the thorniest issue of the 1990s, that of property. In November, after only four hours of debate, 73 of the 93 members of the National Assembly voted to approve the Law of Urban and Rural Reformed Property. Its articles guaranteed formal titles for many of the smallholder beneficiaries of untitled property distribution during the 1980s and 1990s, provided for the indemnification of people who lost property, and stipulated that the major beneficiaries of the "piñata" would have to pay for all houses larger than 100 square meters.[60]

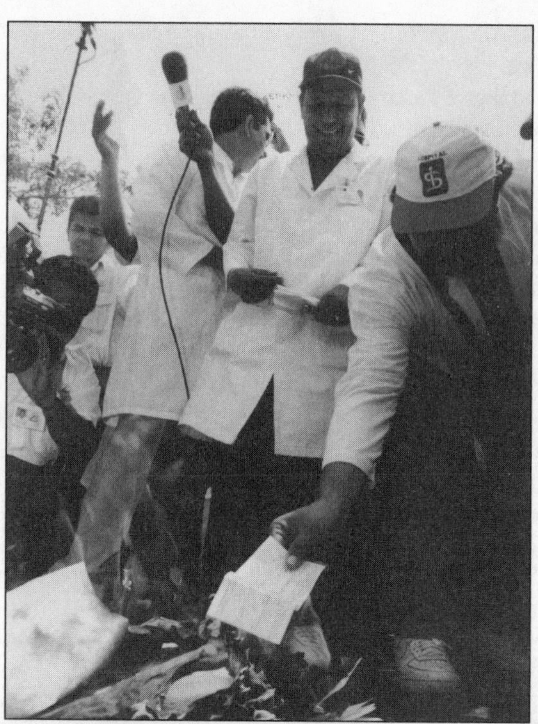

DEMONSTRATIONS IN OPPOSITION TO ALEMAN. *Doctors burn dismissal notices during lengthy doctors strike. Students oppose proposed cuts in government support for higher education. (Photos by and with the permission of Jorge Lopez,* La Tribuna*)*

It is tempting to say that by 1998 and with the settlement of the property issue a "new normalcy" was beginning to emerge in Nicaragua. In a short period the government announced a badly needed program of rural credit for small farmers; the International Monetary Fund agreed to renew support that had been suspended for two years; and an international consultative group consisting of various countries and organizations pledged loans of $1.8 billion over four years to promote macroeconomic stability, the development of agriculture, and governability. In addition, another round of clean (though low turnout) local elections were held in the Atlantic region.

As this was happening, however, the leaders of the two major parties each suffered personal scandals. Alemán was engulfed in escalating rumors of corruption culminating in the "Narcojet" scandal in which traces of cocaine were found in a rented (previously stolen) jet that had been serving as the "presidential plane" since the previous December. For his part, Ortega's thirty-year-old stepdaughter accused him of having sexually abused her over almost twenty years, beginning when she was eleven.[61] Although Alemán was able to avoid direct implication and Ortega clung to his role as leader of the FSLN, both leaders suffered irreparable damage to their prestige.

Late in 1998, hurricane Mitch and its related flooding, deaths, and infrastructure damage created grave problems for Nicaragua's already deeply depressed economy and for the Alemán administration. Much of the north of the country suffered heavily, with heavy damage to areas producing most of the nation's basic grains and coffee. The storm killed over 2,800 people, destroyed or damaged almost 42,000 homes, left 65,000 in shelters, and overall harmed 370,000 people—roughly one Nicaraguan in twelve. The press criticized the government for an insufficient civil defense program and for failing to respond to the disaster with sufficient speed. The president's approval ratings fell to new lows in a November 1998, and signs abounded of political maneuvering connected to the tragedy.[62] As this was being written, Hurricane Mitch appeared likely to have negative long-term consequences for both economy and government.

CONCLUSIONS

Rapid economic growth in the 1960s and 1970s worsened living conditions for the majority of working-class Nicaraguans. This mobilized many people into the political arena in the mid-1970s in search of better working and living conditions or modest reforms. When the Somoza regime brutally cracked down on its critics, the repression caused alliances to be forged among a broad front of opponents, radicalized their originally narrow demands into revolutionary ones, and united the opposition behind the once-weak FSLN. The new rebel coalition marshaled progressively greater resources, whereas those of the regime deteriorated, leading the revolutionaries to power.

The beginning of the revolutionary transformation of Nicaragua in July 1979 was a moment of Central American history no less important than the National War of 1857 or the establishment of the Panama Canal. However, when the Sandinistas consolidated their domination over the revolution, they catalyzed powerful internal and external political forces into more drastic actions in the isthmus. Internal opposition to the FSLN's program developed, and the United States mobilized and financed an armed counterrevolution from abroad. Eventually, the contra war and related programs of economic strangulation caused such economic deterioration and misery that a majority of the Nicaraguan people voted to replace their revolutionary government with one acceptable to Washington.

Nicaragua's transition to democracy, however, did not simply take place, as some would claim, on one day in April 1990. In fact, the country had been going through a stepwise transition begun in 1979 that would continue for some time. The Sandinista period had bequeathed the twin legacies of participatory democracy and formal electoral institutions. These survived through the Chamorro administration and into that of Alemán. Moreover, negotiation and pact making among political elites flourished during the Chamorro period and were still alive under her Liberal successor. However, the negative legacy of hatred and distrust flowing from the revolution and contra war in the 1980s so polarized Nicaragua that democratic consolidation at the close of the century was very difficult. With the end of the cold war, however, the international community was now exerting tremendous pressure for the preservation of democratic forms.

7

INSURRECTION AND REGIME CHANGE IN EL SALVADOR

El Salvador's violent passage from military authoritarian rule to civilian democracy followed a different path from Nicaragua's, but the forces of rapid economic change and repression driving the turmoil and regime change had striking similarities to those underlying the insurrection in Nicaragua. In El Salvador, as in Guatemala (Chapter 8), revolutionaries and power holders struggled in a protracted civil war marked by three regime changes, the last of which was a negotiated settlement that established a democracy that curtailed military power and allowed former rebels to participate in politics.

ROOTS OF CLASS CONFLICT

Income

The economy of El Salvador grew rapidly in the 1960s and 1970s. GDP per capita—a measure of overall economic activity in proportion to population—rose an average of 2.1 percent per year during the 1962–1971 decade, and even increased slightly for the 1972–1978 period to 2.3 percent per year. As noted for Nicaragua, however, the benefits of general economic growth in the Salvadoran economy were very unevenly distributed. Data on consumer prices in El Salvador, which inflated at an average of about 1.5 percent per year for the 1963–1972 decade, are presented in Table 5 (Appendix). Rising oil prices, however, drove consumer prices rapidly upward to an average of 12.8 percent per year from 1973 through 1979.

Did wages, set by the government, rise enough to compensate for this surging inflation? The evidence demonstrates clearly that they did not. An index of real working-class wages in agriculture, manufacturing, transportation, and communication in El Salvador is presented in Table 6 (Appendix). It reveals that real wages rose steadily in the 1960s and early 1970s, but declined sharply in 1974 and 1975, climbed again briefly in 1976, then skidded down even more steeply from 1977 to 1980. Salvadoran workers, thus, lost at least one-fifth of the real purchasing power of their income between 1973 and 1980. Moreover, the base of income of Salvadorans was very low in real terms. Expressed in constant 1986 dollars, per capita GDP in 1960 ($772), 1970 ($958), and 1980 ($1,044) was consistently the second lowest in Central America (Appendix, Table 2). The reader should bear in mind that such averages do not reflect the maldistribution of income. Thus for individuals in the poorer half of the population, the disposable annual income probably ranged from $50 to $150 (Appendix, Table 3), while food and clothing costs were little less than in the United States. Obviously, then, officially set wages for those lucky enough to be employed throughout the CACM boom period steadily lost effective purchasing power.

Employment

Did employment opportunity increase or decrease during the CACM boom? Despite the rapid industrialization and productivity growth of the Salvadoran economy, the capital-intensive production of consumer goods generated relatively few new jobs for the growing work force—just the opposite of what it was intended to do. Moreover, changes in the agrarian economy pushed hundreds of thousands of peasants off the land, also swelling joblessness. Estimates place unemployment in El Salvador at around 16 percent in 1970. By 1978 the unemployment level was estimated to have risen to 21 percent (Appendix, Table 8). After 1980 unemployment rose even more sharply because of the impact of the war; nervous investors closed some plants and disrupted Central American trade forced others to close. All expert observers of the Salvadoran economy concur that unemployment rose markedly during the 1970s, both in the countryside and in the cities.[1]

Wealth

In El Salvador during the 1970s, wealth became concentrated in fewer hands.[2] During the 1950s and 1960s much of the nation's best agricultural land had been converted to capital-intensive cultivation of export crops (in particular cotton) at the expense of subsistence-farming tenants, squatters, and small-holders. During the 1960s, pressure upon the land increased dramatically—the overall number of farms grew by 19 percent, but the land under cultivation shrank by 8 percent. The 1965 agricultural minimum wage law caused the number of *colonos* and *aparceros* (peasants cultivating for subsistence a plot of land donated by the owner) to drop to one-third of the 1961 level by 1971, and the amount of land so employed to drop to one-fifth of the earlier level.[3]

Thus, in the 1960s a dramatic change in Salvadoran rural class relations greatly increased rural poverty. There was a sharp increase in rental and ownership of tiny (less than 2.0 hectares) farms. From 1961 to 1971 the amount of land in rented small plots and the number of renters rose roughly 75 percent. The overall number of small plots of less than 2 hectares rose by one-third, but the amount of land in them rose by only one-fifth, so that the average size of all smallholdings shrank from 0.84 hectares to 0.79 hectares. Despite the increase in the number of small plots, the growing number of newly landless peasants swamped that change—the share of campesinos without land rose from 12 percent in 1961 to 41 percent in 1971. The largest farms (over 50 hectares) shrank in number by 4 percent and in extent by 14 percent.

Apparently many large farmers sold off part of their holdings for capital to invest elsewhere. It has been reported that members of this rural bourgeoisie invested heavily in the fast-expanding industrial sector during the 1960s and 1970s. They invested in technologically modern, mechanized, capital-intensive industries that generated large profits. Industrial production and industrial worker productivity grew rapidly while real industrial wages and level of employment actually declined.

According to experts on the Salvadoran economy, workers' share of the burgeoning national income deteriorated while production and investment became more centralized.[4] Major coffee growers invested roughly four times as much in industry as any other Salvadoran group, and attracted joint ventures with about 80 percent of the foreign capital invested in the country. Moreover, while the total output of Salvadoran industry more than doubled between 1967 and 1975, the number of firms actually producing goods diminished by as much as 10 percent. Orellana estimated that for the 1971 to 1979 period, wages and salaries received 44 percent of national income, while capital received 56 percent of national income as profit, dividends, interest, and rent.[5] Montgomery argued: "The old saying that 'money follows money' was never truer than in El Salvador. . . . These investment patterns not only contributed to an ever-greater concentration of wealth, but confirm that the traditional developmentalist assumption that wealth . . . will 'trickle down' in developing nations is groundless."[6] Orellana agreed: "The majority of Salvadorans, excluded from the benefits of that growth, were prevented from adequately satisfying their basic needs."[7]

Although El Salvador's capitalist elite apparently grew both relatively and absolutely wealthier during the mid-1970s, this pattern changed abruptly in 1979. The Nicaraguan revolution's impact on El Salvador's economy, plus the onset of extensive domestic popular mobilization and political unrest within El Salvador itself in 1978, brought about a sharp decline in investment and economic growth, beginning in 1979 (see Appendix, Table 1). The recession also stemmed partly from falling coffee prices and partly from the breakdown of Central American trade due to the exhaustion of the potential of the CACM import-substitution growth model. El Salvador's 1974–1978 average annual GDP growth rate of 5.3

percent was sharply reversed. The Salvadoran economy experienced a 3.1 percent *decline* in overall production and a 5.9 percent drop in GDP per capita in 1979. In 1980 the economic contraction deepened, with GDP per capita falling 11.7 percent. This severe recession not only harmed the interests of El Salvador's coffee producers and industrialists but also brought massive layoffs among their employees.

In summary, the development model followed by the Salvadoran state under the Central American Common Market increased overall production as well as the share of national wealth controlled by the national capitalist class. Employment and real wage changes reveal that not only did the Salvadoran working classes become relatively poorer during the 1970s, they became absolutely poorer, and markedly so. The purchasing power of working-class wage earners in El Salvador dropped sharply, beginning in 1973. Joblessness and underemployment rose steadily during much of the 1970s and accelerated late in the decade. When one considers the miserable earning power of the average poor Salvadoran, these facts compellingly demonstrate how severely the standard of living of most Salvadorans deteriorated during this period. Such declines in living conditions, measured for most people by such fundamentals as how much food they could put on the table each day, constituted powerful sources of political grievances among large numbers of Salvadorans.

POPULAR MOBILIZATION

Although the military's PRUD-PCN party always controlled the national government, new opposition parties from across the ideological spectrum appeared during the 1960s.[8] An early sign of growing political opposition was the appearance of two reformist parties: the social democratic National Revolutionary Movement (Movimiento Nacional Revolucionario—MNR) in 1959 and the Christian Democratic party (Partido Demócrata Cristiano—PDC) in 1960. The Democratic National Union (Unión Democrática Nacionalista—UDN), a coalition of leftist elements, formed in 1967.[9] The PDC and MNR briefly formed a legislative coalition with dissident deputies from the ruling PCN in the late 1960s. This coalition anticipated a major reform push by the National Opposition Union (Unión Nacional Opositora—UNO), an electoral coalition of the PDC, MNR, and UDN. UNO's presidential candidate, José Napoleón Duarte, apparently won the 1972 election but was denied the office by fraud. UNO reportedly also won the 1977 presidential election, but was again defrauded of victory.

A simmering stew of organizations (from unions to self-help organizations to peasant leagues), many promoted by the Church and by the new political parties, developed rapidly during the late 1960s and the 1970s. The number of cooperatives rose from 246 to 543 between 1973 and 1980.[10] Labor union membership among proletarians and middle-class workers rose steadily from the late 1960s, reaching 44,150 in 1970 and 71,000 by 1977; several unions, especially those of public employees, became more militant in their wage demands.[11] The number and frequency of strikes rose dramatically in 1974 in response to badly deteriorated wages; such disputes diminished in 1975–1976 as wages improved briefly, then escalated again rapidly in 1977–1978 as inflation ate away living standards (see Figure 1).

Development programs sponsored by the Catholic church, PDC, and even the U.S. Agency for International Development (USAID) swelled the number of working-class organizations in El Salvador during the 1960s and early 1970s. Catholic Christian base communities spread widely through urban and rural poor neighborhoods. In the 1970s the CEBs became increasingly involved in making political and economic demands on behalf of the poor. Numerous peasant organizations also developed during this period, in part encouraged by proposals for modest land reform during the regime of Col. Arturo Armando Molina (1972–1977). Peasant leagues began to press the government for land reform and for higher agricultural wages. The United Popular Action Front (Frente de Acción Popular Unida—FAPU), a coalition of labor unions, peasant organizations, university student groups, a teachers association, and the Communist Party of El Salvador (Partido Comunista de El Salvador—PCS), was formed in 1974. FAPU was the first of several such coalitions that would eventually build a very broadly based network of opposition.

Five Salvadoran guerrilla organizations formed between 1970 and 1979 to challenge the PCN regime militarily (see Appendix, Table 10). Each guerrilla group also forged a coalition with unions and other popular organizations between 1974 and 1979. The formation of these five coalitions greatly enhanced opposition capability and resources by permitting increased use of strikes and mass demonstrations and by generating other material resources for the armed opposition.

GOVERNMENT REPRESSION AND THE OPPOSITION

After 1970, the response of El Salvador's PCN military regimes to rapidly swelling popular mobilization became increasingly repressive.[12] A rightist paramilitary organization with direct ties to public security forces, the Nationalist Democratic Organization (Organización Democrática Nacionalista—ORDEN), formed in the late 1960s. ORDEN, whose acronym spells the Spanish word "order," recruited tens of thousands of peasants from among former military conscripts. Its purposes were to suppress peasant organization and to serve as an anti-Communist militia. ORDEN soon began to fulfill its grisly promise. It attacked and killed striking teachers in 1968 and thereafter became increasingly involved in violent repression. One of ORDEN's common techniques was to murder persons involved in organizing workers, peasants, or political opposition to the regime.

Presidents Arturo Armando Molina (1972–1977) and his handpicked successor Carlos Humberto Romero (1977–1979), both military officers, had close links

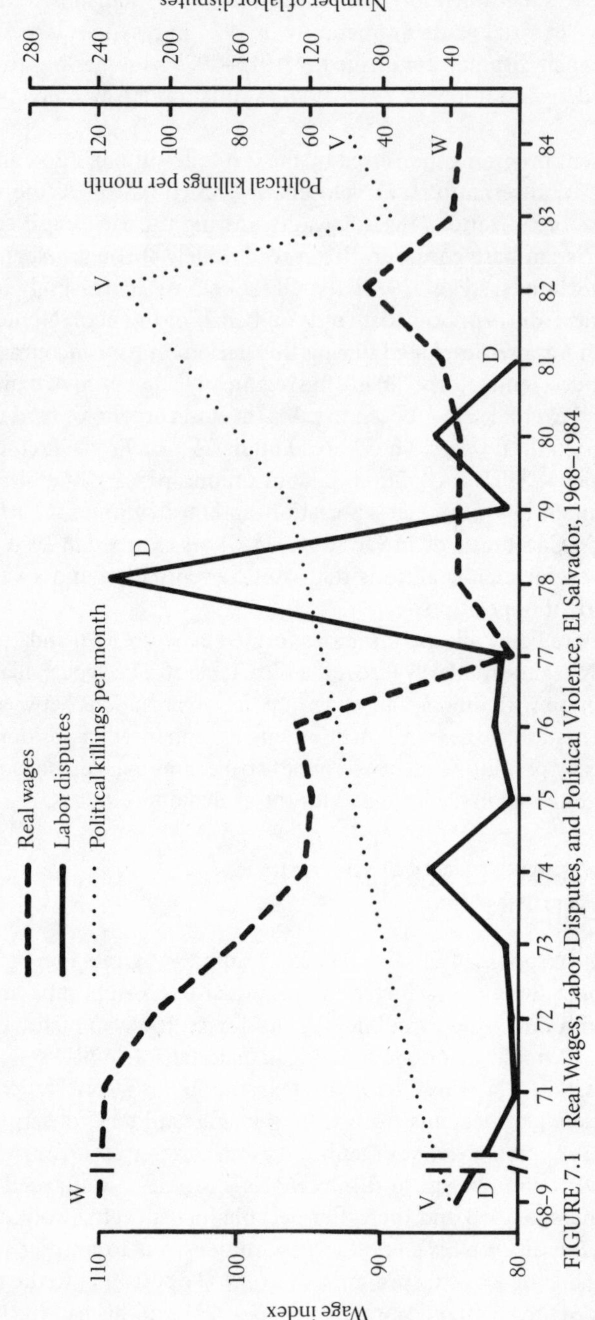

FIGURE 7.1 Real Wages, Labor Disputes, and Political Violence, El Salvador, 1968–1984

to key sectors of the agrarian oligarchy and staunchly opposed political and economic reform. As the first guerrilla actions began to occur and labor and peasant organization membership grew after 1973, regular security forces became much more overtly repressive. In 1974 National Guard and ORDEN forces murdered six peasants and "disappeared" several others affiliated with a Church-PDC peasant league. On July 30, 1975, troops killed at least thirty-seven students protesting the holding of the Miss Universe pageant in San Salvador. Regular government troops in the capital massacred an estimated two hundred of several thousand UNO supporters as they protested fraud in the 1977 presidential election. From 1975 on, "death squads," a label that McClintock characterized as a misnomer employed deliberately to disguise political terror by regular security forces and ORDEN,[13] became increasingly active. Beginning with the public assassination of opposition legislator and labor leader Rafael Aguinada Carranza in 1974, death squads assassinated and kidnapped dissidents, Catholic social activists, and priests and attacked church property. Eighteen Catholic clergy and religious personnel, including Archbishop Oscar Arnulfo Romero, were murdered between 1977 and 1982.[14]

Levels of political repression in El Salvador reached such heights in the late 1970s that official mortality statistics began to reflect the curve of terror. After falling wages led to sharply increased labor disputes in the 1977–1979 period, two separate indicators of violence showed dramatic increases (see Figure 2). The government's own annual tally of violent deaths, reported in official statistical abstracts,[15] rose from normal background levels of an average of 864 murders per year for 1965–1966 to 1,837 in 1977, and then skyrocketed to 11,471 violent deaths in 1980. The other index in Figure 2 is based on the number of political murders per year, reported by a Catholic church human rights agency.[16] Its data record a rise from an average of about 14 political murders per year between 1972 and 1977 to 299 per year for 1977–1978 and to 1,030 by 1979; the number then shot up to 8,024 for 1980, and 13,353 for 1981.

Statistics and graphs do not convey much of the intensity and nature of governmental abuse of human rights in El Salvador. The following violations became commonplace: searches of persons and residences on a massive scale; arbitrary, unmotivated, and unappealable arrests by secret police/military agencies; widespread and systematic use of physical and psychological torture; violent kidnappings; arbitrary and indefinite retention (often without charges) of prisoners; use of illegally obtained "confessions" extracted through torture or intimidation; official refusal to provide information about detainees; judicial corruption; extremely poor prison conditions; systematic impunity for human rights violators; government antagonism toward humanitarian, human rights, and relief agencies; and intimidation and harassment of prisoners or released prisoners and of their families. Among commonplace types of torture used by the military and police of El Salvador are the following:

ELECTION AGAINST THE BACKGROUND OF STATE-SPONSORED TERROR. Alfredo Cristiani and poster during his successful campaign in El Salvador in 1989. (Photo by Electra Press, courtesy of CRIES, Managua.)

> Lengthy uninterrupted interrogations during which the prisoner is denied food and sleep; electrical shocks; application of highly corrosive acids to the prisoner's body; hanging of prisoners by the feet and hands; hooding prisoners [for long periods]; introduction of objects into the anus; threats of rape; disrespectful fondling and rape; threats of death; simulation of death of the prisoner by removing him from the cell, blindfolded and tied, late at night, and firing shots [toward the prisoner but] into the air; all manner of blows; . . . [and] threats of rape, torture, and murder of loved ones of the prisoner. Among the thousands of murdered detainees, the signs of torture reach uncommon extremes of barbarism: dismemberment [of various types], mutilation of diverse members, removal of breasts and genitals, decapitation . . . and leaving of victims' remains in visible and public places[17]

The rapid rise of such government repression in the mid-1970s was followed by the formation of four large opposition coalitions; each linked several labor, peasant, and student groups to one of the guerrilla organizations. FAPU formed in 1974, the Revolutionary Popular Bloc (Bloque Popular Revolucionario—BPR) in 1975, the 28th of February Popular Leagues (Ligas Populares 28 de Febrero—LP-28) in 1978, and the Popular Liberation Movement (Movimiento de Liberación Popular—MLP) in 1979. By joining together and allying with armed rebels, the opposition coalitions' constituent groups committed themselves to revolutionary action. Together these confederations could mobilize hundreds of thousands of supporters into demonstrations and strikes and could raise funds and recruits for the guerrillas. Guerrilla groups also raised large war chests by kidnapping wealthy Salvadorans for ransom. After mid-1979 arms flowed to the guerrillas from private dealers in Costa Rica; other arms came through a sympathetic Nicaragua for a short period during 1980 and early 1981.

Growing opposition mobilization, the escalation of regime and rebel violence, the incapacity of the Romero government to address national problems, career frustration among certain groups of officers, and apprehension about the Sandinistas' victory in Nicaragua in July 1979 led to a first major regime change in El Salvador. A coalition of disgruntled senior officers and reformist younger officers staged a coup d'état that ousted President Romero, a former general. The October 15, 1979, coup temporarily allied these military factions with opposition social democrats of the MNR, the Christian Democrats (PDC), and some business factions. The Carter administration gambled that the reformist inclinations of the junta's members might stem the rising revolutionary tide and immediately endorsed the coup and reformist military regime it established.[18]

This new regime allowed some new civilian players (the MNR, PDC) and ousted some others (especially the PCN's Romero and his allies) and, with U.S. encouragement, proposed socioeconomic reforms. Nevertheless, the new junta failed to stem the rapidly escalating official violence.

Rightist elements soon gained ascendancy and expelled some of the reformers in early 1980. This caused the MNR and a majority faction of the Christian Democrats to abandon the junta. However, the support of the United States added a crucial new element to the political game, continued pressure for socioeconomic reform. The coup thus ushered in a reformist military regime that "signalled the exhaustion of traditional forms of political control and the search for a more viable system of domination. The old power apparatus was severely shaken."[19]

The October 1979 coup briefly raised opposition hopes for reform, but the restructuring of the junta in early 1980 and spiraling official violence quickly alienated much of the center and left and changed the opposition's tactics. Further unification of the opposition occurred quickly in early 1980: The five guerrilla groups joined together into the Farabundo Martí National Liberation Front (FMLN), in order to increase coordination of their political and military actions. Opposition forces then forged the Revolutionary Coordinator of the Masses (Coordinadora Revolucionaria de Masas—CRM) in January 1980 and continued massive strikes, protests, and guerrilla warfare. Several parties and mass coalitions, including the MNR and much of the PDC, then united into the Revolutionary Democratic Front (FDR). The FDR and FMLN soon allied to form the joint political-military opposition organization FMLN-FDR, which increasingly coordinated overall opposition revolutionary strategy, had some 4,000 troops and 5,000 militia, and controlled several zones of the country. The FMLN-FDR adopted a platform for a revolutionary government, began planning programs for the anticipated new regime, and established governmental structures within their zones of control.[20] In recognition of this clear and potentially effective challenge to the sovereignty of the junta, Mexico and France recognized the FMLN-FDR as a belligerent force, increasing the rebels' legitimacy. The FMLN-FDR's representatives operated openly in Panama, Nicaragua, Mexico, Colombia, and, ironically, the United States.

OUTCOME OF THE CHALLENGE TO SOVEREIGNTY

Momentum in the contest over sovereignty was shifting toward the Salvadoran opposition in 1979 and 1980. The rebels had progressively built a massive and cooperative popular base, acquired considerable financial resources, and had several thousand men and women under arms. The October 15, 1979, reformist coup linked the major opposition parties, a reformist military faction, and key middle-sector proponents of democracy in an effort to implement major structural reforms and curtail violence by the security forces. Within weeks, however, rightist elements gained ascendancy within the junta while regime violence actually escalated. This subverted the reformist opposition's tentative accession to power via the October coup and blocked its reform attempts.

The restructuring of the junta in early 1980 closed one middle (and less violent) path to change and drove much of the moderate center-left (the MNR and a majority of the PDC) into an alliance with the armed opposition. On January 30, 1980, Guillermo Ungo and other moderates resigned from the junta and cabinet. When the junta was reconstituted with more conservative elements of the Christian Democrats and government violence continued, the FDR formed (April 1980), followed by the FMLN (October 1980). By late 1980, guerrilla troops had seized effective control of huge areas of Morazán, La Unión, and Chalatenango provinces, so that "1981 opened with the army badly stretched and the undefeated FMLN poised for a major offensive."[21]

The government, in contrast, found its condition and support in disarray. The first junta itself was divided; the agenda of centrist MNR and PDC members for social reform was blocked by the more conservative military members. The junta had little support from the mass organizations and was opposed by most of the private sector. When the PDC joined the junta in 1980, the major organization representing Salvadoran capital, the National Association of Private Enterprises (Asociación Nacional de Empresas Privadas—ANEP) was so outraged that it began to boycott participation in the government. Rightist elements within and outside the military attempted several times to overthrow the regime. The poor performance of the armed forces—with only 15,000 ill-trained men—on the battlefield throughout 1980 suggested that the collapse of the regime was imminent.

The decision of the U.S. government to provide military aid to the failing Salvadoran armed forces profoundly altered the balance of forces between the regime and insurgents. The provision of military aid and advice and of economic assistance during the waning days of the Carter administration began the rescue of the Salvadoran regime. U.S. technical assistance and financing for the government and armed forces escalated rapidly under the Reagan administration. Carter's modest 1980 military assistance grant to El Salvador was $5.9 million. By 1985, U.S. military aid to El Salvador had reached the sum of $533 million. In the twelve years of the Salvadoran civil war, U.S. aid (military plus civilian) totaled about $6 billion.[22]

The Reagan administration, which heavily supported the PDC's Duarte, helped contain rightist opposition to the government and assisted with programs from agrarian reform to constituent assembly elections.[23] The U.S. military assistance (training, arms, munitions, aircraft, and intelligence) held the Salvadoran army together long enough to increase its size and capability so that it could effectively counteract the FMLN. Unlike what had occurred in Nicaragua, U.S. aid in El Salvador rescued the official armed forces and prolonged the conflict.

> The principal reason for the extended nature of the war was the capacity of the junta to hold its piecemeal military apparatus together . . . to ward off guerrilla offensives [and hold] the population in a state of terror. . . . It could only have achieved this or, indeed, survived for more than a few weeks with the resolute support of the U.S., which Somoza was, in the last instance, denied.[24]

FMLN REBELS. An FMLN platoon in eastern El Salvador in 1985 (photo by Tommie Sue Montgomery). Female guerrillas in northern Morazón Province, 1988 (photo by Steve Cagan).

The development and nature of the Salvadoran government after 1979 depended heavily upon the interaction among several major forces—hard-liners in control of the armed forces, major business interests, extremely rightist anti-Communist ideologues of the sort represented by Roberto D'Aubuisson and his Nationalist Republican Alliance party (Alianza Republicana Nacionalista—ARENA), and the Carter, Reagan, and Bush administrations. Indeed, a second change to a civilian transitional regime, marked by the advent of constitutional reform, elections, and formally civilian governments, occurred mainly because of pressure by the United States. The war went badly for the military during the early 1980s, and only massive U.S. economic, military, and technical assistance held off the FMLN.

The right fiercely opposed including moderates in government and much of the proposed reform, but dependence on U.S. aid undermined their resistance. Throughout most of the 1980s, the United States championed the cause of José Napoleón Duarte's faction of the PDC as the only acceptable political force to provide a legitimizing facade to the struggle against the armed opposition. Backed by the immense financial, technical, and political resources of the United States, Duarte was installed in the presidency and the PDC took a majority of the legisative seats via the 1984 presidential and 1985 legislative elections—both of dubious quality.[25] Thus began a new and rather shaky civilian transitional government that would eventually provide the institutional and legal foundation for greater democracy. The short-term goal of the United States in 1984 was to establish new political rules with formal civilian leadership and a broadening spectrum of participants. These political liberalizations would provide enough political space to moderates to keep them from aligning with the FMLN. Although detested as a "Communist" by the Right and distrusted by the military, Duarte with his U.S. backing was indispensible to both because they needed U.S. aid to avoid losing to the rebels. U.S. pressure upon the military and right was sufficient to protect the Duarte/PDC civil government but could neither control radical rightist forces nor compel them to permit social reform. In a very real sense, Duarte formally held the office of president without ever really coming to power.

U.S. presence in El Salvador during the Duarte period, then, created a very unstable and artificial coalition among highly incompatible elements. The Duarte government exercised no effective control over the security forces or the war.[26] Duarte's early initiatives to negotiate with the FMLN-FDR were effectively blocked by disapproval of both the Salvadoran military and the United States. Both wished to win the war rather than negotiate any type of shared power with the opposition. The constitution written in 1982–1983 effectively barred the most needed aspects of agrarian reform—probably the only program that might have removed some of the social pressures that led to the rebellion to begin with. The first civilian transitional government was unable to muster support from the business community or conservative parties for badly needed economic austerity programs, and the PDC's allied labor unions, Duarte's main base of mass support, became increasingly frustrated and reluctant to cooperate with the regime in the late 1980s. The inefficacy and growing corruption of the PDC, aggravated by internal divisions, led to the party's defeat by ARENA in the 1988 legislative elections. On March 19, 1989, moderate-appearing ARENA candidate Alfredo Cristiani won the presidential election, with party strongman Roberto D'Aubuisson discreetly in the background.

Presiding over this second administration in El Salvador's civilian transitional government, "Freddy" Cristiani came from one of his country's wealthiest aristocratic families. A graduate of Georgetown University, diplomatic and fluent in English, he was accepted quickly by the U.S. government and media as a worthy ally in spite of his affiliation with ARENA. In fact, although he was no great champion of social justice, Cristiani proved more moderate than many had expected. Among Cristiani's negatives were that he did little to improve the quality of elections held during his presidency or to clean up the nation's corrupt judiciary. On the positive side, his ARENA credentials helped him with the powerful armed forces and, with the assistance of the Central American Peace Accord and eventual U.S. acquiescence, permitted him to negotiate for peace with the FMLN.[27]

WAR AND PEACE

The situation in El Salvador during the early 1980s was a bloody stalemate. The rebels held their own against and adapted to increasingly powerful and sophisticated military pressure until 1984–1985. The FMLN showed little sign of weakening; indeed, FMLN troop strength reached about 10,000 by 1984. However, U.S. training, aid, and intelligence helped the regime's forces steadily gain ground in the mid-1980s as their transport, logistics, and tactics improved. By 1986 government troop strength had risen to 52,000 from the 1980 level of 15,000. In 1985–1986, rebel strength in the field apparently shrank by as much as half, to about 5,000, where it remained roughly static into the late 1980s.[28] This was partly because the growing government air power had curtailed the size of the guerrilla-controlled zones and because of an FMLN strategy shift.

The war ground on, however, and civilian casualties in rebel-held zones continued to escalate. In 1988 and 1989 the guerrillas revealed new capacity to operate effectively in urban areas. When the ARENA-led congress refused to postpone the March 1989 presidential election in response to an FMLN offer to return to peaceful civic competition, the FMLN attempted to disrupt the election by causing widespread power outages and disruption of transportation.

A dispassionate summary of some of the horror of El Salvador's civil war appears in Table 10 (Appendix). Some 42,000 people died between 1980 and 1982; another 30,000 died before the war ended. Virtually all objective observers blame at least 80 percent of these deaths on the military, the police, and ORDEN.[29] Intensifying pressure from a Reagan administration worried about continued U.S. Congressional support caused the Salvadoran military, police, and ORDEN to curtail sharply the numbers of deaths and disappearances in 1983 and 1984. Despite such efforts—in themselves revealing how much of the repression emanated directly from the security forces—increasing combat operations kept the casualty rate up in the mid-1980s. By 1989 some 70,000 Salvadorans had died in the revolt or repression. More than one in six of that nation's citizens had fled abroad. Even for those untouched by personal losses, the war, migration, and capital flight deepened the nation's depression and increased human misery. From 1980 through 1987 the economy slowed down by almost 10 percent of its 1980 per capita production level (see Appendix, Table 1).[30]

The Central American Peace Accord signed in Esquipulas, Guatemala, in August 1987 raised some hopes for a negotiated settlement of the Salvadoran war but little progress was made until the early 1990s. Starting in late 1982, the rebels had pushed for a compromise settlement rather than outright victory. In their opinion, a direct takeover of the government would have brought the type of U.S.-sponsored surrogate war and economic strangulation they were seeing inflicted on the Sandinistas in Nicaragua.[31] Throughout the 1980s, however, the United States and the Salvadoran Right had opposed a negotiated settlement, opting instead for outright victory over the insurgents.[32] Accordingly, although the Salvadoran government went through the motions of engaging in sporadic negotiation, no real progress took place for some time. Indeed, the Esquipulas agreement simply triggered a sharp upswing in the number of murders by the "death squads"—security forces.

The year 1989 brought things to a head. That spring the FMLN offered to participate in the upcoming presidential elections if the government would agree to postpone them for a six-month period so real democratic safeguards could be put in place. When the government went ahead with the elections as scheduled, the rebels escalated their military operations in outlying areas to demonstrate their strength and convince the government to become serious about negotiating. When this pressure also failed, late in the year the FMLN mounted a major and prolonged military offensive in the capital city, San Salvador. Under the cover of the confusion of this offensive, the military responded by murdering many noncombatants who it felt were sympathetic to the rebels. Most shocking were the murders of six prominent Jesuit priests-intellectuals, their housekeeper, and her daughter on the campus of the Central American University the night of November 16, 1989. Perpetrated by a unit of the U.S.-trained Atlacatl Battalion, this atrocity—according to a U.S. congressional investigation—was authorized the day before by a group of high-ranking officers including the chief of staff of the army and the head of the air force.[33] In the long run, the generals went free while two years later, a colonel and a lieutenant who had apparently acted under their orders became the very first Salvadoran officers to be convicted of human rights violations in the twelve-year history of that bloody war.

Eventually, the strength of the fall 1989 guerrilla offensive, the ugliness and embarrassment of the Jesuit massacre and other atrocities, and the end of the cold

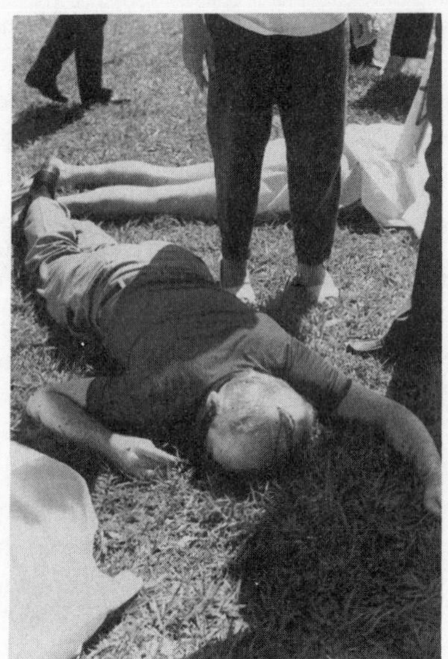

COMING TO A HEAD IN NOVEMBER 1989. The rebel offensive in San Salvador (photo by Arturo Robles, courtesy of CRIES, Managua). A scene from the aftermath of the murder of Jesuit intellectuals at the Central American University by a unit of the U.S.-trained Atlacatl Battalion (photo by Laurel Whitney, reprinted from *envio* with the permission of the Central American University, Managua).

war apparently convinced the United States to opt for a negotiated settlement in El Salvador. As a Rand Corporation specialist who wrote a report on El Salvador under contract to the U.S. Department of Defense put it, "The security concerns that impelled the policy have all but evaporated along with the East-West contest. . . . 'Winning' in El Salvador no longer matters much. A negotiated solution, or even 'losing' would no longer carry the same ominous significance.[34] In any event, the U.S. decision in the early 1990s to support the peace process cleared the way for a marathon and ultimately successful effort by outgoing United Nations Secretary-General Javier Pérez de Cuellar and his staff to bring the warring parties together. Toward the end, U.S. diplomats such as U.N. Ambassador Thomas Pickering and Assistant Secretary of State Bernard Aronson played a key role in pushing the Salvadoran government to make concessions. Finally, even ARENA founder Roberto D'Aubuisson—in a last public gesture before dying of cancer—endorsed the peace proposal.

The 1992 peace agreement began to alter the political landscape of El Salvador by ushering in a civilian democracy that allowed participation by a broad ideological spectrum. Under extensive U.N. supervision, the government drastically reduced the size of the army and made progress in depoliticizing the service, retiring and reassigning senior officers, and reforming military education. The military abolished its U.S.-trained rapid deployment forces (such as the infamous

Atlacatl Battalion), the Treasury Police, and the National Guard. The government dismantled the National Police, replacing it with a new National Civil Police (Polícia Nacional Civil—PNC) under civilian authority and drawing its personnel from both the FMLN and government ranks. A "truth commission" began to investigate the civil war. In return for these and other reforms, the FMLN demobilized by early 1993 and engaged openly in electoral politics.

CONCLUSIONS

El Salvador became a markedly different place after the accord. On the positive side, extensive foreign assistance from the United States and Europe smoothed transition, encouraged the formation of hundreds of civil society organizations, and provided former combatants training for new occupations. The economy improved sharply in the mid-1990s, although working-class wages continued to erode (Appendix, Tables 1, 2, and 6). The FMLN contested elections and won seats in the legislature, mayorships, and city councils posts. Human rights violations declined and monitoring groups operated freely. The press became much more free and able to engage in investigative reporting and commentary critical of the government. On the negative side, the human rights climate remained very imperfect, and several assassinations of FMLN or other leftist organization members revealed the persistence of death squad activities well into the mid-1990s. The restructuring of the police had serious problems, including a protracted period of extreme understaffing of the new PNC in many areas. A crime wave ensued as some demobilized police from the old force took to criminal activities (carjackings, bank robberies, kidnappings) and gang activity escalated among repatriated young U.S.-reared Salvadorans. Efforts began to reform the courts and criminal laws, both in desperate disarray, making punishment of lawbreakers difficult.[35] At the time of this publication, it was still too early to fully assess the balance on this new Salvadoran regime. Much remained to be accomplished with regard to institutional development, individual security, and human rights. Yet the wanton slaughter and material destruction of a decade of civil war had passed, and important steps had been taken toward democratic rules and at least formal reconciliation among formerly violent political competitors.

8

INSURRECTION AND REGIME CHANGE IN GUATEMALA

Guatemala's long and violent passage from military authoritarian rule to civilian democracy followed a different path from Nicaragua's, but one quite similar to El Salvador's. The forces of rapid economic change and repression that drove turmoil and regime change, however, were similar in all three nations. In Guatemala, as in El Salvador (Chapter 7), rebels and power holders fought a protracted civil war marked by three regime changes, the last of which was a negotiated settlement that established a democracy, curtailed military power, and permitted former rebels into the political arena. Unlike El Salvador, Guatemala's military governments were able to keep rebels at bay without much involvement by the United States.

ROOTS OF CLASS CONFLICT

Income

Under the economic guidance of the military-business partnership, Guatemala, too, experienced the same kind of rapid growth in overall economic output seen in Nicaragua and El Salvador. Per capita GDP grew at an average of 3.0 percent from 1962 through 1971, and at an average of 2.6 percent from 1972 through 1980 (Appendix, Table 1). During the CACM boom, per capita GDP in constant 1986 dollars rose from $1,020 to $1,732 between 1960 and 1980, a 70 percent increase and the second highest growth rate in Central America (Appendix, Table 2).

As in Nicaragua and El Salvador, however, the growth of the Guatemalan national economic pie did not mean increased income available to the poor. The average annual change in the consumer price index (CPI) from 1963 through 1972 was only 0.7 percent, but rose to 12.3 percent per annum for 1973–1979 (Appendix, Table 5). It can be seen in Table 6 (Appendix) that real wages did not keep up with inflation. Working-class wages peaked in 1967, then declined throughout the 1970s. In 1979 the effective purchasing power of real working-class wages had declined by over one-fourth of 1967 levels.

Income distribution also became markedly more unequal during the CACM boom. Between 1970 and 1984 income distribution became more and more concentrated in the hands of the wealthiest fifth of the population, whose share of national income rose from 46.5 to 55.0 to 56.8 percent for the years 1970, 1980, and 1984, respectively. The income share earned by Guatemala's poorest fifth of the population shrank from 6.8 to 5.5 to 4.8 percent for the same years. The share of the middle three-fifths of income earners also shrank, from 46.7 percent in 1970 to 39.5 percent in 1980 to 38.4 percent in 1984.[1]

Employment

Official unemployment statistics for Guatemala (Appendix, Table 8), which we can safely assume understate the true rate of joblessness, reveal a steady growth of unemployment even during the years of most rapid CACM-induced growth. Official unemployment rates rose from 4.8 percent in 1970 to 5.5 percent in 1980, and then nearly doubled to 10.0 percent by 1984. Estimated underemployment rates rose from 24.5 percent in 1973 to 31.2 percent in 1980 to 43.4 percent in 1984.[2]

Wealth

Data on wealth distribution have proven more difficult to obtain for Guatemala than for the rest of Central America, but recent studies permit certain inferences.[3] Land has long been very unequally distributed in Guatemala. The agrarian census of 1950 reported that farms smaller than 5 *manzanas* (roughly 3.5 hectares) made up 75.1 percent of the farms but only occupied 9.0 percent of the cultivated land. The 1.7 percent of farms larger than 64 *manzanas* (45 hectares) made up an astonishing 50.3 percent of the cultivated land.[4] The 1979 agricultural census revealed that inequality of landownership in Guatemala had increased, becoming the most extreme in Central America and the second most extreme ever reported in Latin America. The rapid growth of rural population reduced the amount of arable land per capita from a 1950 level of 1.71 hectares/capita to less than half that amount (.79) by 1980.[5]

In the late 1970s Indian agrarian unemployment began to rise while wages deteriorated. This change was accompanied by reports that communally and privately held land in the Indian highlands was being appropriated by Ladinos (mestizos). This concentration of landownership caused people to migrate from those regions to the cities or to public lands newly opened for colonization in the Petén and Izábal. Numerous reports, however, indicate that many small-holders in these departments were being driven off their new plots, especially by military officers and politicians who amassed much land in those zones.[6] To add to the increasing poverty of Guatemala's Indian peasants, the 1976 Guatemalan earthquake devastated the western highlands, sorely harming the living conditions of tens of thousands of rural poor.

Worker productivity in manufacturing grew steadily from the 1950s through the 1970s, yet, as already noted, both real wages and the working- and middle-class shares of national incomes declined sharply during the 1970s. The main beneficiaries of increasing productivity were both foreign and national investors.[7] During the same period the ownership of the means of industrial production became steadily more concentrated in a decreasing number of larger firms, while private sector pressure group organization became steadily more extensive and sophisticated.[8] In some industries modernization of production and growing concentration of ownership displaced many workers.

Although Guatemala's upper classes prospered during most of the 1970s because of the CACM industrialization boom and the relatively high coffee prices of that era, conditions began to deteriorate in 1981, when per capita GDP began a real decline, which continued through 1985. Among factors causing economic contraction in the early 1980s were declining commodity prices, the effect on trade of political unrest elsewhere in Central America, and capital flight. Thus, Guatemala's sharp general recession (as distinct from deteriorating real working-class wages) began around 1981 and deepened sharply in 1982. This slump, lagging four years behind a similar slump in Nicaragua and two years behind the one in El Salvador, seriously eroded the economic position of Guatemalan economic elites and made them critical of the economic management of the regimes of Generals Romeo Lucas García (1978–1982), Efraín Ríos Montt (1982–1983), and Oscar Humberto Mejía Víctores (1983–1986).

POPULAR MOBILIZATION

Reformist elements had promoted important changes under Guatemala's democratic governments of 1944–1954, but after the 1954 coup they suffered badly. The National Liberation Movement (MLN) regime and the armed forces embarked upon a program of demobilization that attacked and decimated the ranks of reformist politicians, unionists, and Indians who had supported the Arévalo and Arbenz governments. Marxist guerrilla opposition to the regime first appeared in 1962 (see Appendix, Table 10), but suffered a severe setback from the heavy general repression and from an intense counterinsurgency campaign in the late 1960s.[9]

Popular mobilization was rekindled in Guatemala during the 1970s as real wages fell and income distribution worsened, but still lagged behind levels in Nicaragua and El Salvador—probably because of heavier regime repression and the problems involved in organizing an ethnically more divided society.[10] The decline of manufacturing wages in the early 1970s was followed by a marked increase in unionization and industrial disputes during the government of Gen. Eugenio Kjell Laugerud García (1974–1978) (see Figure 8.1). When Laugerud momentarily eased repression of the labor movement in 1978, there was a wave of strikes. The 1976 earthquake's damage to lower-class housing had caused the mobilization of slum dwellers into two confederations. These groups pressed for housing assistance and in 1978 organized a transport boycott to protest increased bus fares.

Another factor mobilizing political participation during the 1960s and 1970s was the social Christian movement. The Christian Democratic party promoted hundreds of agrarian cooperatives and a labor union movement during the 1960s in an effort to build a constituency and organizational base. As in El Salvador and Nicaragua, Christian base communities appeared throughout much of poor rural and urban Guatemala during the early 1970s. CEBs helped organize community and labor groups among Guatemala's long quiescent Indian populace as the 1970s came to an end.

From 1970 into the 1980s the Guatemalan presidency remained firmly in the grip of high-ranking military officers, who ruled through the rightist Institutional Democratic party (PID) and National Liberation Movement (MLN). Despite military rule and repression, an explosive proliferation of political parties, factions, and coalitions occurred in Guatemala during that period. Led by the Christian Democrats, reform-oriented political parties of the center and left called for new policies and tried to win power through elections. The opposition was denied presidential election victories three times (1974, 1978, 1982) when the military regimes fraudulently manipulated election returns. Elections so clearly meant next to nothing that popular confidence in the political system ebbed. Abstention from elections rose steadily from 44 percent of registered voters in 1966 to 64 percent in the 1978 national election.[11] When the manipulation of the 1982 presidential election by incumbent president Lucas became publicly known, younger army officers overthrew the Lucas regime and installed Gen. Efraín Ríos Montt as president. This coup marked the onset of a very gradual process of successive regime changes that took fourteen years to complete. The coup's leaders intended for Ríos Montt to begin a process of return to civilian government while sharply escalating repression. The military reformers would soon oust Ríos Montt (1983) when his behavior threatened their reformist project, which was to transform the regime a second time to a transitional civilian regime. This would eventually take place in 1985, with the armed forces exerting extensive but gradually decreasing influence in successive civilian governments.

REPRESSION AND OPPOSITION UNDER REFORMIST MILITARY AND CIVILIAN TRANSITIONAL REGIMES

Guatemalan regimes had employed high levels of repression against labor union activists, students, peasant groups, Indians, opposition parties, and other dissidents during the counterrevolutionary period of the late 1950s. Somewhat re-

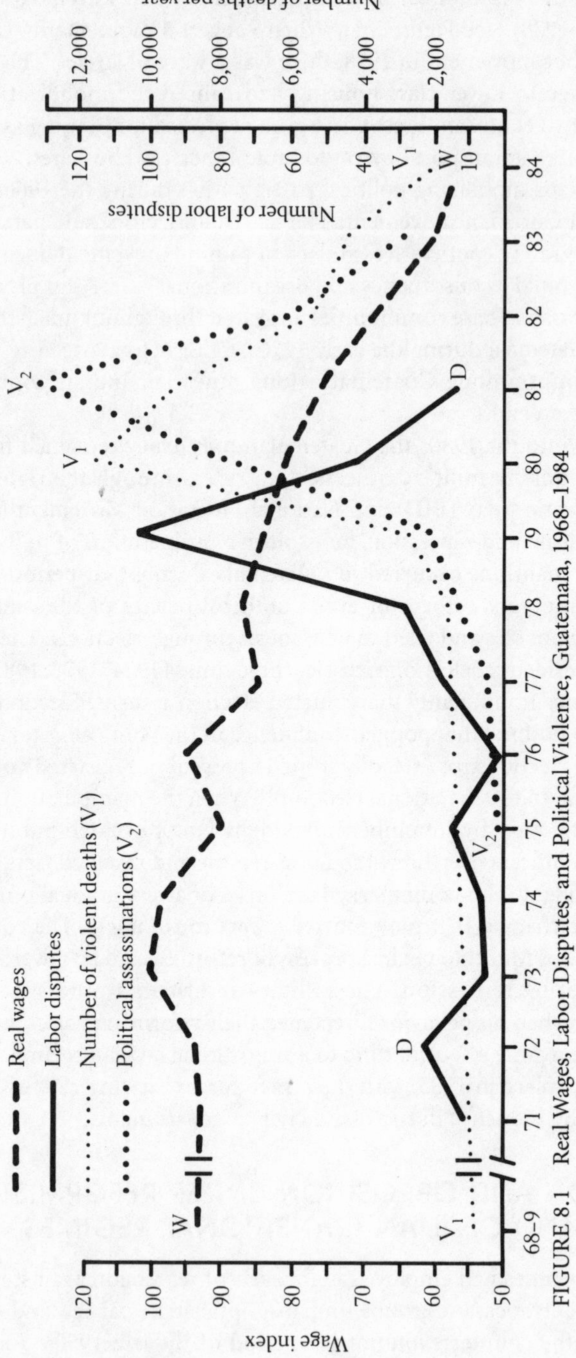

FIGURE 8.1 Real Wages, Labor Disputes, and Political Violence, Guatemala, 1968–1984

laxed during the early 1960s, such repression escalated sharply during the 1966–1970 administration of Julio César Méndez Montenegro (the first civilian president since 1954). In 1966 there appeared both private and public security force death squad terrorism, which consistently took dozens of lives a month. An aggressive 1968–1970 counterinsurgency campaign by the army decimated the Revolutionary Armed Forces (FAR) and the Edgar Ibarra Guerrilla Front (Frente Guerrillera Edgar Ibarra—FGEI) guerrilla movements. During the regimes of Col. Carlos Arana Osorio (1970–1974) and his successor Laugerud García, terror against unions, parties, students, peasant organizations, and cooperatives gradually increased.

Repression of popular opposition escalated to extreme levels in the late 1970s.[12] The 1978 election further stimulated opposition activity, especially to protest a fraudulent vote count that put the candidate of the military's PID, General Lucas García, in the presidency. The government of Lucas sharply escalated repression: It killed many people in response to popular protests about increased bus fares in 1978; death squads and the security forces assassinated tens of thousands of people between 1978 and 1982, including dozens of national and local leaders of the Democratic Socialist, Christian Democratic, and United Front of the Revolution parties. Hundreds of union leaders, university faculty, and student leaders also died or disappeared during the Lucas government.

General Lucas increased repression severely and rapidly (see Figure 2). Since 1960 the U.S. Embassy has tallied Guatemalan political murders. The vast bulk of these murders have been committed by government security forces and rightist death squads.[13] The average political murder rate—drawn from an index based primarily on urban areas—rose from about 30 per month in 1971 to 75 per month in 1979 and then soared to a peak of nearly 303 per month by 1982.[14] The number of rural killings by the army in counterinsurgency operations is thought by some to be much higher, although no reliable numerical measures exist.

As in El Salvador and under the Somozas in Nicaragua, repression of opposition failed to suppress mobilization and eventually generated even more intense opposition. In the countryside, peasant organizations led by the Peasant Unity Committee (CUC) stepped up organizing, and staged a major strike against sugar planters in 1980. In 1978 and 1979 the regrouped FAR and a new revolutionary group made up predominantly of Indians, the Organization of the People in Arms (ORPA) renewed armed actions in the western highlands. Soon afterward the Guerrilla Army of the Poor (EGP), also with strong indigenous support, resumed combat against the regime in the highlands. Estimates placed the number of guerrilla troops at around 4,000 by 1982; the rebels' popular support was widespread.

The armed forces, the backbone of the regime headed by General Lucas, confronted three critical problems in 1982. The first was the apparently massive support for the guerrillas among the large indigenous population in the western highlands and growing unrest in the countryside in general. The second was the economy, which slowed in 1979 and 1980, then contracted very sharply in 1981 and 1982 (Appendix, Table 1). Third, the Lucas government—unable to manage the economy, contain working-class unrest, or arrange successfully for its succession—had rapidly deteriorated, lost many allies, and entered a crisis marked by the fraudulent 1982 election. This crisis led a group of junior military officers to stage the coup that deposed General Lucas, annulled the 1982 election, and put General Efraín Ríos Montt into power.

The coup leaders' apparent dual strategy was to increase repression in order to crush the rebels and demobilize growing opposition while simultaneously reforming the political rules of the game by installing clean elections and eventual civilian rule under military tutelage. The first phase of this reformist military regime was that of Ríos Montt, who swept away the old rules of the game by annulling the constitution of 1965 and the electoral law, dissolving the Congress, suppressing political parties, and imposing a state of siege. Pursuing the political reform agenda, a Council of State wrote a new electoral law and called July 1984 elections for a constituent assembly that would draft a new constitution.

On the military agenda, repression escalated dramatically with the Guatemalan army's new rural counterinsurgency campaign in Indian zones that Ríos Montt's press secretary Francisco Bianchi justified in the following terms: "The guerrillas won over many Indian collaborators. Therefore, the Indians were subversives, right? And how do you fight subversion? Clearly, you had to kill Indians because they were collaborating with subversion. And then they would say, 'You're massacring innocent people.' But they weren't innocent. They had sold out to subversion."[15] The army committed numerous massacres of entire villages and many atrocities against suspected guerrilla sympathizers. The army forced the relocation and concentration of Indians, many of whom were pressed into work on modern, army owned farms producing vegetables to export, frozen, to the United States. The military formed army-controlled, mandatory "civil self-defense patrols" involving virtually all adult rural males. There are estimates that place the death toll from the rural counterinsurgency program as high as 150,000 persons between 1982 and 1985. U.S. Embassy violence statistics have tended not to register such massacres of Indians and other rural dwellers in the counterinsurgency program because embassy staff cannot easily verify the incidents.[16] At least 500,000 persons, mostly Indians, became internal or external refugees because of the counterinsurgency war that many anthropologists view as genocidal.[17]

Unable to detect any meaningful political reform in the violent, institution-wrecking behavior of the Ríos Montt government, groups in Guatemala's political center hunkered down or fled, while those of the leftist opposition attempted to forge coalitions to enhance their power and resource base.[18] The Democratic Front Against Repression (Frente Democrático Contra la Represión—FDCR) appeared in 1979. It included numerous unions and the PSD and FUR. Two years later, several of the FDCR's more radical elements—including the peasant federation CUC—split away from the FDCR and formed the January 13th Popular

Front (Frente Popular 13 de Enero—FP-13). In 1982 both the FP-13 and the FDCR endorsed yet another coalition effort led by a group of prominent regime opponents. This third group was the Guatemalan Committee of Patriotic Unity (Comité Guatemalteco de Unidad Patriótica—CGUP).

The nation's guerrilla groups united into the Guatemalan National Revolutionary Union (Unidad Revolucionaria Nacional Guatemalteca—URNG) in 1982 and issued a revolutionary manifesto challenging the regime's sovereignty. As late as 1989, however, the URNG had still failed to establish further formal links to other popular organizations or to political parties because the process of return to civilian rule had either kept or coaxed such groups back from the legal political arena. Labor unions, for example, were very reluctant to form any sort of political links that might jeopardize their legal status—even to legal political parties.[19]

One reason that broader coalitions between opposition groups and the rebels failed to form in Guatemala, as they had in Nicaragua and E1 Salvador, was that the military reformist regime began to succeed—at least in its efforts at political change. Rightist terrorism in urban areas was sharply curtailed after 1982, despite the intensification of rural counterinsurgency. President Ríos Montt's increasingly erratic public behavior, including links to evangelical Protestants, soon embarrassed the military reformists. They deposed him in August 1983 and replaced him with General. Oscar Humberto Mejía Victores, who carried forward political reforms. The electoral registry was reformed and a new voter registration undertaken. The constituent assembly elected in 1984 labored for a year and produced a new constitution that took effect in May 1985. Mejía Victores immediately called for elections, and some long-suppressed political forces of the center-left were allowed to resurface and contest the election.

Elections for president, congress, and municipalities were held in late 1985. Although the parties of the far left did not participate in the 1985 elections, centrist parties did take part. Even the social democratic PSD, which rightist terrorism had driven underground a few years before, tested the legal political venue once again. Though held against a backdrop of three decades of brutal and bloody demobilization, the election itself was generally free from the rightist terror against opposition parties. The Christian Democrats, led by presidential candidate Vinicio Cerezo Arévalo, won the presidency and a majority of the congress in clean elections in November and December 1985.[20]

Representatives of Guatemalan political parties admitted that they took part in the 1984 and 1985 elections and the constituent assembly because they believed the military seriously intended to reduce its role in governing.[21] Although doubts remained until the elections themselves were over, as the polling date drew nearer in October 1985, civilian political circles reported increasingly frequent signs of the military's determination to permit an open and fraud-free election. The military regime's opening to civilian politicians in the mid-1980s—especially its curtailment of terror against the centrist opposition and refusal to engage in electoral fraud in 1985—thus helped prevent the opposition parties from allying with the revolutionary Left. The marriage between the democratic center and leftist guerrillas in neighboring El Salvador had been a key step in the radicalization of the opposition.

The 1985 election ushered in the second of Guatemala's critical regime changes in its long, military-managed liberalization and culminated in a civilian transitional regime with new electoral rules and institutions for competing for public office and with a broader spectrum of political actors allowed into the arena. Powerful economic sectors that once supported military rule, reeling from three more years of miserable economic performance, began to embrace the prospect of a government and economy managed by elected civilians. Citizens noted the new arrangements and demonstrated expectations for an end to Guatemala's long, violent political nightmare by voting in the elections. In comparison to turnout in earlier elections (e.g., 1982's 46 percent), there were sharp increases in voter turnout in the elections of 1984 (78 percent) and 1985 (69 percent), especially in urban areas. This increase in electoral participation reflected widespread popular hope for peaceful change, at least among the urban populace, which had experienced diminished violence and increased political freedom.

THE CIVILIAN TRANSITIONAL REGIME AND THE CIVIL WAR

The civilian transitional regime confronted two critical, interconnected problems. The first was the civil war, a contest over the right to rule Guatemala in which President Cerezo and his successors had limited power over its antagonists, the armed forces and the URNG. The second was the consolidation of civilian rule and further progress toward democracy. In order to consolidate civilian, constitutional rule, the war had to end in a way that would both pacify the rebels and reduce the armed forces' enormous power in national political life. The various constituencies supporting the war needed to be persuaded to accept civilian constitutional rule. An additional grave problem was the continued deterioration of the economy. Progress on these fronts was halting and often seemed elusive.

The August 1987 Central American Peace Accord, which President Cerezo actively promoted, provided a rough, internationally endorsed blueprint for action by promoting political reconciliation and dialogue as well as formal democratization. Developments in Cerezo's effort to end the civil war, however, were discouraging because the military and rebels failed to cooperate fully. Cease-fire talks with the URNG, held in Madrid, were immediately suspended. The required National Reconciliation Commission was criticized as inefficacious by some of its own members, and dialogue between the government and other national political and economic forces was limited. The Guatemalan guerrilla war heated up in late 1987 as both the URNG and the army sought to improve their positions. Combat operations in early 1989 continued at a level that belied the military's claim of virtual victory over the URNG.[22]

These military developments and the gradual political changes wrought by the reformist military and civilian transitional regimes began to alter the resource balance between the parties to the war. Despite the fact that Guatemala's economic and military assistance from the United States remained a tiny fraction of that received by El Salvador (Appendix, Table 4), the military's and government's institutional capabilities remained fairly high. Political reform helped isolate the rebels from a broader political coalition while the army's brutal rural counterinsurgency program increasingly denied them access to their Indian supporters. Moreover, the military's retreat from executive power, the election of a new government, and new initiatives to improve the abysmal human rights situation (enactment of *habeas corpus* and *amparo* laws, a human rights ombudsman, and judicial reforms)[23] increased the government's domestic and external legitimacy. Economic performance improved markedly after 1987 (Appendix, Table 1). A better economy and increased legitimacy brought the Cerezo government additional resources that—at least for a while—rallied popular support. These factors, combined with the military's increased concentration on security matters, strengthened the government's position.

Despite a promising beginning, the Cerezo administration performed poorly in many areas. Business groups, opposition parties, and labor criticized Cerezo and the Christian Democratic party (Partido Demócrata Cristiano de Guatemala—PDCG) for a laundry list of ills: corruption, indecision and policy errors, economic problems, failure to address the needs of the poor, and lack of effective progress on human rights. Social mobilization increased. Several external human rights monitors and the government's own human rights ombudsman denounced escalating human rights abuses by the army and police against labor activists, union members, homeless street children, students, human rights advocates, religious workers, political party leaders, and foreigners (including two U.S. citizens—Diana Mack Ortiz, a nun, and businessman Michael Devine—and Salvadoran Social Democratic party leader Héctor Oqueli).[24]

This dismal record badly handicapped Cerezo's Christian Democratic party in the 1990 election. Neither did it seem particularly helpful to the PDCG at election time that—after twenty-five years of civil war—the government and the URNG began tentative peace negotiations in Oslo, Norway, in April 1990. By the mid-1980s, the URNG had changed its ultimate objective from outright military victory to the achievement of a negotiated settlement. In the early 1990s, several factors reinforced that decision: the high costs of continued fighting while cut off from its indigenous base and from more moderate allies, the collapse of the Soviet bloc, and the electoral defeat of the Sandinistas in Nicaragua. The army's new willingness to negotiate reflected a reported erosion of support for the military among the bourgeoisie, increasing criticism of military human rights violations, and the continuing attrition of the war.

The 1990 election was relatively free and clean, although the left remained excluded. Only about half of Guatemala's dispirited voters (a major decline from

1985) turned out for the two rounds of 1990 elections—a general ballot and a presidential runoff between two conservatives, newspaper publisher Jorge Carpio Nicolle and engineer Jorge Serrano Elías. Voters soundly rejected the discredited PDCG and elected Serrano, a Protestant with a populist flair who had promised to push the peace negotiations.

Serrano, a former minister in Ríos Montt's cabinet, appointed numerous military officials to his government. However, he responded with unexpected vigor to the escalation of human rights violations by detaining and prosecuting military officials, and he energetically pursued government negotiations with the URNG. The economy continued to worsen in 1991, however, leading Serrano to impose hard austerity measures.[25] The unhealthy economy and austerity measures led to slow growth and a contraction in real wages that mobilized popular protest, to which the security forces replied with a typical barrage of human rights abuses.

Serrano plunged the civilian transitional regime into a major political crisis on May 25, 1993, when (with the apparent acquiescence of part of the military) he responded to his multiple difficulties by attempting an *autogolpe* ("self-coup"). He illegally dissolved the Supreme Court and Congress (to "fight corruption"), censored the press, restricted civil liberties, and announced his intention to rule by decree. Most Guatemalan citizens, civil society organizations, and governmental institutions responded to this unconstitutional maneuver (called the *Serranazo*) with energetic protests. External actors such as the United States and Organization of American States made clear to Guatemalan political actors, including the military, that they and their international financial institutions—essential to Guatemala's economic recovery—would look with great disfavor on a deviation from constitutional practice.[26]

The combination of internal resistance and external pressure undermined the Serranazo and kept the civilian transitional regime on its constitutional track. The Court of Constitutionality, backed by an institutionalist military faction, ruled against Serrano and ousted him under provisions of the 1985 constitution. Congress elected Ramiro de León Carpio, the human rights ombudsman, to serve out the balance of the presidential term. President de León, unaffiliated with a political party but backed by a broad array of civil organizations, then pushed for a package of constitutional reforms enacted by Congress and ratified by popular referendum in January 1994. This initiated the election of a new Congress in August 1994 to serve out the rest of the term. The new Congress had large contingents from two parties that had campaigned against corruption, the right-wing populist Republican Front of Guatemala (Frente Republicano de Guatemala—FRG) headed by the infamous Efraín Ríos Montt and the center-right National Advancement party (Partido de Avance Nacional—PAN) of Guatemala City mayor Alvaro Arzú.[27]

The peace negotiations—stymied throughout most of 1993 by the Serranazo, restoration of constitutional rule, and foot-dragging by de León and the military—gained forward momentum in 1994 when they resumed under the mediation of the United Nations.[28] A January "Framework Accord" established a timetable and provided for an Asamblea de la Sociedad Civil (Assembly of Civil Society—ASC) that included almost all political parties and a diverse array of nongovernmental organizations, including women's and indigenous groups, to advise negotiators. Progress came steadily thereafter: In March 1994 negotiators signed a critical human rights accord that established a United Nations human rights monitoring mission; it began to operate in November. There followed agreements on the resettlement of displaced persons and on a historical clarification commission to study the long-term violence (both in June 1994) and a critical accord on indigenous rights (March 1995).[29]

As negotiations continued into 1995, another national election took place. Alvaro Arzú of the PAN and Efraín Ríos Montt of the FRG announced their candidacies for president. The Ríos candidacy prompted a protracted political flap because the constitution barred participants in prior de facto regimes from becoming president. The election tribunal ruled against the former dictator. After considerable initial bluster about running despite the ruling, Ríos and the FRG ran a stand-in candidate, Alfonso Portillo.

One key sign that change was afoot in Guatemala came when a coalition of leftist groups in the ASC formed a political party, the Frente Democrático Nueva Guatemala (New Guatemala Democratic Front—FDNG) to compete in the election. This was evidence of the left's growing confidence in its ability to participate in the system. The URNG suspended military actions during the final weeks of the campaign. In the November 1995 general election the FDNG took 6 of 80 seats in Congress, the PAN 43, and the FRG 21, with turnout up from the 1990 election. The FDNG and various indigenous civic committees captured several important mayoral races, including Quetzaltenango. In the presidential race neither Arzú (who favored peace negotiations) nor Portillo (the FRG and Ríos Montt openly opposed peace negotiations and promised if elected to rule with an iron hand) won a majority, prompting a January 1996 runoff, which the PAN's Arzú won by a scant 2 percent.[30]

Alvaro Arzú took office under worsening political portents: the URNG's resumption of military operations, labor protests, and soaring human rights abuses, including the assassination of two FDNG activists and an army attack on indigenous refugees.[31] The new president moved decisively to advance peace by shaking up the army high command and police, meeting with rebel leaders, and embracing negotiations. There ensued an indefinite cease-fire between the URNG and the army in March 1996, an accord on socioeconomic and agrarian issues (May 1996), and another—critically important—on civil-military relations (September 1996) that would increase civilian control of the armed forces, limit military authority to external defense, and replace the violent and corrupt national police.

On December 29, 1996, the government and the URNG signed the Final Peace Accord in Guatemala City, ending thirty-six years of civil war.[32] This agreement on new political rules for the nation, embracing the reforms of previous accords, marked the establishment of a new civilian democratic regime in Guatemala. The armed forces came under increased civilian authority and found their responsibilities curtailed. Police reform commenced. The rebels of the URNG, many groups of the left, the new FDNG, and indigenous peoples—previously repressed or otherwise excluded—had gained access to the political system as legal players. The URNG agreed to demobilize and participate within the constitutional framework. A wide array of civil society organizations, including those representing the bourgeoisie (heretofore ambivalent about the peace process and new democratization), embraced the new regime.

CONCLUSIONS

Guatemala still had far to travel before consolidating its new civilian democratic regime. The historic peace accord notwithstanding, turmoil of every sort persisted into the Arzú administration. With institutional reforms and continued removals of top police and military officials, human rights abuses declined but by no means disappeared. The president himself attempted to squelch press criticism and coverage. Police reform and the dismantling of the civil self-defense patrols in the short run actually reduced public security protection, contributing to a crime wave and the appearance of vigilantism by citizens.

Arzú's economic program of neoliberal reforms (privatization of electricity and telecommunications, budget cuts, fiscal reforms, trade and foreign exchange liberalization, and reduction of regulation) appeared destined to promote new economic growth but at the cost of short-term worsening of the nation's highly unequal distribution of income and increased poverty.[33] The civilian democratic regime and Arzú administration faced the daunting challenges of simultaneously rebuilding the economy under a neoliberal model while increasing socioeconomic equity and alleviating poverty sufficiently to permit meaningful popular participation in politics. There remained considerable potential that violent forces antagonistic to the democratic project and needed socioeconomic reforms might undermine the new regime.

Nothing more clearly revealed the challenges of the consolidation of civilian democracy in Guatemala than the murder of Auxiliary Archbishop Juan Gerardi Conedera on April 26, 1998. Two days after the Catholic church's Human Rights Office issued a report on civil war political violence to Guatemala's Historical Clarification Commission, Bishop Gerardi—one of its authors—was bludgeoned to death. Police quickly arrested an unconvincing suspect. Not long afterward, however, *Jaguar Justiciero*,[34] alleged in the report to be a death squad long connected to the presidential guard, claimed credit for the murder and began intimidating other Catholic human rights workers.[35]

In sum, although enormous progress toward peace and democracy had been made as this was being written, such a cold-blooded attack on such a visible actor in the peace process suggested that Guatemala might prove to be the most challenging case of democratic consolidation in Central America.

9

MAINTAINING STABILITY IN COSTA RICA AND HONDURAS

Costa Rica and Honduras suffered important negative effects from the Central American Common Market growth boom and the ensuing political and economic turmoil of the 1980s and 1990s. Both nations nevertheless managed to escape the violent upheaval and civil strife of the rest of the region and did so in spite of their very different political systems—Costa Rica already democratic, Honduras at first ruled by the armed forces. Despite the differences in their regime types at the outset, Costa Rica and Honduras owed their relative stability since the 1970s to the employment of a similar general strategy. That strategy involved government policy that alleviated some of the effects of eroding popular living standards and that either avoided or ameliorated brutal political repression.

SOURCES OF CLASS CONFLICT

Economic growth in both Honduras and Costa Rica was accelerated by the investment and industrialization booms associated with the Central American Common Market (see Appendix, Table 1). Costa Rica's per capita gross domestic product rose at an average annual rate of 3.4 percent during the 1962–1971 decade, and at an annual average of 2.6 percent from 1972 through 1979. Per capita GDP in constant 1986 dollars almost doubled, from $1,332 to $2,222 between 1960 and 1980. Among Central American nations, Costa Rica had the largest share of its work force (16 percent) in manufacturing by 1983. By 1987, Costa Rica (at 23 percent) ranked second in the isthmus in terms of manufacturing contribution to domestic production.[1] The agricultural sector work force shrank from 51 percent to 29 percent between 1960 and 1980. Commerce, services, and the government sector all expanded in Costa Rica as the nation rapidly modernized and urbanized.

Honduras was the nation of Central America least altered in social and economic structure by the common market. In the late 1970s, Honduras still reminded many observers of what the rest of the region had been like several decades before. Honduras' economic performance was certainly the least successful of the five CACM nations in terms of overall growth. Much of its new investment went into agriculture. Honduras' agricultural sector remained the largest in the isthmus (Appendix, Table 2), having only declined from 70 percent to 63 percent of the work force between 1960 and 1980. Even though its work force in manufacturing more than doubled (from 6 to 13 percent) between 1950 and 1983, the Honduran manufacturing sector remained the smallest in Central America.

Despite its relative slowness within the region, Honduras did experience a sustained period of overall economic growth. Per capita GDP growth averaged almost 1.5 percent per year between 1962 and 1971. As a consumer but not an exporter of manufactured consumer goods, Honduras quickly developed trade imbalances with other CACM nations and particularly with neighboring rival El Salvador. These trade imbalances and resulting economic difficulties worsened sharply after the 1969 war with El Salvador. These setbacks helped depress Honduran economic growth, which slowed to only 0.4 percent from 1972 through 1979. Overall, however, per capita GDP (in constant 1986 dollars) in Honduras rose from $575 in 1960 to $886 by 1980, a 54 percent increase. After 1980, the slow but sustained per capita GDP growth of 1960–1980 reversed, declining an average of 1.2 percent a year to $775 annually in 1990.

Income

The prevailing theory about the onset of rebellion in Central America argues that severe declines in real working-class wages and living conditions play an important role in mobilizing many people into labor, political, and protest organization and activity.[2] Because many urban and rural wage earners in Central American societies live on earnings that give them little or no margin of safety or surplus, a drop in their real earnings (wages corrected for inflation) can have catastrophic effects on their ability to survive. A rapid erosion of life chances can be a powerful impetus to join political or labor groups seeking redress of such problems.

Wage data on Costa Rica and Honduras reveal that wage workers in both countries lost ground relative to other income earners in the mid-1970s, but recovered much of their purchasing power by 1978–1979. The index of working-class wages in Table 6 (Appendix) shows that Costa Rican workers' wages fell in 1975 and 1976, but recovered and then began to exceed earlier levels significantly by the late 1970s. Wages dropped again in 1982 but began an immediate recovery in

1983–1984. Costa Ricans' real wages remained relatively high through the rest of the 1980s. In Honduras, wages fluctuated somewhat but experienced no sustained declines like those occurring in Guatemala, El Salvador, and Nicaragua at the same time. Honduran working-class wages fell in 1974 and 1975, recovered in 1976, fell again in 1977, and then rose to above 1973 levels again in 1978 and 1979. Real working-class wages in Honduras declined again in 1981, recovered in 1982, but then declined every year afterward into the early 1990s, sparking considerable labor unrest in the 1990s. In sum, while working-class earnings and living standards did decline in Honduras and Costa Rica during the mid-1970s, they were less severe and sustained than those in neighboring countries, apparently because the governments of both countries permitted real wage rates to recover much of their earlier purchasing power.[3] Since 1982, however, Honduran workers have lost ground again, whereas their Costa Rican peers more or less held their ground against inflation.

Income Distribution

Another way to examine the amount of economic class disparity in Honduras and Costa Rica is to explore shifts in the distribution of income among classes. One measure of changing income inequality pattern during the 1970s is the share of national income paid out as employee compensation. A decrease in the level of employee compensation would indicate a relative shift of income away from salaried and wage-earning workers and toward investors and entrepreneurs. Data on both Honduras and Costa Rica in Table 7 (Appendix) reveal that between 1970 and 1975, the employee-compensation share of all national income fluctuated somewhat, but tended to increase. Costa Rican levels remained well above the 1962 index-year level. Honduran employee compensation improved markedly in the early 1970s. If we assume that the working-class wages indices reported in Table 6 (Appendix) suggest trends beyond the end of the data in Table 7 (Appendix), we may conjecture that the wage and salary income share in Honduras and Costa Rica continued to rise after 1975, at least until the early 1980s.

Various studies[4] indicate that during the 1960s and early 1970s, Costa Rican public policy had redistributed income toward the middle three-fifths of the populace, mainly at the expense of the richest fifth.[5] Unfortunately, there are no comparable data on income distribution available for Honduras.

In summary, Costa Rica and Honduras present a clear contrast to Nicaragua, El Salvador, and Guatemala in both relative and absolute income trends. In the former two, wages fluctuated during the 1970s and early 1980s, but tended toward cycling back up after sharp declines—at least to recover lost purchasing power within a year or two. As shown in Chapters 6, 7, and 8, however, in the latter three countries real and relative income for working-class citizens suffered sustained and severe declines.

Wealth

Honduras and Costa Rica also diverged sharply from the marked increases in class inequality observed to have occurred in Nicaragua, El Salvador, and Guatemala during the 1970s. Although both nations were members of the CACM and experienced the rapid energy-driven consumer price increases of the mid-1970s, data reveal that these factors affected wealth distribution in Honduras and Costa Rica less than in the rest of the isthmus.

Costa Rica's social democratic political system and low military expenditures brought that nation into the 1970s with an extensive social welfare system that attenuated the impact of inflation on popular living conditions. Data comparing Costa Rican spending on social programs to that of other isthmian nations appear in Table 12 (Appendix). In the 1970s and early 1980s Costa Rica's ratio of spending for social services versus defense was between four and five times greater than that of its nearest competitor among the other Central American countries. The positive effects of these policies on living conditions are evident in Costa Ricans' higher levels of literacy, greater longevity, and lower mortality rates.[6] As noted above, income distribution in Costa Rica became modestly but measurably less unequal during the 1960s and 1970s, helping to prevent the rapid movement of wealth toward the upper classes, as occurred in Nicaragua, Guatemala, and El Salvador.

In Costa Rican agriculture, concentration of landownership grew steadily in the 1960s and early 1970s, but the availability of some colonizable land until the late 1960s and the still-growing banana industry absorbed much of the surplus agricultural work force. Moreover, during the 1974–1978 period, Costa Rica developed an aggressive and successful land reform program that distributed land to numerous peasants and staved off the deterioration of living standards for many.[7] Additionally, the growth of employment opportunities in the urban service and manufacturing sectors absorbed a substantial proportion of the surplus agricultural population and prevented the sharp growth of rural unemployment and poverty through the late 1980s (Appendix, Table 8).

Honduras, the least industrialized nation in the CACM, underwent the least dramatic changes in socioeconomic structure in the first two decades of the CACM. During the 1970s, therefore, Honduras experienced wealth and income inequality increases less severe and rapid than those affecting Guatemala, El Salvador, and Nicaragua.[8] As noted above, working-class wages tended to recover from inflation in the late 1970s and income distribution did not sharply disfavor wage and salary earners. Honduran governments vigorously encouraged the growth of export agriculture in the 1960s and 1970s, and colonizable agricultural land continued to be available until the late 1970s. Both of these factors helped to prevent a rapid growth of rural unemployment. Because of widespread peasant organization and mobilization during the 1960s and 1970s, the government began an ambitious agrarian reform program.[9] From 1975 to 1979 the Honduran program distributed some 171,480 hectares to roughly 10 percent of Honduran landless and land-poor campesino families.[10] Although the agrarian reform distributed only about one-fourth of its goal and has been widely criticized as insufficient and co-optative, it was nevertheless a major transfer of wealth toward campesinos. Since 1980, peasant organizations, facilitated by the 1970s reform legislation, have invaded much additional land, in what amounts to an informal or quasi-legal redistribution program.[11] Efforts by the government of Rafael Leonidas Callejas to scale back agrarian reform land transfers sharply in 1991 provoked violent clashes between peasants and the government. The government quickly restored the program.

POPULAR MOBILIZATION

In Costa Rica popular mobilization also appears to have increased markedly during the 1970s.[12] Indeed, many communal self-help organizations there were organized by social promoters employed by the government itself. Although the union movement (including industrial workers, service workers, and white-collar public employees)[13] was highly divided among competing, party-affiliated confederations, union membership grew during the 1970s.[14] Industrial disputes rose sharply during 1975–1976 when wages went down but subsided when wages recovered strongly in the late 1970s (see Figure 4). Wage disputes rose again in 1982 after real wages fell sharply in 1982, but leveled off in 1983 and 1984 as working-class earnings once again recovered purchasing power. Economic austerity measures including public employee layoffs and sharp consumer price increases (Appendix, Table 5) in the late 1980s and early 1990s were followed by numerous strikes and demonstrations in 1990 and 1991. These again were quelled in part by wage concessions.[15]

The political party system of Costa Rica remained stable in the 1960s and 1970s; the social democratic National Liberation party (PLN) remained strongest but alternated in power with a coalition of moderately conservative parties under the Unity banner. Radical left parties won a few seats to the Legislative Assembly, but remained weak outside the union movement. The Catholic church was generally quiet during this era. Overall, mobilization of demands by a broad array of Costa Rican groups increased, and there was some terrorism by tiny conspiratorial groups often connected to foreign conflicts.[16] The traditional Unity coalition of conservative parties was reorganized under the banner of the Social Christian Unity party (Partido de Unidad Social Cristiano—PUSC) in 1985 and won the 1990 elections. In sum, although there was increased organizational activity, no dramatic increase in opposition organization or coalition formation developed from the late 1970s through the early 1990s.[17] No significant challenge to the sovereignty of the Costa Rican state occurred.

In Honduras,[18] popular mobilization generally increased during the 1960s and 1970s.[19] The greatest growth in unionization came among peasant wage workers

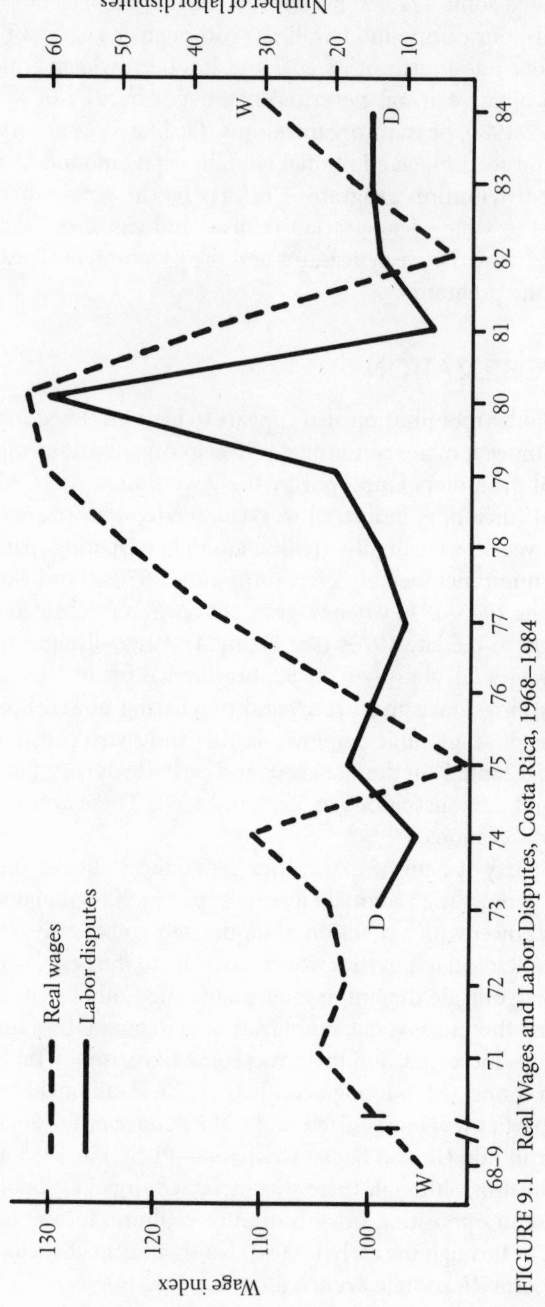

FIGURE 9.1 Real Wages and Labor Disputes, Costa Rica, 1968–1984

and landless peasants organized into land occupation movements by several federations. The Catholic church took a modest role in mobilizing such rural activism in the 1960s but generally retreated from it in the 1970s. The Liberal party remained out of power during military rule from 1963 through 1981. The National party collaborated with the first López Arellano regime in the 1960s but was frozen out afterward. Two small new centrist parties developed during the 1970s. These were the Christian Democratic Party of Honduras (Partido Demócrata Cristiano de Honduras—PDCH) and the Innovation and Unity party (Partido de Inovación y Unidad—PINU). When elections resumed in 1979, however, neither PINU nor the Christian Democrats had captured a major share of the support of the Liberal or National parties. Business and private sector organizations also multiplied and became more active in pressing policy demands upon the state during the 1960s and 1970s.

Several small leftist guerrilla groups appeared in Honduras during the 1970s and early 1980s (see Appendix, Table 10).[20] In 1960 a pro-Castro splinter from the Honduran Communist party (Partido Comunista de Honduras—PCH) formed the Morazán Front for the Liberation of Honduras (Frente Morazanista para la Liberación de Honduras—FMLH), a guerrilla group sporadically active in the 1960s and early 1970s. In 1979 the FMLH reappeared. In 1978, the PCH spun off more dissidents who formed the Popular Movement for Liberation (Movimiento Popular de Liberación—MPL), known as the "Chichoneros." The MPL's most spectacular action was the taking hostage of eighty San Pedro Sula business leaders in 1982. The Lorenzo Zelaya Popular Revolutionary Forces (Fuerzas Populares Revolucionarias "Lorenzo Zelaya"—FPR), founded by a pro-Chinese faction of the PCH, appeared in 1981 and conducted various acts of urban political violence. The Revolutionary Party of Central American Workers of Honduras (Partido Revolucionario de Trabajadores Centroamericanos de Honduras—PRTCH), the Honduran branch of a regional revolutionary group, was founded in 1977. In 1983 the guerrilla groups formed the National Directorate of Unity (Dirección Nacional de Unidad—DNU) to coordinate their activities on the revolutionary left. Despite the rise of armed opposition, insurgent violence in Honduras remained at a very low level compared to that of neighboring nations.

One new guerrilla group, the Army of Patriotic Resistance (Ejército de Resistencia Patriótica—ERP-27), appeared in Honduras in 1989. However, reconciliation efforts and a government amnesty program for political prisoners and exiles resulted in the release of more than 300 persons from jail in 1991. Several exiled guerrilla leaders from four different groups also returned to Honduras from exile, and four Chichoneros announced their intention to abandon armed struggle and form a new political party.[21]

Overall, then, the levels of popular mobilization of various sorts increased in Costa Rica and Honduras during the 1970s. Indeed, in both nations some violent political participation occurred in protest of regime policies, and in Honduras the violence reached the level of incipient guerrilla struggle by various leftist factions. In neither nation, however, was legitimate mass mobilization repressed to the point of triggering armed resistance as a last resort, as had been true in Nicaragua, El Salvador, or Guatemala.

GOVERNMENT RESPONSE TO POPULAR MOBILIZATION

The response of Central American regimes to popular mobilization in the 1970s varied substantially. We have already seen the violently repressive responses of the Salvadoran, Guatemalan, and prerevolutionary Nicaraguan regimes to swelling popular organization and protest. Although they were very different regime types, Costa Rica and Honduras responded in a strikingly different fashion from the other three Central American governments.

Costa Rica: Accommodation and Democracy

Costa Rica kept an open, constitutional regime characterized by electoral honesty and considerable popular access to public officials. Costa Rican officials generally responded to mobilization of demands by accommodating pressure group initiatives of many sorts. Even when such demands escalated to include civil disobedience, demonstrations, strikes, and riots, the government generally responded with study and compromise to defuse conflict. For instance, violent civil disturbances—land invasions in the early 1970s, the Limón riot of 1979, banana workers' strikes in 1980, 1981, 1982, and street vendors' strikes in 1991—were met with very modest official force, so that deaths were very rare.[22] Efforts to somehow accommodate those pressing the demands were also made—the government negotiated with protesters or strikers, formed panels of inquiry, or made conciliatory policy gestures.

In the early 1980s, Costa Rica experienced a severe economic crisis. As living standards of a majority of Costa Ricans plummeted, public approval of the government declined. Nevertheless, efforts to forge a militant general nationwide labor confederation failed. Voting for leftist parties—long considered a bellwether of protest—actually declined in the 1982 and 1986 national elections. Costa Rica's more radical party and labor groups became increasingly divided in the early and mid-1980s. Polls revealed that even in the midst of a severe recession, most citizens remained loyal to the regime.

The Costa Rican economic crisis continued into the late 1980s and 1990s, but patterns of government-citizen interaction continued much as in the early 1980s. American economic assistance, given generously in the early and mid-1980s for Costa Rican cooperation with the United States' harrassment of the Nicaraguan contras (Appendix, Table 4), had somewhat eased the persistent economic crunch. However, when president Oscar Arias Sánchez derided the Reagan administration by engineering the Central American Peace Accord of 1987 and reducing cooperation with the contras, the United States retaliated by sharply cutting economic aid to Costa Rica. This slowed Costa Rican economic output and increased inflation (Appendix, Tables 1 and 5).

Successive governments in San José responded—under the pressure of international lenders—by adopting a neoliberal economic model (public sector wage cuts and layoffs, privatization, and reductions in public services) that deviated from the social democratic development model in place since the 1950s.[23] These policy changes, too, generated citizen mobilization and protest, but as before the Costa Rican government responded with ameliorative measures: repression remained low, real wages were kept up (Appendix, Table 6), and social assistance and housing subsidization programs were sharply increased. Income distribution among classes remained fairly stable into the 1990s despite the economic turmoil. Voting for leftist parties remained very low, and the PLN-PUSC domination of elections persisted. Outside of protest mobilization, the most significant signs that the persistent economic difficulties angered Costa Ricans were two: First, voters ousted the governing party in successive elections in 1990, 1994, and 1998. Second, and perhaps more significantly, voter turnout in the 1998 election dropped from the usual level of 82 percent to only 71 percent.[24]

Thus, even though particular PLN and PUSC administrations were unable to succeed themselves in office through this difficult period, the constitutional democratic regime established in the late 1940s and early 1950s remained solidly in place. Even when forced to adopt the austere and distributively stingy neoliberal economic model, Costa Rican governments found ways to ameliorate the economic difficulties of the citizenry. The democratic regime retained the support of diverse social forces, elites, and mass political culture, and thus successfully weathered two decades of severe economic turmoil.[25]

Honduras: Accommodation and Political Reform

From 1963 through 1982, Honduras was governed by the armed forces rather than a civilian democratic regime like Costa Rica's. The military authoritarian regime of the 1960s and 1970s harbored among its leadership groups with developmentalist and populist orientations and showed somewhat less inclination to control all aspects of national life than the militaries of El Salvador and Guatemala. For instance, during the early 1970s the second military government of Gen. Oswaldo López Areliano (1971–1975) accommodated burgeoning campesino mobilization and developed a populist agrarian reform program. López was deposed for the second time in 1975 by a conservative faction of the armed forces led by Col. Juan Alberto Melgar Castro. Labor repression then increased, marked by a massacre of fourteen protesters at Los Horcones in 1975. In an astounding departure from what would have happened in neighboring nations, army officers implicated in the massacre were tried in civilian courts, convicted, and imprisoned.[26]

Violent regime repression of opponents (illegal detentions, disappearances, and murders) rose significantly in Honduras in the early 1980s, but still remained quite moderate by Central American standards. For instance in 1982, a year when Guatemala and El Salvador each had over ten thousand political disappearances and murders, Honduran human rights activists reported a total of only forty assassinations and "permanent disappearances."[27] Political parties, unions, peasant leagues, and a free press operated openly. They no doubt helped to restrain human rights violations by vigorously denouncing government abuses of authority.[28]

Honduran security forces took numerous measures to curtail armed opposition, including forming rural militias called Civil Defense Committees (Comités de Defensa Civil—CDCs) in several areas, and stepped up counterinsurgency efforts. Right-wing elements, apparently involving some Nicaraguan exiles and enjoying military complicity, began to murder and to kidnap and torture suspected subversives and critics of the government in the early 1980s. By 1982, "extrajudicial action [had become] standard operating procedure for the Honduran armed forces in dealing with violent opposition. The methods include[d] disappearances, torture, use of clandestine detention centers, and . . . execution of prisoners."[29] Although human rights violations increased markedly in the 1980s;[30] they remained well below levels observed in El Salvador and Guatemala.

One key aspect of the Honduran case was the process by which the armed forces returned formal power to civilians. Despite the growing institutional strength of the military during the 1960s and 1970s, the Honduran armed forces did not become nearly as repressive or aggressive in expanding their power within and hold over the state apparatus as did neighboring militaries. As the punishment of military officials for the Los Horcones massacre revealed, the Honduran military had not placed itself completely above accountability to the law and constitution.

A series of problems in Honduras and neighboring nations eventually persuaded the military authoritarian regime, headed by then-president General Policarpio Paz García, to voluntarily embark on a project of political reform—not the repressive project undertaken by the rulers of Honduras's three immediate neighbors. Popular unrest had grown in the mid- and late 1970s, and its repression by the army and military-dominated police, the Public Security Forces (Fuerzas de Seguridad Pública—FUSEP) brought increasing pressure for reforms from the Carter administration. The blatant corruption of the military government had become an increasing embarrassment, and the military's traditional National party allies had become somewhat disaffected from the military-authoritarian regime. Finally, deeply troubling to the military regime were events unfolding elsewhere in the isthmus in 1979: Nicaraguan revolutionaries ousted the repressive Somoza, destroyed his National Guard, and began a revolution. Popular mobilization and growing violence in El Salvador portended similiar problems there.

Rather than face the possibility of civil war, revolution, or destruction of the military, General Paz García and the senior military officers' council decided to return power to civilians, ushering in a brief reformist military regime. The change to a civilian transitional regime was swift. General Paz García called an election for a constituent assembly in 1980. The Liberal party, long mistrusted by the armed forces, captured a near majority of the constituent assembly. With Paz García holding the provisional presidency to maintain military ascendancy, the Liberals drafted a new constitution, which set elections for a new, civilian government for 1981.

Confounding the expectations of many observers, the armed forces permitted both traditional parties (including the Liberals' social-democratic Left) and the two new groups (PINU and the Christian Democrats) to take part in a generally free and open 1981 election. Moreover, again contrary to widespread expectations, the military did not rig the 1981 elections on behalf of its longtime National party allies. Liberal candidate Roberto Suazo Córdova won a clear majority in a clean election, and General Paz García relinquished the presidency in early 1982.[31]

So began the transitional civilian democratic regime in Honduras, engineered by the armed forces to prevent the anticipated catastrophes of civil war and further institutional deterioration of the military itself. For well over a decade the military would remain very powerful in the transitional civilian regime, resistant to civilian control and feared by civilian politicians. Military power remained largely exempt from civilian control until the mid-1990s, blocking transition to full formal democracy. Indeed, during the 1980s, the Honduran military's power and resources actually increased despite its eschewal of the formal reins of power. U.S. military assistance to Honduras during the 1980s increased dramatically, ballooning from $3.1 million per year for 1977–1980 to $41.5 million annually for 1981–1984 and eventually to $57.7 million per year for 1985–1988 (Appendix, Table 4). The United States provided this military aid (and copious economic assistance) in exchange for the Honduran armed forces' help with U.S. efforts to contain revolutionary movements in neighboring El Salvador and Nicaragua. In trade for effectively ceding control over much of southern Honduras to the Nicaraguan contras, cooperation with the U.S.-advised Salvadoran armed forces against the FMLN, and a heavy U.S. military presence, the Honduran military waxed rich in U.S.-built bases and U.S.-supplied equipment and training. Human rights abuses by the army and FUSEP increased during the mid-1980s.

The prospects for civilian rule in the early 1980s, therefore, appeared dim.

One of the most striking weaknesses of the Honduran government's prospects for democracy, surprisingly, was President Suazo himself. In an apparent attempt to retain power, he precipitated a constitutional crisis in 1985. Suazo failed in his effort when the armed forces, labor movement, and United States applied counterpressure to block his efforts to amend the constitution. The military's adherence to constitutional rule was a positive development for civilian democracy.

The chaos resulting from Suazo's maneuver, however, led to the adoption of a Uruguayan-style combined party primary-presidential election in 1985 in which the majority party's front-runner would take office. This brought about the confusing result that José Azcona Hoyos, the leading Liberal candidate, became president in 1986, despite having won fewer total votes than the leading National party candidate, because the Liberal candidates together drew the most popular votes. The Liberals lost a clean election in 1990 and passed power to Rafael Callejas of the National party.

This peaceful transition of power from a ruling party and president to a victorious opponent in 1990 constituted another positive development for democracy in Honduras. However, the prospects for transition to a fully civilian democratic regime still remained in question for many observers. Among continuing obstacles to civilian, constitutional rule were the military's great power, elite commitment to democracy that sometimes appeared desultory, and increasing repression and human rights violations by the military and FUSEP. Popular anger grew over Honduran support for the U.S.-backed, anti-Sandinista contras, leading to protests. There were also growing economic difficulties that included cutbacks in U.S. economic and military aid, a sharp contraction in GDP per capita (1989–1991), rapid increases in consumer prices, and declines in real wages (Appendix, Tables 1, 4, 5, and 6).[32]

As the contras withdrew from Honduras in 1990 and 1991 following the 1990 Nicaraguan election and peace accord, Honduran anger about the contra problem subsided. An amnesty law passed in 1991 allowed members of armed insurgent groups to abandon their violent opposition; some eventually rejoined legal politics, effectively dismantling the tiny revolutionary left. However, the Callejas administration's neoliberal austerity program, adopted to address spiraling inflation, provided a new source for extensive labor unrest and popular protest. Although the security forces were often heavy-handed in repressing such mobilization, the military and the Callejas government also exercised some restraint. Human rights abuses were investigated and some perpetrators punished. In late 1990 the military high command replaced its own chief with a new commander who made efforts to control and punish abusive behavior and to reconcile with guerrilla group leaders and with some peasant and labor sectors.[33]

In November 1993 Honduras held another election, won by the progressive Liberal Carlos Roberto Reina, a lawyer with a human rights background who campaigned on a promise to curtail the power of the armed forces and clean up corruption. The Liberals also captured control of the Congress. For a second time the incumbent government relinquished power to a victorious opponent, another step forward in democratic consolidation. However, the military commander, General Luis Discua, immediately manifested the military's displeasure with Reina's proposals to end the draft, cut the military budget, and transfer the police agency FUSEP to civilian control. Despite military objections, Reina and Congress eventually passed and ratified the constitutional reform transferring FUSEP to civilian control, a process that began in late 1996. As it had in El Salvador and Guatemala, the police reform process led to a crime wave in the major cities of Tegucigalpa and San Pedro Sula. The military draft law was revised and the draft allowed to lapse, causing a decline in military force levels. This reduction in military power constituted a critical political game rule change and effectively reduced the military's role within the regime. It thus marked 1996 as the year of Honduras's long awaited final transition to full civilian democracy.[34]

As Reina's successor, Liberal Carlos Roberto Flores Facussé took office in January 1998 after yet another clean election, Honduras showed some signs of the consolidation of civilian rule. The military's influence had been reduced and some reforms were instituted to improve its human rights performance. The government had established civilian authority over the police. Civil society, especially human rights and indigenous groups, increasingly and energetically denounced the human rights abuses of the 1980s and 1990s. The government initiated an investigation of past military rights abuses, including the seizure by a judge of files of military intelligence and counterintelligence services that implicated numerous high ranking officers. But there was also distressing evidence that serious problems remained. Human rights problems persisted, marked by renewed activity by death squads and the assassination in February 1998 of Ernesto Sandoval, a leader of the Human Rights Committee of Honduras (Comité de Derechos Humanos de Honduras—CODEH), Honduras's leading human rights agency.[35]

SUMMARY AND CONCLUSIONS

During the 1970s, both Costa Rica and Honduras at least partly ameliorated the growing inequalities affecting working-class victims of rapid economic change, while employing either a low or a moderate level of repression. There are, however, important differences between the two cases that bear further attention. First, although political repression was very low in Costa Rica, it was substantially higher in Honduras under both the military governments of the late 1970s and the Suazo and Azcona governments in the 1980s. Such repression notwithstanding, the Honduran security forces voluntarily transferred nominal control of executive and legislative power to a constitutional regime, a political reform of symbolic significance to Hondurans. Second, the public policies of Costa Rica and Honduras during the 1970s differed sharply in specifics, but the net effect in both cases was to permit working-class wages to recover previous purchasing power after declines, and to shift some wealth and income to certain lower-class groups.

Thus, although Costa Rica and Honduras were quite different, in each case key political elites and the state made modest concessions to working-class needs and restrained (at least some of the time in Honduras) draconian efforts to curtail political mobilization.

The combination of modest socioeconomic reforms to ameliorate the effects of growing poverty with restraint in repression and the accommodation of pressures for political reforms was the formula that saved Costa Rica and Honduras from falling into the abyss of internecine violence like their neighbors. The combination enabled them to maintain relative political stability, although the two countries were so different that the similarity in their strategies was somewhat difficult to recognize at first glance.

Costa Rica's democratic government adjusted wages and resisted repression and thus remained stable through a turbulent two decades. Honduras's military governments of the 1970s and early 1980s also ameliorated poverty with wage increases and land distribution. Most interestingly, the Honduran armed forces successfully employed two quick regime changes, from military-authoritarian to reformist-military to incipient civilian democratic, within a three-year span (1979–1982) as its major accommodation of mobilization. The Honduran armed forces exercised comparative restraint in repression. We call this restraint, despite the military's hands accumulating the blood of some 1,000 victims during the 1980s and 1990s. It was *relatively* restrained—indeed, it paled in comparison to the sanguinary repression wreaked by the security forces of Somoza's Nicaragua, El Salvador, and Guatemala, who together took at least 250,000 Central American lives in the 1970s and 1980s.

These similarities in amelioration of poverty and the creative management of state response to mobilization by Costa Rica and Honduras, nations otherwise quite distinct from each other, strongly suggest that the slaughter and chaos of insurrection, revolution, and civil war were not inevitable in the Central America of the late 1970s. A relatively poor, military-dominated regime and a somewhat more prosperous democracy each responded to the growing tide of opposition mobilization with policy choices that almost certainly saved many thousands of lives.

10

POWER, DEMOCRACY, AND U.S. POLICY IN CENTRAL AMERICA

If Central American politics are in part the product of the unique internal social, economic, and political evolution of each of the republics, they are also heavily influenced by the United States. The proximity of the United States, as well as the gross disparities in population and national wealth between the region's major hegemon and its tiny neighbors, has meant that U.S. policy has long had a profound impact on the region. All too often, that impact has been detrimental to the well-being of Central Americans. We believe that, especially during the cold war, U.S. policy toward the region was particularly ill advised and destructive. Indeed, in the introduction to a paper he gave at a U.S. Department of State conference on Central America in March of 1979, one of the authors asserted that Washington's

> apparent definition of interest [in Central America]—and certainly its strategies for achieving them—are outdated, shortsighted and fundamentally flawed. . . . U.S. goals . . . are short-termed, reactive, and excessively concerned with stability and, hence, the maintenance of an elite-dominated status quo. These policies pose a grave threat to long-range U.S. interests by contributing to the continuation of socially unjust systems and thereby increasing the probability of civil and regional conflict and stimulating an ever-growing feeling of anti-Americanism among the peoples of the region.[1]

If anything, U.S. behavior toward the isthmus in the dozen years that ensued from 1979 until the end of the cold war only served to underscore the validity of that pessimistic observation. The U.S. defense of the forces of status quo in El Salvador, Guatemala, and Honduras, its promotion of counterrevolutionary reaction in Nicaragua, and its preference in the 1980s for military rather than negotiated solutions contributed significantly to an unprecedented escalation in violence. By the early 1990s that violence had taken between 200,000 and 300,000 lives (mainly civilians), displaced millions, left countless others jobless, orphaned, or physically or psychologically maimed and had nearly ruined the economies of the region. Although U.S. policy was not the only cause of the Central American tragedy, it was a very important contributing factor to the onset and evolution of the violence.[2]

In the preceding chapters we have presented specific information about U.S. policy toward the individual countries. This chapter emphasizes the nature and problems of U.S. policy in the region. Although the tactics and style of U.S. policy toward Central America occasionally change, its overall objective remains remarkably constant. That objective is to protect U.S. economic and security interests by keeping as much influence as possible over events and policies in Central America. The traditional U.S. way of assuring such influence has been through the maintenance in power of friendly, "moderate"—read pro-U.S., traditional, elite-dominated—regimes.

In the twentieth century the United States went from the policy of the big stick, in the first three decades, to that of the good neighbor, under Franklin D. Roosevelt and Harry Truman. This was followed by cold war interventionism, under administrations from that of Dwight Eisenhower through that of Gerald Ford. Interventionism was then interrupted by a tenuous promotion of human rights during the first years of the Jimmy Carter presidency but resumed at the end of the Carter administration and continued throughout that of Ronald Reagan and part of that of George Bush. Throughout those ninety years and even in the post-cold war period, however, a major concern has been with maintaining control in "our backyard." Even in times of lofty rhetoric about good neighborliness, the Alliance for Progress, human rights, or democracy, U.S. policies clearly revealed an overarching concern with maintaining stability and control.

One colorful but troubling example of the U.S. preoccupation with control and security is that of President Franklin Roosevelt, who described Anastasio Somoza García of Nicaragua as an "S.O.B.," but maintained cooperative relations with the dictator because he was "*our* S.O.B." President John F. Kennedy promoted the Alliance for Progress to encourage economic and social development and democracy in order to undercut the appeal of communism in the hemisphere. Often at cross-purposes with promoting democracy and development, however, was the simultaneous increase in U.S. military aid and training throughout Latin America. Intended to increase the counterinsurgency capability of Latin America armed forces, the military aid helped soldiers topple several democratic regimes and abuse human rights. President Carter, despite his evident concern for human rights, tried hard in 1978 and 1979 to keep the Sandinistas out of a new government in Nicaragua. He even attempted to preserve Somoza's brutal National Guard and corrupt Liberal Nationalist party intact after the dictator's departure.

THE PROBLEM OF POWER

Any serious discussion of the problems of U.S. behavior in Central America should address the critical relationship between power and democracy. Power is the basic currency of politics. Simply put, groups within a given polity generally receive benefits and attention from their government and political system in rough proportion to the amount of power they can bring to bear on that system. The powerful receive the most; the powerless, little or nothing. Charles W. Anderson argued that the traditional "power contenders" in Latin American society—the Church, the military, the rural and urban economic elites—allow new groups to enter and receive benefits from the political system only when these groups demonstrate their own "power capabilities."[3] We argued in Chapter 5 that regime changes in Central America—especially struggles for democratization—have involved conflict and the reconfiguration of relationships among traditional power contenders and new groups from the middle and working classes.

Power capabilities vary from group to group. The Church exercises authority through the traditional belief systems and moral suasion. The military has a near monopoly of the means of violent coercion. Economic elites use their economic resources for influence. In contrast, lower-class groups have far fewer resources. To some extent they can wield power by organizing, and by carrying out strikes, protests, and the like. But the incontrovertible fact about Central America is that the majority of the people—illiterate or semiliterate peasants, urban and rural workers, and slum dwellers—usually lack the organization that would give them real power capabilities. During the cold war, when they attempted to develop power through peaceful collective activity and organization, they were often seen as subversive, labeled "Communist," and violently repressed. Accordingly, because Central America's poor majorities have held little power, public policy was usually unresponsive to their social plight. We have seen how this lack of responsiveness generated grievances, and how repression was applied, thus causing violence to become the people's recourse of last resort.

It was the gross disparity in power between a relatively small privileged group—the upper class and emerging middle sector—and the underprivileged and impoverished majority that generated the Central American crisis of the late twentieth century. As we noted in earlier chapters, power relationships in the five countries had deep historical roots. It is no accident that Costa Rica, the country that developed the most egalitarian society, and Honduras, which—due to its status as an economic backwater—never developed a highly cohesive and exploitative elite were least affected by recent turmoil. Conversely, it is also not surprising that Guaternala, El Salvador, and Nicaragua, the countries with the greatest historically rooted power disparities, experienced the highest levels of violence. The elites in those three countries, long accustomed to their lopsided monopoly of power, showed little inclination to share power or to make the sacrifices needed for the genuine development of all sectors of society.

DEMOCRACY

There is no doubt that democracy is one of the most powerful bases of legitimacy for contemporary governments. Seldom do we find a regime of any type anywhere in the world that does not claim to be democratic. The problem lies in the fact that there is much disagreement over the meaning of the term *democracy.* Socialist theorists tend to stress economic and social criteria, whereas those from the industrially developed West emphasize political—often narrowly procedural—characteristics. In the United States, one definition with which few would quarrel is that democracy is "government of, by, and for the people." However simple this definition may sound, it sets forth two conceptual elements fundamental to democratic theory: first, that the system should be as participatory as possible, and, second, that it should facilitate the general well-being.[4]

In the 1980s the United States promoted "civilian rule" and proclaimed the birth of "democracy" in its client states, Guatemala, El Salvador, and Honduras, and condemned its alleged absence in the revolutionary state of Nicaragua. Only in 1990, when the besieged Nicaraguan people elected the U.S. approved Violeta Chamorro president, was Nicaragua finally added to Washington's list of democracies. However, if we honestly apply the criteria set forth in the last paragraph, it is very difficult to sustain those conclusions.[5] All four countries held nationwide, internationally observed elections. And it is true that, except in the case of El Salvador, they were internationally acclaimed as procedurally clean. But democracy requires much more than simply holding procedurally correct elections or establishing civilian rule. A critical issue is popular participation in elections and in other political affairs.

The elections in Guatemala in 1985 and 1990 as well as those in El Salvador in 1982, 1984, 1988, 1989, and 1991 were held against a background of state-sponsored terror that had taken tens of thousands of lives and had disarticulated most mass-based civic and political organizations. By default, candidates usually ranged from center to far right and media outlets genuinely critical of the system were nonexistent. Citizen participation in formal national politics was confined—typically by government repression—largely to the formal act of voting by most citizens and to campaign involvement by a tiny minority of center and right-wing party activists. In Nicaragua in 1984 and 1990, however, there was no program of state-sponsored terror. On the contrary, many organizations representing the poor majority had been encouraged to develop, grow, and make demands on their government. The major international human rights organizations all concur that the practice of systematized torture, murder, and disappearance of political opponents—massively institutionalized in Guatemala and El Salvador—was not a problem in Nicaragua. Though the right-wing Coordinadora Democrática coalition chose not to participate in Nicaragua in 1984, three parties on the right as well as three on the left challenged the Sandinistas. What is more, even then the antiregime Nicaraguan media (including *La Prensa* and Radio Católica), though lightly censored, carried a sharply anti-Sandinista message to the voters, as did the six participating opposition parties in extensive uncensored free time-slots on state-sponsored radio and television.

The U.S. application of the term *democracy* in Central America during the cold war is also called into question if we ask in each case, Is this a government "for the people?" In whose interest does it rule? By 1984, the social achievements of the Nicaraguan government were so significant that even the Kissinger Commission felt obliged to admit that "Nicaragua's government has made significant gains against illiteracy and disease."[6] Had it chosen, the commission might also have mentioned advances in agrarian reform, housing, social security, and the status of women. Even after the contra war forced the diversion of large amounts of funds out of the social and into the military budget, the Sandinistas continued as best they could to combat pressing social problems. By the time of the 1990 election, however, most such programs had been weakened due to the high cost of defense. Nicaragua's disastrous economic and political situation in 1990 persuaded the citizenry to use the democratic election system established by the revolutionary regime to vote the FSLN out of office and end the revolution. Thus the transition in 1990 to the civilian democratic regime drew upon democratic rules of the game already in place to choose a new set of rulers.

In El Salvador and Guatemala, in contrast, the process of regime change toward democracy during the last decade of the cold war followed a path different from Nicaragua's. In both countries, the reformist military regime that overthrew the authoritarian military regime engaged in such violent repression that to many observers it appeared at the time that no meaningful transformation of the political systems was under way. When each country's reformist military regime ceded rule to a transitional civilian government, skepticism abounded about how much real power these elected civilian rulers had as long as their repressive militaries still held veto power over key policy matters. The civilian politicians, however, gradually gained independence from the armed forces as cold war threats diminished, and formerly excluded power contenders were eventually allowed to take part. Honduras followed a similar path of gradual transition to democracy, albeit without the presence of a civil war or such high levels of repression.

Eventually all four countries established formal civilian democratic regimes, but the quality of their democracies remained to be determined. Some would argue that not only must formal rules of democracy and popular participation without massive repression exist but, more important, qualitative and socioeconomic foundations must be put in place as well. The poor majority of citizens, the reasoning goes, need the fundamental human and political resources provided by socioeconomic well-being—sufficient income, health, and education—to truly participate and thus have some chance to influence decisions in a formally democratic country. By the late 1990s Nicaragua, El Salvador, Guatemala, and Honduras all had formal civilian democracies, but poverty and maldistribution of income and wealth left poor citizens in each with few of the socioeconomic requisites of an effective democracy. Thus elites—albeit a broader circle of power contenders than in the 1970s—continued to dominate the polities.

MOBILIZATION

The decades following World War II were marked by a growing awareness that something was seriously wrong in Latin America. Those who viewed mass poverty as rooted in an extremely unequal distribution of power began advocating a greater diffusion of power. In the 1940s and 1950s, social democratic and Christian democratic parties talked of "penetrating" the masses, of creating and fortifying party-oriented labor, peasant, and neighborhood organizations that would unify and express the interests of the masses. From the 1950s onward, educators such as Paulo Freire of Brazil, aware that mass empowerment would require the emergence of a socially, politically, and linguistically literate citizenry, began promoting, through adult education, consciousness-raising programs that encouraged poor people to examine and question their social condition.[7]

In the wake of the victory of the Cuban revolution in 1959, the United States was jolted into a period of support for reform in Latin America. Thus the Alliance for Progress was created in 1961. The Peace Corps, inaugurated the same year, promoted community development throughout the Third World, and particularly in Latin America, by mobilizing, educating, and empowering poor people to solve their own problems. For a while, thousands of idealistic U.S. citizens lived among and worked with Latin America's urban and rural poor and promoted collective self-help programs.[8] Inspired by the old saying that it is better to teach a hungry person to fish than simply to give him a fish, Peace Corps community action promoters helped poor communities form legal community action committees, which, in turn, elected their own leaders, identified needs felt in the community, and tried to mobilize resources to address those needs. Through community action, thousands of schools, soccer fields, clinics, roads, bridges, housing projects, and small electrification and potable water projects were built. Ultimately, many hundreds of thousands, perhaps millions, of ordinary Latin Americans experienced a surge in democratic participation.

Before long, however, a strong reaction set in. Ill-equipped or disinclined to respond to the legitimate demands of newly articulate poor people, and annoyed in some cases that community groups ignored or bypassed traditional politicians, some Latin American elites came to see the community action movement as a nuisance or a threat. Local elites chided Peace Corps volunteers for associating with what the latter often called "those Communists"—the poor people in the community action organizations. Eventually, when the central governments, too, conveyed their displeasure to U.S. diplomats, the Nixon administration officially terminated Peace Corps involvement in community action. This graphically illustrates how the maintenance of good relations with pro-U.S. regimes was far more important to Washington than was the continuation of efforts to promote the democratization of Latin American society through increased popular participation.

Others also became interested in popular participation and mass mobilization. Programs similar to community action were started by the Costa Rican government, for example. However, the most extensive government-sanctioned mobilization effort occurred in revolutionary Cuba. Spurred into action, at least in part, by an awareness of an impending CIA-sponsored counterrevolutionary invasion, Fidel Castro and his associates began to mobilize the Cuban people early in 1961. A huge literacy crusade, with significant politically socializing content, was begun, and common citizens were encouraged to form grassroots Committees for the Defense of the Revolution. By the time the United States launched the Bay of Pigs invasion in April 1961, Cuba was prepared to resist. Because of revolutionary mobilization, the counterrevolutionary effort to topple Castro failed dismally.

Clearly the most extensive mobilizing activity in the hemisphere in the 1960s was begun by the Latin American Catholic church. Even in the 1950s, some important Latin American Church figures such as Dom Helder Câmara of Brazil had begun calling for social justice and an uplifting of the oppressed majority. By the end of that decade and the beginning of the next, they found a powerful ally in the Vatican as Pope John XXIII embarked on his pivotal aggiornamento, or updating, of the Catholic church. Part of this process of change, as expressed in pronouncements of the Second Vatican Council, was the new focus on the problems of Latin America, by then the largest single segment of world Catholicism. This, in turn, stimulated Latin American Catholics to engage in an even deeper examination of the human problems of their region.

The high-water mark of such concern came at the Second General Conference of Latin American Bishops at Medellín, Colombia, in 1968. Focusing on the problems of poverty and exploitation in Latin America, the bishops used a form of structural analysis not unlike the "dependency" explanation we discussed in our second chapter.[9] As we noted in Chapter 4, they argued that Catholic clergy should make a preferential option for the poor and that, in order to carry out this option, priests and nuns should create Christian base communities (CEBs), or grassroots organizations, in which people of all classes would discuss the social problems of their community or country in light of the social gospel. In addition, natural community leaders or lay delegates of the word would be trained to preach the social gospel and act as community organizers.[10]

The impact of Medellín on Latin America in general, and especially on Central America, was greater than anyone might have dreamed in 1968. No doubt to the astonishment of many conservative bishops who had perfunctorily signed the high-sounding Medellín declarations, thousands of priests and nuns—and even a few bishops—began implementing the ideas of the conference almost immediately. By the 1970s, extensive grassroots mobilization was taking place through newly created CEBs in the four countries of northern Central America. Poor people by the tens, possibly hundreds, of thousands were becoming aware of themselves as human beings made in the image of God and having a right to be treated by their government and employer with dignity and justice. Though the objectives and tactics of the CEB movement were nonviolent, the elite-dominated governments of the region predictably viewed them as highly subversive. Again the label "Communist" was applied and, eventually, tens of thousands of Catholics, including dozens of priests and nuns and even one archbishop, died in the repression that was mounted to reverse their mobilizing effort.

By the mid- to late 1970s, the social mobilization process had become massive and extremely widespread throughout northern Central America. Peasants had mobilized into unions and federations and created cooperative organizations concerned with production and marketing. Urban workers had expanded the labor movement. Teachers, medical personnel, students, and women had all become more organized and active. As we noted in earlier chapters, the Honduran regime chose to accommodate or, at worst, only mildly repress the mobilization process. Such relative moderation is probably one of the major reasons why Honduras avoided open insurrection. In Nicaragua, Guatemala, and El Salvador, however, the much more entrenched and powerful elites chose violent demobilization rather than accommodation as the tactic for dealing with newly articulated popular demands. In all three countries, repressive violence begot responding violence, as previously moderate citizens in increasing numbers opted for insurrection or guerrilla warfare. In Nicaragua, the process of mobilization, repression, and insurrection ultimately led to the victory of the revolutionary coalition in 1979. In Guatemala and El Salvador, in contrast, the unprecedented scale and cruelty of state-sponsored terrorism (with heavy U.S. material support for the Salvadoran regime in the 1980s and for the Guatemalan regime from the early 1960s through 1977) curtailed or reversed the process of civilian mobilization and stalemated the rebels on the battlefield.

The process of mobilization that had brought about the Nicaraguan revolution continued and was encouraged by the new government thereafter. Prior to the victory, Catholics from the Christian base movement had joined with nationalist Marxists from the FSLN and others to organize a variety of grassroots organizations. These included the Rural Workers' Association (Asociación de Trabajadores del Campo—ATC), the Sandinista Workers' Federation (Confederación Sandinista de Trabajadores—CST), the Association of Women Confronting the National Problem (Asociación de Mujeres Frente a la Problemática Nacional—AMPRONAC), the Civil Defense Committees (Comités de Defensa Civil—CDCs), and the Sandinista Youth (La Juventad Sandinista).[11] After 1979 the CEB movement also continued and other grassroots organizations, such as the National Union of [small] Farmers and Ranchers (Unión Nacional de Agricultores y Ganaderos—UNAG), emerged. By 1984, the U.S. Embassy in Managua estimated that between 700,000 and 800,000 Nicaraguan citizens—around half of the adult population—were in such organizations.[12]

The grassroots organizations performed a variety of functions. They helped defend the revolution. They were a device for political socialization. They helped mobilize volunteer participation to carry out several ambitious social programs. And, most important, they provided an avenue for political and governmental participation, which ordinary people had never experienced previously. The local organizations held internal elections, discussed the community's most pressing needs, organized to solve those needs, successfully petitioned their government for everything from material and financial support to major changes in government policy, and named representatives to local, regional, and national planning boards of government economic and social service entities.[13] Sometimes such organizations abused their power or engaged in petty corruption, but overall they gave many ordinary Nicaraguan citizens the first opportunity in their lives to participate meaningfully in the political process.

In addition to the grassroots organizations, the Sandinista-led government used education as a vehicle for advancing participation and democracy in Nicaragua. Relying in large part on the techniques of Catholic educator Paulo Freire and the labor of tens of thousands of volunteers, the revolutionary government carried out a basic literacy crusade within its first year in power. The drive significantly lowered rates of adult illiteracy and won Nicaragua the United Nations (UN) prize for the best literacy crusade of the year. Thereafter, continued attention was paid to maintaining and increasing literacy and generally improving the educational level of all Nicaraguans. In addition to building the skills of the workforce and socializing Nicaraguans to support the revolution, a central motive for the heavy emphasis on education was to "empower" the people—to create a citizenry capable of intelligent self-government.[14]

Costa Rica is the only other country in Central America where significant and sustained governmental efforts have been made to mobilize the populace. In the 1960s and 1970s the Costa Rican government promoted hundreds of local citizen self-help organizations through its National Community Development Directorate (Dirección Nacional de Desarrollo de la Comunidad-DINADECO) and through health, education, welfare, agricultural, and housing agencies. There developed many community development, nutrition, health promotion, and economic groups (especially cooperatives) that engaged thousands of citizens in making demands on the political system and in working together to solve local problems.

THE ROOTS OF U.S. POLICY IN CENTRAL AMERICA

At least until the end of the cold war, the United States had real, legitimate, and widely agreed-upon security interests in Central America. Virtually all agree that it was in the interest of the United States that no Soviet bases, troops, advanced weapons, or nuclear arms be present in the isthmus and that no country in the

GRASS-ROOTS MOBILIZATION. A protest march in San José, Costa Rica (photo by John Booth). Adult education in Nicaragua as depicted in a revolutionary mural (photo by Thomas Walker).

region form a military alliance with the Soviet Union. It was and remains in the interest of the United States that Central American societies enjoy sufficient economic prosperity, democracy, and political stability that their citizens not be driven massively into exile or refuge. Similarly, it was and remains in the interest of the United States that Central American nations be at peace among themselves and that their military forces be neither excessively large nor out of balance with each other. An arms race or increased intraregional conflict might have caused a war in Central America, sparked direct U.S. military intervention there, or threatened the security of the Panama Canal or important trade routes.

However, many critics of U.S. policy in Central America believe that U.S. actions during the cold war actually harmed rather than advanced these interests. In order to understand how this came about, we must review the roots of U.S. policy.

U.S. interests in Central America have evolved over time and have sometimes been subject to intense debate within the United States. During the nineteenth century, encouraging trade, coping with massive British naval power, and transit across the isthmus were important U.S. concerns. As U.S. sea power supplanted British dominance in the late nineteenth century and as the United States rapidly industrialized, the desire to establish and control a transisthmian canal led to U.S. intervention in Panama in 1903. Once canal construction and operation were under way, the United States used troops in Panama and Nicaragua to assure a canal monopoly and protect the canal itself. U.S. diplomats (sometimes assisted by the marines) energetically and often heavy-handedly promoted U.S. business and geopolitical interests throughout Central America in the early twentieth century. During World War II, the United States, through cooperative security arrangements with Central American governments, sought to protect the Panama Canal from Axis interference.

During the cold war, U.S. interests in Central America continued to focus upon economic and security concerns. A desire to contain Soviet-inspired communism was a major force driving U.S. policy. Contrary to common belief and despite the boom brought about by the common market, U.S. investments in Central America remained quite modest compared to those in most other parts of the world. Nevertheless, promotion of a "healthy business climate" in Central America also heavily influenced U.S. policy choices.

From the U.S. perspective, the effervescent mobilization that took place in Central America throughout the second half of this century was problematical. Although a cause for hope for millions of poor people and a step toward true, socially rooted democracy, mobilization worried some of Central America's entrenched elites. They viewed the process with alarm and responded with state terror to discourage participation. Hearkening to their cries of "Communist subversion," Washington, too, joined the fray. It is interesting to consider why the government of the United States—whose people tenaciously defend their own right to participate in myriad civic and interest organizations—allied itself with the privileged minority in Central America in its campaign against participatory mobilization. Perhaps the most basic reason for this behavior is that U.S. policy—especially in our backyard—often responded more to domestic political fears, misperceptions, and rhetoric in the United States than to careful analysis of the situation in the isthmus.

As a capitalist country, the United States made consistent efforts to promote capitalism and to protect U.S. business interests both at home and abroad. Policymakers in the White House, State Department, and Congress tended to formulate national security—especially in Central America and the Caribbean—as much in terms of nurturing business interests and trade as along military and geostrategic lines. Radical and even merely reformist political doctrines, commonly (but often incorrectly) labeled "Communist" by local elites were usually viewed as anathema to U.S. interests.

From the early twentieth century on, the impulse to contain this "threat of communism" to the United States and to capitalism motivated conservative politicians and cowed and intimidated their critics. U.S. politicians feared being depicted by their adversaries as having "lost ground" to communism. After World War II, and especially with the Cuban revolution, the fear of Soviet-inspired communism in our backyard shaped U.S. policy in Central America. Thus even U.S. politicians and policymakers sympathetic to the need for socioeconomic reform and democracy supported demobilization in Central America when pressures for reform were labeled "subversive" by Central American elites or by interested U.S. observers.[15]

Much of the U.S. preoccupation with communism in Central America, however, was tragically ill founded and largely inappropriate.[16] (We examine communism in Central America below.) Ill advised or not, the strong belief in the threat of communism held by most U.S. administrations since the 1940s was transmitted to Latin American military establishments as part of the doctrine of national security. This doctrine, in turn, served to justify a systematic and widespread demobilization campaign in Central America.

As taught in war colleges and military training centers around the hemisphere, the doctrine of national security was a product both of U.S. anticommunism and Latin American elaboration. It originated in an elaborate national security apparatus (CIA, National Security Council, and so forth) created in the United States in the late 1940s. In 1950, National Security Council document "NSC-68" described an expanding Communist menace and urged huge increases in military expenditures. Even though George Kennan, the originator of the concept of containment of communism, by then felt that the threat described in "NSC-68" was exaggerated, that document nevertheless became the blueprint for U.S. behavior in the early part of the cold war. Its ideas were spread to Latin America through training programs that the United States expanded or initiated with virtually all of the military establishments of the hemisphere.

Latin America in the 1950s and 1960s was fertile ground for the growth and elaboration of cold war concepts of national security. Though local Communist parties were weak and there were few, if any, obvious external threats to the security of any of the elite-based governments, the privileged classes and their military allies found it very convenient to interpret popular mobilization and protest as subversive and part of a grand, Moscow-controlled plot. In this setting, national security ideas from the United States were quickly adapted, elaborated, and refined into a full-fledged ideology, complete with training centers, native military philosophers, literature, and even meetings held annually by the Latin American Anti-Communist Confederation.

The ideology that emerged was geopolitical. National and international politics were seen as a zero-sum game between communism and the "free world." Whether in foreign or domestic affairs, a loss of territory, allegiance, or influence for one side was seen as a gain for the other. Internal politics became a battlefield. The whole issue of social, economic, and political justice was largely irrelevant or seen as a point of entry for threatening ideological influences.

The national security doctrine was also inherently elitist. Its believers argued that the military was uniquely capable of understanding the national good and, therefore, had the right to run the state and make decisions for society as a whole if, in the judgment of armed forces leaders, civilian politicians were not doing a good enough job. Democracy was directly equated, in the doctrine, with a visceral anticommunism. Accordingly, strange as it may seem, the harshly authoritarian anti-Communist "national security states" created under this ideology were often described by their apologists as "democratic."

All opposition to national security states—and most forms of civilian organization except those on the right—were viewed as subversive and "Communist" or "Communist inspired." The most brutal forms of demobilization and atomization of civilian society were accepted as appropriate. As we noted in Chapter 5,[17] there is now substantial hard evidence that U.S. personnel played an active role in promoting the use by their Latin American colleagues of what was euphemistically called "counterterror" (the widespread use of extralegal arrest, torture, and murder designed to quiet so-called "subversive" groups). The armies, national guards, and police of virtually all Latin American countries received advice, technical and material assistance, and training involving the use of manuals that instructed Latin Americans in the techniques of counterterror. It is not surprising, therefore, that the tactics, devices, and patterns of torture, murder, and disappearance employed by security forces and government-sponsored death squads were similar from country to country. What is more, their methods were practically identical to the those used by the U.S. CIA and its operatives in the late 1960s in Vietnam in Operation Phoenix, which, according to the estimates of U.S. and South Vietnamese government officials, featured the execution without trial of between twenty and forty thousand Vietnamese civilians suspected of being part of the support base of the Vietcong.[18]

By the late 1960s and early 1970s, countries, such as Brazil, Uruguay, and Guatemala, with the most brutal demobilization programs—complete with death squads, torture, murder, and disappearance—also happened to be ones in which the U.S. Agency for International Development's benignly titled Office of Public Safety had established very close links with local security forces.[19] In the early 1970s these links became a public scandal in the United States and throughout the world. The U.S. Congress investigated the links between U.S. government programs and state-sponsored terror in Latin America. In 1974, Congress formally terminated U.S. police and internal security aid programs and ordered the U.S. Department of State to submit yearly reports on the human rights performance of all states to which the U.S. government supplied aid.

But these measures did not solve the problem. In practice, State Department human rights reports seemed to be influenced and colored more by the status quo–oriented policy goals of Washington than by the objective reality of the countries supposedly being described.[20] And though some of the most objectionable U.S. links were discreetly terminated, state-sponsored terror and direct or indirect U.S. material aid to rights-violating regimes and forces continued. Starting in 1982, the Reagan administration began successfully petitioning an increasingly red-baited Congress to make exceptions to the 1974 prohibition against U.S. assistance to police and internal security forces for El Salvador, Guatemala, and Honduras.

COMMUNISM IN CENTRAL AMERICA

Because so much U.S. policy turned on the question of communism in Central America, it is essential to explore in some detail the meaning and influence of communism. It is true that most Central American insurgents and many of the area's intellectuals found Marxist and, in some cases, Leninist analysis to be useful in understanding the reality around them. Nevertheless, it is misleading to equate the intellectual acceptance of those analytical tools with a commitment to a Communist agenda or political subservience to the Soviet-oriented international Communist movement. Most Central Americans were far too pragmatic and nationalistic to accept such control.

Indeed, Soviet-oriented Communist parties fared poorly in Central America. Communists, socialists, and anarchists—many of them European exiles—influenced Central American intellectual life and labor movements in the early twentieth century. The Communists, followers of Karl Marx, received a boost over their leftist competitors because of the Soviet revolution in Russia. Although always targets of repression, Communists gained leadership roles in Central American labor movements in the 1930s. The Soviet alliance with the West during World War II gave the region's tiny Communist parties and their more successful unions a brief political opening the early 1940s. Although repression of the left resumed in most countries after 1945, brief exceptions occurred in Costa Rica in the 1940s and Guatemala in the early 1950s, where Communist elements were junior partners with more conservative parties in government coalitions.

Communist parties fared poorly because of the Soviet practice of limiting the flexibility of local parties to pursue national solutions. Rigid attempts to justify the Stalin-Hitler pact of 1939 discredited Communists in Central America, as it did their copartisans in the United States. Soviet insistence in later years that Latin American Communists seek accommodation with local dictators tarnished their already poor image. Moscow so restrained local Communist parties that, in the 1960s, less patient advocates of sociopolitical reform resigned in disgust and emulated Castro's successful insurgency.

Throughout most of the history of their existence, therefore, the small, Moscow-oriented communist parties of Central America generally were viewed with mistrust and even contempt by local nationalists—including most other Marxists. Most Central American revolutionaries and intellectuals remember that the Cuban communist party, in its determination to follow Soviet orders to peacefully coexist with Fulgencio Batista, actively opposed Fidel Castro until just a few months before the rebel victory. Costa Ricans are well aware that their local communist party, the region's largest, backed the regime of strongman Rafael Calderón Guardia, who later tried to manipulate the 1948 election fraudulently. That episode sparked the civil war of 1948 in which anticommunist rebel social democratic forces were eventually victorious. Since then the Costa Rican communists have never won more than five of the fifty-seven seats in the legislature, and in the last decade their representation has fallen to only one.

Nicaraguans remember that the communist-led labor movement collaborated with the Somoza dictatorship in the 1940s. They recall that the original founders of the FSLN broke away from the pro-Soviet Nicaraguan Socialist party precisely because the latter offered no national solutions to Nicaragua's problems. They also recall that only just before the FSLN victory did the local Communists join the rebel cause. Even in El Salvador, local Communists joined the insurrectionary effort just shortly before the would-be "final offensive" of late 1980 and early 1981. In Nicaragua after the rebel victory, none of the Moscow-oriented Communist parties played more than a peripheral role in the new government. Furthermore, in the election of 1984, the three Communist parties, which had lambasted the FSLN for allegedly selling out the revolution to conservative forces, garnered a pitiful combined vote representing barely 3.8 percent of the total.[21] From 1984 onward, Nicaragua's traditional Communists remained in the opposition, acting more as an irritant to the FSLN than as a source of brotherly support.

In summary, during the cold war traditional Communist parties in Central America exercised their greatest influence on labor movements and in brief periods of limited participation in rule in Costa Rica and Guatemala. However, at their strongest they remained weak, conservative, and generally unpopular.

In comparison to the ideology, intentions, and significance of traditional Communist parties, those issues with respect to Central America's Marxist revolutionary movements are more complex. Most of the principal leaders of

Nicaragua's FSLN, El Salvador's FMLN, and Guatemala's URNG were Marxist-Leninists. They shared a strong predilection for socialism's emphasis on distributive justice as an answer for the injustices they saw in their societies. They adopted a revolutionary strategy similar to that implemented by Castro in Cuba—guerrilla warfare against regime and armed forces—supplemented by tactical alliances with other social and political forces. Marxist-Leninist rebels, as we noted earlier, gained popular support and power largely because of the repressiveness of the regimes of Nicaragua, El Salvador, and Guatemala. In Nicaragua, the Sandinistas built their base of popular support and their broad coalition because they became the only viable alternative for reform for individuals and mobilized groups brutally attacked by the Somoza regime. Moderate, centrist options for reform and redress of grievances were foreclosed in El Salvador and Guatemala by brutal repression, driving many to swell the ranks of Marxist-led guerrilla movements.

Marxist-Leninist rebels regarded Cuba as a friend and ally and received some, albeit limited, Cuban aid in their struggles. Soviet and Eastern bloc assistance to these insurgents was limited, in keeping with Moscow's skepticism about their chances for success. Once the Sandinistas won power in Nicaragua, however, their links to the Soviet bloc became overtly friendly and Moscow became more cooperative. After the West refused Nicaragua military assistance in 1979, the Sandinistas turned to Cuban and Soviet arms and advice for reorganizing their security forces, all the while anticipating increased U.S. hostility.[22] As U.S. pressure on and antagonism toward Nicaragua mounted in the early and mid-1980s, Nicaragua rapidly strengthened its links to the Eastern bloc to counter an expected invasion, fend off the contras, and replace embargoed Western aid, trade, and credit (Appendix, Table 9).

Despite such links of necessity, the Sandinistas were pragmatic in almost all their policies. Instead of imposing Soviet-style Stalinist centralism and one-party political monopoly of the revolution (as Castro did in Cuba), they remained committed to a mixed economy and political pluralism. The Sandinistas were very proud of the originality and independence of their revolution. In a 1990 interview in *Paris Match,* Daniel Ortega even asserted that "it is the Sandinista Revolution which invented perestroika." Recalling a 1985 conversation with Mikhail Gorbachev, he commented: "At that time he [Gorbachev] was not even talking about perestroika. For three hours I had explained the specific policies we were following in Nicaragua. How, for example, we had distributed individual plots of land to peasants so that they would become landowners. He responded that . . . that was the right path to follow and that we, the Sandinistas, should absolutely avoid committing the errors that they, the USSR as well as the Eastern Bloc countries, had committed."[23] Thus, although the Sandinistas never tried to hide the fact that they found some elements of Marxist and Leninist analysis useful, they dramatically demonstrated by means of their social, economic, and political policies that they were pragmatic and nationalistic rather than orthodox Communists.

Though Nicaragua's critics made much of the friendly relationship that the Sandinista government developed with the Socialist bloc, that link should be put in perspective. Nicaragua increased not only its ties to the Eastern bloc but also ties with many non-Communist regimes. Nicaragua increased trade, aid, and diplomatic relations with governments as disparate as those of Brazil, Canada, Chile, France, Libya, the People's Republic of China, the Scandinavian countries, and Spain. It is true that Nicaragua frequently voted with the USSR in the United Nations. But Nicaragua sometimes abstained (e.g., on votes on Afghanistan and the Korean Airlines shoot down) or voted against the USSR on important UN issues (e.g., the matter of sending a peacekeeping force to Lebanon). Indeed, Vanderlaan's careful examination of Nicaragua's UN voting record from 1979 through 1985 revealed that although Nicaragua often voted against U.S. positions and with positions backed by the USSR, it agreed almost as often with the majority of Latin American countries. In fact, it was in agreement with Mexico even more frequently than with the USSR.[24] Likewise, although it is true that Nicaragua eventually came to rely almost exclusively on the Socialist bloc as a supplier of military equipment, it should also be remembered that the Sandinistas first asked the United States to help standardize its military equipment and that in spite of Pentagon endorsement of that idea, the Carter administration—facing a conservative, cold war opponent in the 1980 election campaign—chose the politically safe option of rejecting that request.[25]

Like the Sandinistas, other Central American insurgents appeared to be Marxist-Leninists with respect to revolutionary strategy, but pragmatic and nationalistic in concrete policy matters. They recognized that U.S. influence in the isthmus would probably doom any purely Communist regime or government, especially one that allowed Soviet troops or missiles within its borders. Moreover, evidence of the failure of Stalinist political and economic centralism abounded throughout the socialist world in the 1980s. To assume that the Sandinistas or Central America's other Marxist rebels would ape failed systems was unrealistic indeed.

Thus, though the United States had been intently worried about communism in Central America for four decades, its concerns about the influence of Communists were overblown. Communist parties were weak. Marxist-Leninist guerrillas had not prospered in Honduras and Costa Rica, where regimes were not excessively repressive. The excessive concern of the United States about communism had led to misguided and counterproductive policies—especially in the form of assisting repressive regimes in their campaigns of demobilization.

DEMOBILIZATION IN CENTRAL AMERICA

Though there was some death squad activity in Honduras starting in the early 1980s, systematic programs of mass demobilization in Central America occurred largely where traditional elites were the most powerful and entrenched—

Guatemala, El Salvador, and Nicaragua under the Somozas. In Guatemala and El Salvador, demobilization took the form of state-sponsored terror. In Nicaragua it came in two forms: state-sponsored terror prior to the Sandinista victory of 1979, and U.S.-sponsored contra terror from 1981 onward. Whatever the form, the objective seems to have been constant—to atomize and make docile the ordinary citizenry of Central America. This would promote and facilitate rule by traditional, conservative, pro-U.S. elites or, where necessary, their replacement with friendly, if ineffective, reform-oriented moderates.

The demobilization process—or at least the U.S. link to it—had its longest and most brutal history in Guatemala.[26] It started immediately after the U.S.-sponsored overthrow of elected reformist President Jacobo Arbenz in 1954. Scant hours after Carlos Castillo Armas was imposed as president, a mysterious Committee Against Communism—comprised, in fact, of CIA personnel—seized Guatemalan government, political party, and labor and peasant union documents and began compiling what would soon become known as the Black List. Before the year was out, the names of an estimated 70,000 individuals connected with the former government or with grassroots or political organizations from that era were included on that list of suspected Communists. That August, the Castillo Armas government issued a Law Against Communism, which declared, among other things, that anyone included on the Black List, or "register," as it was formally called, was henceforth banned from public employment and subject to indefinite imprisonment without trial.

Though the Black List ultimately became a death list, this did not happen immediately. The major reason appears to be that the Arévalo and Arbenz governments had been reasonably successful in their attempt to train the Guatemalan security forces to respect human rights. However, in the ensuing decade the U.S. government became increasingly involved in Guatemalan affairs, blocking a return to democracy in the early 1960s and providing ever-escalating doses of security assistance, advice, and training. Meanwhile, previously nonviolent politicians, frustrated by the closing of the democratic option, turned inevitably to open rebellion. By the late 1960s, the insurgents and the opposition in general were labeled "terrorists" and a program of state-sponsored "counterterror," was begun. Featuring the torture, murder, and disappearance of thousands of suspected Communist subversives, this demobilization program was carried out both directly by uniformed security forces or indirectly by government-sanctioned death squads.

By the early 1970s, the rural areas had been "pacified." Terror now moved to the cities as Gen. Carlos Arana Osorio, former coordinator of the rural pacification effort and now president, began eliminating alleged "subversives" (e.g., party leaders, intellectuals, media persons, and labor organizers) among the urban population. The mid-1970s brought a period of eerie calm. But soon, as corrupt military officers began taking over traditional Indian lands and peaceful Indian protests were met with violence, the whole cycle began again. Indians came to support reemerging guerrilla groups, and the regime responded with unprecedented terror in rural areas, particularly in the early 1980s.

It is true that from the 1977 through the mid-1980s, the United States cut off military aid to the Guatemalan regime because of human rights abuses. However the significance of that fact is more apparent than real. Military training continued, and under the Reagan administration, some U.S. material aid to the Guatemalan military, aid that previously had been listed as military, was relabeled nonmilitary. What is more, Israel—the biggest recipient of U.S. aid in the world—took up much of the slack as a supplier of military equipment and training to the Guatemalans during this period.[27]

The demobilization campaign of the late 1970s had not eradicated leftist rebels, and the growth of corruption in the Guatemalan military authoritarian regime and deepening economic difficulties led to the 1982 coup that established a reformist military government. Under its first leader, General Ríos Montt, violent demobilization increased sharply, but the economy eroded further and some of the military's former allies distanced themselves from the regime. The military's leaders then ousted Ríos Montt, replaced him with General Mejía Victores, and decided to return at least nominal control of the executive and legislative branches to civilians. Washington approved of the Guatemalan armed forces' plan to allow the formal transfer of power to a civilian president and congress and energetically supported the election of 1985 and the resultant civilian transitional regime. The Reagan administration had been frustrated by the refusal of the U.S. Congress to authorize funds for direct military aid to Guatemala's unsavory prior military regimes, so the White House viewed the government of elected president Vinicio Cerezo as providing a useful cosmetic change. It would prove easier for Washington to provide military and economic assistance to even such a shaky and weak civilian regime.

For two presidential terms, the civilian transitional government in Guatemala made only very slow progress toward controlling the armed forces, ending the civil war, and reducing the demobilization campaign of the armed forces.

Moderate Cerezo had to promise before taking office not to prosecute military personnel guilty of human rights violations. Although rights abuses continued, no one was prosecuted, and Cerezo refused to allow the International Red Cross to open a Guatemalan office. Moreover, powerful economic groups successfully fought proposed socioeconomic reforms, and some business interests conspired unsuccessfully with right-wing radicals within the military to overthrow the regime. Elected in 1990, Conservative President Jorge Serrano Elías made little progress in addressing social problems, curbing human rights abuses by the military, or conducting peace talks with the rebels. Serrano then attempted the disastrous self-coup of 1993 and was ousted from office by Congress and the judiciary. The resolution of this constitutional crisis broke the logjam and strengthened the hands of those seeking deeper democracy in Guatemala. Serrano's replacement, Ramiro de León Carpio, made progress on peace negotiations. Elected in 1995, de León's successor, Alvaro Arzú, completed peace negotiations, began curbing the military, and instituted a more inclusive, formal civilian democratic regime.

As we noted earlier, El Salvador, too, suffered a process of demobilization in the 1970s and 1980s in which the United States played a major role. Admittedly, demobilization was nothing new to that country. Tremendous violence against poor people had been carried out by the military on behalf of El Salvador's elite in the early 1930s, when the effects of the world depression had set off mass-based pressure for reform. The "Slaughter" (*la Matanza*) had taken the lives of around 30,000 people. But the violence of the late twentieth century achieved new levels of cruelty and carnage that were estimated by normally cautious U.S. media sources as having exacted a toll by 1988 of at least 70,000 dead and 500,000 displaced.[28]

The demobilization campaign was clearly a response to the unusual burst of mobilization of the early to mid-1970s. At first the campaign was carried out at relatively low, but nonetheless well-publicized, levels by the military regimes of Arturo Molina and Humberto Romero. The international attention focused on these abuses, however, made it impossible for the normal flow of U.S. military assistance to continue to the regime in the early part of the vocally human rights-oriented Carter administration. However, when the Somoza regime was overthrown by revolutionaries in Nicaragua, a sense of urgency swept Washington, and a decision was made almost immediately that military aid to El Salvador, the next country likely to "fall," would have to be resumed. Such an apparent reversal of policy, it was suggested, could be made palatable only if a civilian-military, reformist government were to come to power. Washington viewed the most acceptable civilians as the Christian Democrats.[29] Meanwhile, reformist elements in the Salvadoran armed forces, private sector, and opposition parties that shared Washington's concern with blocking a revolutionary outcome began plotting to oust General Romero.

The coup d'état that would largely fulfill the wishes of both the U.S. government and these Salvadoran groups took place on October 15, 1979. The civilians who filled positions on the first civilian-military junta and in the government following the coup were reformist Social Democrats, Christian Democrats, and unaffiliated moderates. But the junta was rapidly transformed. Conservative interests blocked the reformists, and human rights abuses by the armed forces actually accelerated. Less than three months later, the first civilians resigned in protest over the powerlessness of their role and left in place a reformist military regime still determined to repress popular sector and leftist mobilization. The slots of the civilians quitting the junta were then filled by individuals from the conservative wing of the Christian democratic movement, and hard-liners from within the military replaced moderate officers in the junta.

Meanwhile, U.S. military aid to El Salvador was resumed immediately after the October coup. Despite much fanfare about moderation and reform, torture, murder, and disappearance soared to heights never seen during the previous two military governments.[30] In February 1980, U.S. Chargé d'Affairs James Cheek met with Christian democrats in the government and urged that El Salvador institute what he called "a clean counter-insurgency war." This war could be facilitated, he argued, by giving the armed forces much greater leeway in dealing with suspected subversives. Though some Christian democrats were cool to the idea, Cheek's suggestions were fully implemented in March through the promulgation of Decree 155, which imposed a harsh state of siege and gave the military draconian powers in dealing with civilians.[31]

Throughout the rest of the Carter administration and for several years into the Reagan period, grassroots party and interest organizations were systematically dismantled, with almost total disregard for human rights. In public statements, U.S. officials blamed the tens of thousands of killings, first, on "violence of the right and the left," and later, when that rhetoric wore thin, on the work of "right-wing death squads." The government and even the military were falsely depicted in the United States as composed of moderates earnestly trying to bring historically endemic violence under control.

Eventually pressure mounted in the U.S. Congress to reduce the shocking level of human rights abuse in El Salvador. In 1982 and 1983, with congressional approval for further military aid hanging in the balance, the Reagan administration sent a series of emissaries to San Salvador to pressure the Salvadoran government and military and to curtail the killings.[32] As a result, for the next several years—though the aerial bombardment of civilian populations in rebel-controlled areas actually escalated—the so-called death squad killings declined. But by then, the demobilization had been largely accomplished. The leadership and much of the membership of most grassroots party and interest organizations to the left of the conservative minority of Christian democrats who had stuck with José Napoleón Duarte had been killed, driven underground, or forced into exile. The two opposition newspapers had been terrorized into extinction. And the Catholic church, having suffered the martyrdom of Archbishop Romero and numerous clergy and lay activists, had been cowed into a much less critical posture.

Criticism of the reformist military's exceedingly violent record in the early 1980s made continued U.S. economic and military aid to El Salvador progressively less certain in the U.S. Congress. This brought pressure from the Reagan administration to move toward an elected, constitutional government and recognition within the regime itself that civilian rule would be expedient. The junta called an election in 1982 for a constituent assembly that would draft a new constitution. With terror at its apogee, parties of the extreme right won the bulk of the votes and a majority of seats in the constituent assembly. U.S. pressure brought a slackening in the violence, and Washington essentially forced the right-dominated constituent assembly to appoint a moderate figurehead, Alvaro Magaña, as interim president. In 1984, with terror somewhat curtailed, Salvadorans cast their presidential vote for the U.S.-funded and endorsed center-right Christian Democratic candidate, José Napoleón Duarte, who, as reformist ex-mayor of San Salvador, was a popular figure. This ushered in a civilian transitional regime, but one that for years would be severely limited in its power over public policy. Duarte's ability to rule effectively and promote reforms was completely hamstrung by the constitution written by the rightist-dominated constituent assembly and by the overweening power of the armed forces.

By the time of the 1988 legislative elections, President Duarte was dying of cancer and his administration had proven to be as corrupt as it was weak. In the wake of the signing of the Esquipulas peace accord in August 1987, death squad terror once again escalated as the right attempted to sabotage its implementation, at least in El Salvador. Not surprisingly, the voters in the 1988 and 1991 legislative and 1989 presidential elections abandoned the Christian Democrats and moved sharply to the right.

Nicaragua, as we noted above, suffered demobilization both before and after the revolutionary victory of 1979. The first wave was conducted by the Somoza regime from 1975 through July 1979. The second was carried out by U.S.-backed contras from 1981 through mid-1990. Together, these demobilizing activities resulted in the deaths of over 80,000 people; around 50,000 in the earlier period and almost 31,000 in the latter. Though some of the deaths counted here were those of combatants, the bulk were civilians.

The barbarity of the Somoza regime in its efforts to pacify Nicaragua and perpetuate itself in power is so well documented that it need not be belabored here.[33] What is important, however, is the close relationship that existed between the U.S. government and Somoza's National Guard. In 1979 Somoza's guard had more U.S.-trained personnel than any other military establishment in Latin America, not just proportionally, but absolutely.[34] More Nicaraguan officers and men had been trained in the United States or at the U.S.-run School of the Americas in Panama than officers of any other Latin American country, including a comparative giant like Brazil, with almost forty times the population of Nicaragua. What is more, U.S. military aid and the training of Nicaraguan military personnel ceased fully only after guard massacres of civilians in several cities in September 1978. As in the case of Guatemala, Israel immediately picked up the slack, supplying the guard with badly needed automatic weapons and other military equipment. In addition, U.S. military attachés remained in Nicaragua until a few months before Somoza fell, and as we noted earlier, the CIA used cargo planes disguised with Red Cross markings to spirit many of Somoza's officer corps into exile in the confused first days of the rebel victory.

The instrument the Reagan administration chose for the demobilization of Nicaragua under the revolution was the contras. This counterrevolutionary force, pulled together from remnants of the National Guard by agents of the Argentine military soon after the Sandinista victory, received a massive infusion of funds when President Reagan signed National Security Decision Directive Number 17 in November 1981. Although young people who had never served in Somoza's

DEMOBILIZATION. Scene at a Somoza National Guard body dump on the outskirts of Managua in the summer of 1979 (photo courtesy of *Barricada*). Views of two regime/death squad body dumps in El Salvador: "La Puerta del Diablo," about three miles southeast of the capital, May 1982, and "El Playón," approximately twenty miles west of the capital, March 1983 (photos and copyright by Tommie Sue Montgomery, 1982, 1983).

National Guard eventually came to constitute the majority of the lower ranks, the contra officer corps was comprised largely of ex-Guardia officers.[35] The United States manipulated and funded the contras from the early 1980s on, but the force was more than a creature of Argentina and the United States. Revolutionary agrarian policies and military recruitment alienated enough peasants to turn the contras into a strong social movement. This deeply worried the revolutionary government and armed forces.[36]

The tactics of demobilization employed by the counterrevolutionaries and their U.S. backers shifted over time. At first, there was a naive belief that the contras might serve as a catalyst around which disgruntled Nicaraguans would rally and overthrow their government. Some in the CIA clearly believed that the contras could serve as authentic and ultimately successful guerrillas. However, when the contras in their first two years followed their Guardia instincts and behaved like crude terrorists rather than like a guerrilla vanguard, the CIA became alarmed and commissioned its famous manual for contra officers, *Psychological Operations in Guerrilla Warfare.*[37] Although criticized in the United States for its instructions on the selective assassination of government officials and for its cold-blooded ideas on the hiring of professional gunmen to create martyrs from among the opposition at antigovernment rallies, the overall thrust of the document is actually one of relative moderation. The manual was intended to teach the contras to focus their terror narrowly and intelligently. Though selective assassination was advocated, the contras were not to terrorize the population as a whole. Instead they were to behave respectfully and thus win a civilian base, which, in the long run, would help them isolate and defeat the Sandinistas.

A few contra units actually seem to have followed the tactically sound CIA advice. Pockets of civilian support developed in remote, lightly populated regions in the central departments of Boaco and Chontales and in the north. But by and large, the contras failed to achieve the discipline desired by the CIA and behaved quite brutally.[38] This, coupled with their widespread image in Nicaragua as U.S. mercenaries and as the direct linear descendants of Somoza's hated Guardia Nacional, meant that by the mid-1980s it was clear to most informed observers that the contras could never rally enough popular support to overthrow their government.

Although the contras grew in numbers in the mid-1980s as they recruited more and more disgruntled peasants, their military accomplishments remained limited. The contras forced the Sandinista army to quickly improvise its own counterinsurgency strategy. This prevented the rebels from taking or holding territory but also eventually contributed to disrupting the economy and undermining support for the government. As CIA awareness of the contras' limitations for toppling the FSLN from power grew, contra tactics changed. The idea of spawning a guerrilla-led popular insurrection against the Sandinistas was abandoned. The new strategy was to employ terror and sabotage to disrupt the economy, government, and social life of the nation. Terror and sabotage against human and material infrastructure—which, in fact, had been practiced by most contra units from the start—became the principal and most effective instrument of demobilization. Contra units attacked (1) rural social service infrastructure such as schools, health clinics, day care centers, and government food program storage facilities; (2) economic infrastructure such as cooperative or state farms, sawmills, tobacco drying facilities, bridges, power lines, and trucks; (3) cooperative or grassroots organizations such as the small farmers association (UNAG); and (4) persons employed by, associated with, or receiving benefits from those three. Among the nearly 31,000 Nicaraguans killed in the contra war were 130 teachers, 40 medical personnel, and 152 technicians.[39] In addition, starting in the mid-1980s, the contras began planting powerful antitank mines on remote rural roads, an action resulting in the destruction of vehicles of all types and the death and mutilation of hundreds of civilians. The purposes of these activities seem to have been to destroy the rural economy of Nicaragua and hence to inflict economic hardship on all citizens of that agriculturally dependent country, to cut off the delivery of innovative government social services to remote rural populations, to disrupt grassroots organizations such as the peasants' (UNAG) and rural workers' (ATC) associations and village CDSs, and to force heavy government defense spending in order to undermine social services, cause inflation, and seed popular discontent with the Sandinistas.

The terror and sabotage campaign of the late 1980s bore fruit. Social services were curtailed throughout the country and cut off completely in some remote rural areas. Nicaraguan agricultural output declined, the economy went sour, and inflation went through the roof. Membership in grassroots organizations, which had climbed early in the contra war (1982–1984), stagnated in 1985 and 1986. Mass organization membership then declined sharply in 1987 and 1988, as discontent over the economic situation rose and finding ways to make ends meet occupied more and more of the time of ordinary Nicaraguans. As opposition protests and union resistance to austerity programs grew in 1986–1987, the government itself repressed its opponents and curtailed civil liberties.

By the time of the February 1990 elections, the U.S.-sponsored program of demobilization had so undercut the legitimacy of the Sandinistas and so intimidated the Nicaraguan people that the victory of the U.S.-endorsed candidate, Violeta Chamorro, should not have come as a surprise. It is probably true that a plurality—perhaps even a majority—of those who voted for Chamorro had opposed the revolution all along; even in the comparatively good times of 1984, the opposition had received nearly one-third of the vote. But another significant segment of the Chamorro voters was made up of citizens who had become disillusioned with the Sandinistas as they watched government programs deteriorate and the economy collapse in the latter half of the 1980s. Apparently either unaware of or unconcerned with the role the United States had played in generating that decay, these voters sincerely and angrily blamed the Sandinistas. Finally, it appears that another segment was composed of people who, although they favored the revolution, were simply unwilling to face the punishment the United States had signaled would continue should the FSLN win. Typical of this group was a generally pro-Sandinista woman who, on the day following the election, was berated by an army veteran for having betrayed the Fatherland in voting for UNO. She was the mother of two draft-age boys, and she responded indignantly that she was not going to sacrifice her boys "for the fucking Fatherland!"[40] Thus, the latter two blocks of votes, which very likely provided the winning UNO margin, appear to have been a product of U.S. policy.

THE COST OF U.S. COLD WAR POLICY IN CENTRAL AMERICA

U.S. policy in Central America during the cold war was not only destructive and ill advised but, more important, counterproductive to the interests of the United States, as well as to those of the peoples of the isthmus.

Responding more to domestic political pressures in the United States and to outmoded conceptions of security and economic interests than to the concrete reality of Central America, it jousted with a vastly overblown threat of communism for more than four decades. As a result, the United States sided with a tiny exploitative elite in demobilizing strategies that took the lives of between 200,000 and 300,000 people. Furthermore, U.S. policy did violence to both the concept and the practice of democracy in the region. Power and democracy go hand in hand. As long as U.S.-advised military forces used counterterror to quiet and exclude from the political arena a wide spectrum of civil society, the transition to civilian democratic regime types was made impossible.

U.S. POLICY IN THE POST-COLD WAR PERIOD

The end of the cold war at the beginning of the 1990s brought a dramatic shift in U.S. foreign policy. Since the Soviet Union and the socialist bloc no longer existed as a perceived threat to U.S. interests, Washington could begin responding to Central American reality on its own terms. Accordingly, the United States immediately reversed its policy toward the civil wars in El Salvador and Guatemala. U.N.-backed efforts at achieving negotiated settlements between guerrilla forces and the governments of those countries—long opposed by the United States—were now enthusiastically endorsed. In Nicaragua, though cold war policy lingered a bit longer, President Clinton eventually appointed a new U.S. ambassador, John Maisto, who quickly observed that it was time for the United States to leave the "hangups of the cold war" behind and treat all civilian forces in that country—including the Sandinistas—as legitimate.[41]

The post-cold-war shift in U.S. policy toward the region greatly facilitated the achievement of negotiated peace settlements in El Salvador (1992) and Guatemala (1996) and the various intra-elite accords on modifying the rules of the political game that took place in Nicaragua in the mid-1990s. This ushered in civilian democratic regimes and bolstered the prospects for the consolidation of civilian democratic regimes in those war-ravaged countries.

Other aspects of U.S. policy, however, had not changed—principal among them, the promotion of a strongly capitalist economic model. Using heavily U.S.-influenced international lending agencies—the International Monetary Fund, the World Bank, the Inter-American Development Bank—to wield both carrot and stick, Washington insisted on harsh "structural adjustment" policies which, though they resulted in overall growth, also tended to concentrate income and hurt the poor majority. Thus, by the late 1990s, the dynamic contradictions between income-concentrating neoliberalism and the consolidation of civilian democracy—both promoted by the United States—were coming to the fore.

11

REFLECTIONS AND PROJECTIONS

We have now come to the point in this volume where it is logical to reflect and project: to reflect on patterns and truths that have emerged from our examination of Central America in the last three decades and to project or speculate about the region's possible future. Decades of involvement with the subject have taught us that it is far easier to sum up than to predict. We freely admit that our individual and joint writings—like those of most other observers over the years—are strewn with faulty predictions. Be that as it may, we will now have another go at it.

REFLECTIONS: REPRESSION, MOBILIZATION, AND DEMOCRATIC TRANSITION

The Crises

As we have noted previously, the crises in Central America in the latter half of the twentieth century arose from several factors: (1) centuries of socioeconomic formation; (2) rapid economic growth in the 1960s followed by a sharp economic crisis in the mid-1970s; (3) elite and government intransigence in the face of mobilization driven by the economic crisis; and (4) international cold war politics—notably the behavior of the United States. We disagree with the Kissinger Commission report of 1984, which argued that the violent upheavals of the 1970s and 1980s occurred mainly because of Soviet bloc/Cuban meddling in "our backyard."[1]

Clearly the crises of the twentieth century can, in part, be traced to the early social and economic formation of what are now the five major Central American countries. In the colonial period, Guatemala, El Salvador, and Nicaragua developed relatively strong, largely Hispanic ruling classes, which used the majority nonwhite, largely Indian masses to produce primary export products. Inequality and harsh exploitation were established from the start, and elite factionalism became intense by the end of the colonial era and in early independence. Thus both the political and economic pressures encouraged violent, military-dominated polities. In the other two countries, less-exploitative systems developed, but for different reasons. In Costa Rica, where Indians had either been killed or driven out of the central highlands, there was practically no racially distinct underclass to exploit. Moreover, divisions among elites were minor. So civilian rather than military government became the norm for long periods, and military rule when it occurred was an aberration. Honduras, on the other hand, a poor backwater of the region, never really developed the type of powerful, self-confident, and therefore exploitative elite minority seen in all three neighboring countries.

These differing patterns of social formation meant that, in the twentieth century, the governing elites of these five countries essentially became conditioned to respond differently to local sociopolitical crises. As we saw, the Honduran and Costa Rican elites responded with relative moderation and accommodation whereas those of Guatemala, El Salvador, and Nicaragua exhibited intransigence and employed violent repression. Where accommodation or even mere cooptation—as was frequently the case in Honduras—prevailed, social peace was preserved. Where intransigence and repression ruled the day, insurgent forces emerged, gained legitimacy, and either toppled the government (Nicaragua) or held government forces at bay in protracted civil wars (Guatemala and El Salvador).

It was at this juncture that external interference actually exacerbated a problem it was intended to solve. Seized by inflated cold war fears of Soviet penetration into Central America, the United States misinterpreted mobilizing popular demands for social justice and democracy. Listening almost exclusively to the voices of an intransigent local elite and a foreign policy establishment deeply suspicious of the left, Washington rallied to the trumpets of anticommunism. Thus, in the 1950s—at the height of McCarthyism at home—the CIA worked successfully to overthrow Guatemala's first experiment in socially progressive democracy. It then beefed up the military and police establishments of all four of the local dictatorships and began to train local security forces to implement repression and counterinsurgency. This began in Guatemala and Nicaragua in the 1960s, in El Salvador in the 1970s, and in Honduras in the 1980s. In the face of such increasingly violent intransigence, and with democratic avenues of redress closed, guerrilla movements began to form or expand—first in Guatemala and Nicaragua, then in El Salvador, and still later in Honduras. We believe that, had local dictatorships been less protected by U.S. arms, less encouraged by U.S. support, and more constructively responsive to the demands of mobilized civil society and the needs of the suffering majority, accommodation might have taken place and thus obviated the conversion of opposition and mobilized demand making into insurrectionary movements.

Central America's Unique Patterns of Transition

Central America is a remarkable laboratory for the study of democratic transition in that it presents several types of regime change. Of the five countries, Honduras—with its fragile state and weak elite—historically oscillated between military and civilian rule. Under pressure by the Carter administration to become democratic and with top military officers keenly aware of both the Nicaraguan revolution next door and the growing institutional cost to the military of remaining in power, Honduras moved quickly from military authoritarian to reformist military to transitional civilian democratic regimes in the early 1980s. This occurred just as the Reagan administration chose Honduras as a staging ground for attacks on the Nicaraguan revolution and Salvadoran insurgency. Ironically, for a few years in the early 1980s repression perpetrated by certain military units escalated dramatically while the elected government took a back seat to the U.S.-supported military. But such extremism was out of character and by the mid-1980s the military had brought its own excesses somewhat under control. The early and tentative years of the transitional civilian democratic regime in the 1980s gave way to full civilian democracy with greater civilian control of the military and armed forces reform by 1996.

Costa Rica, on the other hand, had gone through a long process of building toward democracy in the early twentieth century that drew upon several factors: the institution of universal education just before the turn of the century; expansion of working-class organizations and other civil society that gained considerable momentum during the 1930s; a tradition of civilian rule and elections—albeit elitist and often fraudulently manipulated; and a critical division of the ruling cafetalero elite in the 1940s. This culminated in the brief civil war and democratic revolution of 1948–1949. Its resolution, the constitutional revision of 1949, and a working agreement among political elites from the 1950s on provided the bases for a continuing and successful civilian democratic regime. Although buffeted by the turmoil and violence that convulsed the region in the 1970s and 1980s, Costa Rica maintained its stability and democratic practices throughout with accommodation of opposition, good human rights performance, and public policy that improved middle- and working-class living standards.

In the other three countries transition from dictatorship in the 1970s to democracy in the 1990s took place literally at gunpoint. In each country economic strains in the 1970s led to opposition and popular mobilization for change, to which each government responded with violent intransigence. For Nicaragua, El Salvador, and Guatemala in the 1970s, there appeared no viable option to insurrection.

In Nicaragua, the FSLN overthrew the Somoza dictatorship in 1979 and instituted eleven years of revolutionary regime. Moderate in comparison to other Marxist-led regimes, the Nicaraguan revolution moved from de facto rule

(1979–1984) to institutionalized, elected government (1984–1990); implemented grassroots participatory democracy; built election institutions and held formal elections (1984 and 1990); and produced a new constitution (1987). In 1990, after the economic and political damage of the contra war and revolutionary policy had polarized and virtually beggared the country, Nicaraguans availed themselves of their electoral institutions to reject the revolutionary regime and institute more conventional civilian democracy.

Guatemala and El Salvador passed from military authoritarian regimes through military reformist regimes and civilian transitional regimes and ultimately to civilian democracy by way of civil war and elaborately negotiated peace settlements. Although they originally dreamed of overthrowing their respective dictatorships and establishing revolutionary regimes, both the FMLN of El Salvador (by 1982) and the URNG of Guatemala (by 1986) had discarded that objective as unrealistic. They could see what the United States was doing to the revolutionary government of Nicaragua. They became convinced that for them, in the words of Rubén Zamora (the leader of the Salvadoran FMLN's political wing), outright "victory would be ashes in our mouths."[2] The United States, and hence, its two client governments, would resist negotiated settlements until after the end of the cold war. The United States and key elites in El Salvador and Guatemala, including the armed forces, thus pursued a moderate, reformist strategy of using elections and transition to civilian government to enhance governmental legitimacy and deny rebels a broader coalition. In the post–cold war environment and with the Nicaraguan revolution over, Washington and local actors became willing to accept peace agreements very similar to those envisioned by the guerrillas a decade earlier. Thus civilian democratic regimes, with former rebels included in the political arena and reformed militaries, emerged from decades of violent conflict.

The legacy of "transition at gunpoint," as seen in Nicaragua, El Salvador, and Guatemala, appeared mixed. On the one hand, all three countries now had at least formally democratic political institutions, and civil and political conditions were far better than those that had existed prior to the onset of guerrilla activity. In addition, since all three transitions (especially that in Nicaragua) had required considerable grassroots participation, democracy in the 1990s (especially in Nicaragua) would feature broad involvement on the part of ordinary people. This situation stood in marked contrast to that of the countries of the Southern Cone of South America where, in the immediate post-transition period, ordinary people, who had been completely demobilized by previous dictatorships, were very hesitant to participate in normal institutions of civil society.

There was, however, a negative aspect to this type of transition. The rapid demobilization of tens of thousands of fighters on both sides in all three countries and the abundance of arms left over from the period of strife produced high levels of armed delinquency—and in Nicaragua, sporadic renewed insurgency—which threatened both individual and state security. For several years the police,

RECURRENT INSURGENCY IN POST–1990 NICARAGUA. *In 1998, a Recontra woman hands in her weapon and a Recompa man kisses his Sandinista kerchief in yet another round of ceremonies for demobilizing insurgents. (Photos by and with the permission of Jorge Lopez,* La Tribuna*).*

undergoing extensive reforms because of the regime transitions or peace accords, could not cope with the resulting surge in violent crime. Moreover, as in all civil wars, the fratricidal armed conflict of the 1970s and 1980s and accompanying personal loss and black propaganda had left a legacy of deep polarization and partisan hatred that would likely impede the normal functioning of civil politics for years to come.

Finally, the legacy of bitter competition between the United States and the three revolutionary movements during the 1970s and 1980s would likely play a role in post–cold war politics for some time to come. For instance, in the 1996 Nicaraguan election, when the gap in the polls between conservative Arnoldo Alemán and his FSLN opponent Daniel Ortega suddenly narrowed, State Department spokesman Nicholas Burns strayed from Washington's official policy of neutrality and made off-the-cuff statements indicating U.S. disapproval of Ortega. Although later ambiguously retracted, this expression of apparent U.S. preference may well have influenced the vote.[3] This phenomenon raised an important question: Would perceived U.S. disapproval of old cold war enemies act as a barrier to the normal alternation in power in potentially emerging two-party systems in Nicaragua and El Salvador?

PROJECTIONS: PROSPECTS FOR DEMOCRATIC CONSOLIDATION

The External Setting

This brings us to an examination of the prospects for democratic consolidation in Central America. As we note below, most of the theoretical literature on this subject focuses on domestic considerations that promote or impede consolidation. In Central America, however, we would argue that it makes little sense to discuss such factors as if these countries existed in a vacuum. In fact, Central America's international environment, particularly, the behavior of the United States, is—and long has been—one of the most important factors shaping local regime types. This should not be surprising because the United States emerged from World War II as the world's most powerful nation and by the end of the century had become the world's only superpower. Washington exercised tremendous influence over the tiny nearby Central American republics through its diplomacy, aid programs, demonstrated willingness to project military power into the region, close relationships with local military institutions, and virtual veto power over the decisions of critically important international lending agencies such as the International Monetary Fund, the World Bank, and the Inter-American Development Bank.

Although it is probably true that most U.S. policymakers throughout the twentieth century would have preferred democratic forms,[4] it is also clear that this preference had frequently taken a back seat to the practical politics of pursuing

U.S. economic and security interests. This was especially true during the cold war when concern with containing a perceived communist threat overwhelmed any squeamishness U.S. policymakers may have had about Central American dictators.[5] Even when the Reagan and Bush administrations pushed for the election of civilian governments in El Salvador and Guatemala, they continued to support local military establishments whose campaigns of "counterterror" against a wide spectrum of civil society made such elections far from democratic. What is more, until the end of the cold war, the United States opposed (and hence delayed) negotiated settlements that would have allowed for greater civil rights and fuller democracy.

With the cold war over in the 1990s, the United States reversed policy—promoting peace settlements and much freer and more meaningful democratic processes. For example, U.S. aid helped finance and provided technical assistance for the Nicaraguan election of 1996. With this type of U.S. backing, democracy in Central America had an unusual window of opportunity. However, because there was no telling whether or how long this propitious international setting would last, it was especially important that Central American democracy be consolidated internally. Accordingly, it is appropriate at this point to discuss domestic components of democratic consolidation—both in theory and in the concrete reality of Central America at the end of the 1990s.

Internal Factors

All the Central American nations now have elected, civilian, constitutional regimes, a circumstance that would have seemed inconceivable as recently as 1980. This remarkable change from military authoritarian to civilian democratic regimes in Central America aroused much interest among scholars.[6] As we have so frequently argued in the preceding pages, Central America's old (Costa Rica) and new (all the rest) civilian democratic regimes all face difficult political and economic challenges. The new democracies, in particular, stand at a critical juncture where their political actors must work to conserve their fledgling democratic regimes from powerful and often unpredictable forces.

In practical terms, the preservation of democracy in Central America requires the four newer democratic regimes to devise predictable and widely acceptable political structures and processes more like those that have existed in Costa Rica since the 1950s. These must be able to sustain citizen participation and protect the individual political rights that guarantee the participation of civil society. This process of preserving the new democracies of the isthmus is *democratic consolidation.*[7]

Students of the consolidation of democracy, some focusing specifically on Latin America, have identified several important consolidation factors. Among the most important is (1) the development of an elite settlement, a consensus among a broad array of elites (the leadership of major social, economic, and political forces) to accept and accommodate each other's participation in the political game, to accept democratic procedures, and to allow the mass public and civil society to take part in politics.[8] Such accords, typically shaped by what Larry Diamond and Juan Linz call "founding democratic leadership,"[9] may derive from explicit pacts among elites or may simply evolve over time. However such settlements initially occur, they must allow for some evolution so the regime can adjust to changing circumstances and accommodate new power contenders.[10]

Another very important element is (2) the emergence of an autonomous civil society (political participation and organized interest activity). Such participation by the civil society—especially in matters of economic policymaking—is essential to communicate citizens' needs to government and to restrain state power.

Among other factors that contribute to democratic consolidation are the following: (3) the development of a mass culture of support for democratic norms; (4) strong but moderate political parties; (5) a strong legislature; (6) a strong and effective government; (7) a small military that is allegiant to civilian leadership; (8) some deconcentration of wealth or amelioration of poverty; (9) moderate economic growth; and (10) as noted above, the support of important external actors.[11]

To evaluate each of these ten points for all five Central American countries would necessitate another entire volume and is well beyond the scope of this chapter. Nevertheless, a brief review of several of them will tell us something useful about the prospects for democratic consolidation Central America.

Prospects

We have already noted how very important we consider the last of these consolidation factors—the support of external actors for democracy—so we need not detain ourselves further with it other than to reaffirm that the United States will play a major role here. As long as U.S. foreign policy values and reinforces democracy in Central America, local elites will operate within important constraints that will make it easier for them to play by democratic rules. Since the 1980s other key outside actors, of less influence than the United States but nevertheless of import, have also encouraged democracy in Central America. Indeed, several of these, including most European countries and the Catholic church, favored and contributed in various ways to democratization and democratic consolidation. These pressures appear likely to continue for the middle term.

Elite Settlement. To what extent had there emerged broadly inclusive interelite agreements about democratic rules of the game? Costa Rica's elite settlement has been in place for decades, a cornerstone of that nation's political stability. Progress toward elite settlement in the other countries, however, has aroused much debate. In the late 1980s and mid-1990s John Peeler, author of a definitive study of Costa Rica's elite settlement, remained skeptical about the progress toward democratic elite settlements in the other countries of the isthmus.[12] On the positive side, numerous specific accords and pacts have been signed among formerly warring elites in Nicaragua (ending the contra war in 1990), El Salvador (the 1992 peace accord), and Guatemala (various deals culminated in the 1996 peace accord). Nominally democratic rules were put in place, formerly excluded players were allowed into the legal political arena, clean elections were being held, power was regularly being transferred peaceably from incumbents to opponents. Many key actors in each country appeared willing to play by these rules.

On the negative side, Nicaragua's former combatants (both ex-contras and ex-army soldiers) repeatedly broke agreements to demobilize and took up arms again, sometimes because the government failed to meet previous promises and other times apparently angling greedily for better deals or engaging in banditry. The broad general peace agreements in El Salvador and Guatemala seemed to be holding, but periodic assassinations of political and human rights activists and candidates for office in both countries (and in Honduras) clearly revealed that some political actors wished to intimidate some players, disrupt the accords, or destabilize the democratic regimes. In summary, the willingness of Central American elites to play by democratic rules had reached a historic high level as this went to press, but there remained doubts and pockets of resistance. We simply may not know for many years whether this situation will allow elites to trust each other and thus evolve into smoothly cooperative settlements like Costa Rica's. On balance, however, middle-run prospects for democratic elite settlements appeared reasonably good.

Civil Society and Participation. How much autonomous civil society and political participation had developed in Central America? Turning first to political participation, recent surveys of urban citizens in all Central American nations (summarized here) reported a wealth of voting and registration, electioneering, contacting of public officials, organizational activism, and communal self-help in all five nations. The range and breadth of political activity among urban citizens was remarkable, especially given the turbulence in some countries. Indeed, in the early 1990s the factor that most curtailed participation was high national levels of repression. Because repression declined dramatically in several countries in the 1990s after peace deals were signed and military and police reform implemented, we suspect that citizen participation should increase.

With respect to civil society (activism within groups), there was strong evidence that such associational participation increased Central Americans' support for democracy and political activity. Moreover, higher national levels of civil society activism contributed to higher levels of democracy within the region.[13] Overall, then, these studies of participation and civil society suggested reason for optimism about democratic consolidation in Central America. Especially in a climate of reduced repression, citizens increasingly participated in politics and in organizations that conveyed demands to government and strengthened democratic performance.

Mass Culture. Did the broad general public of Central America support democratic rules of the game? The same urban surveys just mentioned explored citizen support for various kinds of participation and for citizens' rights and liberties. In summary, Central Americans generally strongly favored democratic liberties in the early 1990s. As was the case for political participation, high levels of repression reduced popular support for democratic liberties. However, the recent waning of state repression with peace and the emergence of democratic regimes suggest that, other things equal, citizen support for democratic liberties should be on the increase in the isthmus.

Party Systems. To what extent did Central America approach the model of other stable democracies in having two strong but moderate (ideologically centrist) political parties? Costa Rica clearly filled the bill with its dominant main parties, the social democratic PLN and the moderate conservative PUSC. Honduras also had two strong moderate parties that between them had effectively dominated the political arena for decades—the center-right National party and the center-left Liberal party. In Costa Rica and Honduras the dominant pair of parties regularly traded off ruling power through elections.

Two other countries had strong parties, but they were more ideologically polarized than centrist and less evenly matched than in Costa Rica and Honduras. El Salvador's ARENA, once on the far right, moderated somewhat after the mid-1980s and dominated the presidency and legislature from the Cristiani administration (1988) into the late 1990s. The Salvadoran Christian Democratic party declined and virtually vanished by the 1990s. On the Salvadoran left was the former guerrilla insurgent coalition FMLN, which had joined the legal political struggle and (though much weaker than ARENA) made large gains in the legislature and city council elections of 1998. In Nicaragua the FSLN somewhat moderated its leftist stances in the early 1990s and remained relatively strong but lost two successive elections (1990 and 1996) and developed serious internal strains and leadership problems. The Liberal Alliance in 1996 had reconstituted a strong Liberal coalition and appeared likely to become a very powerful party. Other Nicaraguan parties were tiny and highly centrifugal, personalistic, and fractious.

Guatemala had a several small and medium-sized ideological or personalistic parties of varying ages. The Christian Democrats of Guatemala, once a candidate for a strong, centrist role, failed to consolidate their position of electoral leadership during the presidency of Vinicio Cerezo Arévalo and declined badly after their 1990 election defeat. President Alvaro Arzú's PAN won the 1995 election in a runoff. The PAN, however, and the URNG and FDNG (both emerging as leftist electoral parties as this was being written) were too new to assess. Guatemala's party system was the most fragmented in the region.

In summary, only Costa Rica and Honduras clearly met the two-party, centrist model. El Salvador and Nicaragua were developing into two-party polarized polities (both had other very small parties). Although there remained real questions as to whether the ex-guerrilla organizations FSLN and FMLN would ever be able to win sufficient votes to capture their respective nations' presidencies, they had taken part effectively in legislative and municipal contexts. To the extent that the two-party, centrist model might contribute to democratic consolidation, Costa Rica and Honduras appeared to have an advantage. Something similar could develop in El Salvador and Nicaragua should the polarized big parties further moderate their politics and continue to learn to work together in the legislative and municipal arenas. Anyone familiar with the viciousness of Nicaraguan partisan political rhetoric, however, would feel little cause for optimism in that particular case.

Armed Forces. To what extent were the region's militaries small and loyal to civilian rule? In the Central American isthmus as recently as 1990 this question was risible, but by the late 1990s there had been significant progress. In 1990, only one government approached the criterion of having a small and allegiant military—Costa Rica had dismantled its army in 1949—but all the other countries had large armies swollen by war (or in Honduras by foreign aid to support U.S. geostrategic goals in the region). After 1990, though, change came rapidly. After settling the contra war in 1990, the new Nicaraguan government reduced the EPS's size by 80 percent, civilianized the police, passed a new military code, and professionalized and renamed the army (now the Nicaraguan Army). Nicaraguan military behavior after 1990 suggested a growing willingness to accept civilian control. With the end of the Salvadoran and Guatemalan civil wars the armies of both countries underwent substantial force cuts and came under increased civilian influence, and top officers were retired and reassigned. In the mid-1990s the long truculent Honduran military, too, submitted to reforms that included abolition of the draft, reassignment of officers, and civilianization of the police.

No one familiar with the history of Central America's recently reformed militaries could be wholly sanguine about their prospects for loyalty to their civilian governments, but by the late 1990s armies of the isthmus were out of power, discredited by their past abuses and poor performance as rulers, and lacking the former financial and political support of the United States (demobilization was no longer a major issue for Washington). Central American militaries had become smaller, less human rights abusive, and more cooperative with civilian officials. We view these changes as unrequited goods and a positive augury for democratic consolidation in the middle-term future.

CONCLUSION

On balance, then, there were positive signs for the consolidation of formal civilian democracies in Central America as the twentieth century drew to a close. In political terms, collectively the citizens of the isthmus enjoyed more human rights and greater political freedom than ever before. Their political elites were playing by democratic rules, and key institutional and external factors seemed likely to continue to support democratic regimes. The great experiment of the Nicaraguan revolution—a regime that pushed for much more participatory democracy and greater social justice than the polities that survived it—had failed under a combination of fierce U.S. pressure and its own errors.

The extant democracies of Central America were derided by critics as "low intensity" or "light" democracies, and there was some merit to the implicit criticism. Formal democratic rules and procedures in a socioeconomic context of enormous inequality and widespread poverty would provide only modest influence over public policy to the legions of poor and disorganized Central Americans. The great neoliberal economic experiment imposed upon all five countries of the region by international financial institutions and major donor nations, at least in the short run, exacerbated inequality and poverty. Thus the only long-run hope for increased resources for the poor majority under neoliberal development models—and thus for increased popular political power and the deepening of democracy—appeared to be for the economies of the region to produce sustained and rapid growth. The realistic prospects for such growth appeared to range from modest in the countries with more robust economies (Costa Rica and El Salvador) to grim in the nearly prostrate Honduras and Nicaragua.

On the other hand, low-intensity democracy was, we believe, far better than no democracy at all, especially in one regard well known to all Central Americans. Civilian governments—especially with curtailed militaries—intimidate, imprison, maim, and kill much less than military regimes. Inequalities and economic limitations notwithstanding, citizens able to organize, contact officials, vote, and protest, can defend and pursue their interests more effectively than those who cannot. In this sense, through the democratization of their polities in the traumatic 1970s, 1980s, and 1990s, millions of ordinary Central Americans won the right to become protagonists in their own political reality. Social justice and deeper democracy certainly remained a distant goal and illusion for many in the region. Some 300,000 lost their lives to authoritarian repression during the decades-long struggle for formal democracy. We consider it a singular advance that under Central America's civilian democratic regimes, few will suffer similar fates.

APPENDIX

TABLE 1 Percent Growth in Per Capita Gross Domestic Products, Central American Countries, 1950–1997

	Costa Rica	*El Salvador*	*Guatemala*	*Honduras*	*Nicaragua*
1950	–1.0	–	–3.0	0.5	13.6
1951	–2.4	–0.9	–1.9	2.7	3.8
1952	7.0	4.6	–1.2	1.1	13.9
1953	10.6	4.3	0.4	5.2	–0.6
1954	–4.3	–1.8	–1.4	–8.4	6.3
1955	6.5	2.2	–0.8	–0.1	3.7
1956	–8.0	5.0	5.8	5.4	–3.1
1957	3.4	2.4	2.3	1.9	5.4
1958	7.3	–0.7	1.4	0.5	–2.6
1959	0.2	1.6	1.6	–0.2	–1.5
1960	5.2	1.2	–0.9	3.0	–1.3
1961	0.7	–0.2	1.8	–0.6	4.8
1962	2.6	8.3	1.0	2.6	8.2
1963	5.1	0.6	7.0	0.5	8.2
1964	1.4	5.6	2.1	2.0	9.0
1965	5.6	1.7	1.9	5.4	6.8
1966	4.3	3.4	3.0	2.6	0.6
1967	2.6	1.7	1.6	2.4	4.3
1968	4.2	–0.5	6.3	2.7	–1.4
1969	3.2	–0.2	2.2	–2.4	4.0
1970	4.1	–0.7	2.7	–1.1	–2.5
1971	4.1	1.5	2.6	0.1	1.4
1972	–1.7	2.6	4.3	0.2	0.3
1973	5.5	2.1	3.5	1.0	1.7
1974	3.0	3.5	3.1	–3.2	9.0
1975	–0.3	2.5	–1.2	–5.2	–1.1
1976	0.3	1.0	4.2	2.6	1.6
1977	6.3	2.8	4.6	2.0	2.8
1978	3.3	1.4	2.4	4.1	–10.2
1979	1.8	–5.9	1.9	1.4	–27.2
1980	–1.8	–11.7	0.8	–0.4	7.4
1981	–5.0	–9.6	–1.8	–2.4	2.0
1982	–9.7	–6.5	–6.1	–4.9	–4.4
1983	0.0	–0.2	–5.4	–3.9	1.3
1984	5.1	0.5	–2.8	–0.3	–4.8
1985	–1.7	0.1	–3.7	–1.8	–5.9
1986	–8.6	–0.6	–2.5	2.4	–4.0
1987	0.7	0.9	–0.4	0.9	–1.7
1988	0.6	–0.4	0.8	1.8	–15.5
1989	2.8	–1.3	1.0	–1.1	–5.7
1990	0.8	2.7	0.1	–3.2	–3.0

(continues)

TABLE 1 *(continued)*

	Costa Rica	*El Salvador*	*Guatemala*	*Honduras*	*Nicaragua*
1991	–0.5	1.5	0.7	–0.2	–3.3
1992	4.6	5.2	1.9	2.7	–3.0
1993	3.4	–1.4	0.9	3.9	1.3
1994	1.9	10.4	1.1	–4.5	0.9
1995	0.0	3.9	2.0	0.6	1.7
1996	–2.8	0.6	0.1	0.0	2.8
1997	1.0	1.7	1.3	2.0	2.3

SOURCES: Wilkie and Haber (1981: Table 22–3); CEPAL (1985: Table 2; 1986: Table 3); Inter-American Development Bank (1988: Tables A-1, B-1; 1990: Table B-2; 1997: Table B-2; 1998).

TABLE 2 Selected Economic Data for Central America, by Country, 1950–1996.

	Costa Rica	*El Salvador*	*Guatemala*	*Honduras*	*Nicaragua*	*Region*[a]
Gross Domestic Product (GDP)[b]						
1960	1,646	1,985	4,045	1,112	1,461	10,249
1970	2,932	3,437	6,911	1,905	2,849	18,034
1980	5,975	4,723	11,987	3,243	2,950	29,978
1990	6,313	6,334	12,923	3,985	2,587	32,143
1996	7,777	8,783	16,412	4,855	3,010	40,837
GDP per capita[c]						
1960	1,332	772	1,020	575	879	891
1970	1,694	958	1,373	725	1,388	1,207
1980	2,222	1,044	1,732	886	1,065	1,393
1990	2,094	1,210	1,404	775	663	1,209
1996	2,218	1,488	1,501	832	660	1,346
Percent change in GDP/capita						
1960–70	27	24	31	26	58	35
1970–80	31	9	26	22	–23	15
1980–90	6	16	–18	–13	–38	–13
1990–96	6	23	7	7	0	11
Percent[d] employed in agriculture						
1960	51	62	67	70	62	63
1980	29	50	55	63	39	47
c. 1992	27	40	60	62	44	50
Percent[d] employed in manufacturing						
c. 1950	11	11	12	6	11	10
1983	16	14	15	13	15	15
Percent GDP from manufacturing						
1960	14	15	13	12	16	14
1980	22	18	17	16	25	18
1996	19	21	14	15	16	17
External debt[e]						
1980	2,737	915	1,166	1,486	1,172	7,746[f]
1990	3,772	2,132	2,778	3,480	10,676	22,838[f]
1996	3,667	2,672	3,262	4,494	5,964	20,059[f]
Debt as a percent of GDP						
1970	11.5	5.2	3.6	9.5	10.9	8.2[g]
1982	110.3	42.0	17.6	69.4	121.5	72.2[g]
1991	73.0	36.7	29.8	118.9	649.1	181.5[g]
1996	51.2	36.0	32.6	119.0	290.2	105.8[g]
Debt service ratio						
1990	15.4	13.0	11.2	18.0	58.3	23.8[g]
1996	6.2[h]	5.6[h]	5.0	12.6	54.2[h]	16.7[g]

[a]Weighted averages unless otherwise specified.

[b]In millions of 1986 U.S. dollars; regional value is sum for all nations.

[c]In 1986 U.S. dollars.

[d]Of economically active population.

[e]Disbursed total external debt, in millions of U.S. dollars.

[g]Unweighted mean.

[h]Estimate based on prior year.

SOURCES: Booth and Walker (1993: T. 2); Inter-American Development Bank (1983: Tables 3 and 58; 1988: Table E-1 and country tables; 1992: Tables B-2, E-11 and country tables; 1997: Tables B-1, B-2; B-10, E-1, and country profiles); U.S. Central Intelligence Agency (1993: country reports).

TABLE 3 Selected Social Data for Central America, by Country, 1960–1998.

	Costa Rica	*El Salvador*	*Guatemala*	*Honduras*	*Nicaragua*	*Region*[a]
Population (in 1,000s)						
1960	1,236	2,570	3,964	1,935	1,493	11,198
1980	2,284	4,525	6,917	3,662	2,771	20,159
1998 (est.)	3,672	6,159	11,572	6,489	4,486	32,078
Population density estimate (persons/km^2)						
1998	72.3	293.8	106.3	55.2	39.4	80.5
Mean annual population growth						
1961–70	3.4	3.4	2.8	3.1	3.2	3.3
1970–80	2.8	2.3	2.8	3.4	3.0	3.0
1980–90	2.8	1.6	2.9	3.4	3.4	2.8
1990–96	2.4	2.2	2.9	3.0	2.5	2.7
Percent indigenous population						
1978	1	2	60	2	2	14
Percent urban population						
1960	33.2	36.4	34.0	22.5	41.7	33.6
1996	49.3	48.4	41.8	48.6	74.1	50.2
Percent literate						
1960	86	42	40	30	32	42
c. 1995	95	77	63	73	65	72
University enrollment[a]						
1980	2,433	1,172	736	724	1,249	1,263[b]
1995	2,919	1,932	755	985	947	1,508[b]
Primary school enrollment ration						
1990	93	78	79	108	98	89
Life expectancy at birth						
1980–85	73	57	59	60	60	60
1995	76	66	65	66	67	67
Infant mortality/1000 live births						
c. 1993	14	40	62	49	56	55
Religious identification c. 1985 (percent)						
Catholic	97	93	79	94	88	90
Protestant	3	4	6	3	8	5
Average income for population strata (c. 1980)[c]						
Poorest 20%	$176.7	46.5	111.0	80.7	61.9	95.3[d]
Next 30%	$500.8	155.1	202.7	140.0	178.2	235.4[d]

[a]Per 100,000 population.

[b]Unweighted average for region.

[c]In constant 1970 U.S. dollars.

[d]Unweighted averages.

SOURCES: Booth and Walker (1993: Appendix Table 2); IADB (1988: 384, 408, 416, 440, 464; 1992: country tables; 1994: country tables; 1997: Table A-1 and A-2); Gallardo and López (1986: Tables 2, 4, 7, 8, and 10; Barry and Preusch (1986: 129); U.S. Central Intelligence Agency (1993: country reports); and UNESCO (1997: Tables 1.2 and 3.9).

TABLE 4 Mean Annual U.S. Military and Economic Assistance to Central America, 1946–1992.

	Costa Rica	*El Salvador*	*Guatemala*	*Honduras*	*Nicaragua*	*Region*[a]
			Military Assistance[b]			
1946–1952	–	–	–	–	–	–
1953–1961	.01	.03	.19	.14	.24	.62
1962–1972	.16	.72	3.31	.90	2.36	7.45
1973–1976	.03	2.08	.83	2.23	.28	5.45
1977–1980	1.25	1.60	1.25	3.13	.85	6.98
1981–1984	3.95	98.85	.00	41.48	.00	144.28
1985–1988	3.93	112.78	5.20	57.73	.00	179.64
1989–1992	.10	63.10	2.35[c]	25.60	.00	91.15
Overall mean, 1946–1992	.83	23.86	1.63	12.38	.69	38.24
			Economic Assistance[b]			
1946–1952	1.00	.40	1.65	.42	1.03	4.50
1953–1961	5.80	1.23	13.48	3.90	3.73	28.14
1962–1972	9.41	11.95	14.52	8.42	12.95	56.07
1973–1976	14.10	6.10	19.60	24.43	26.90	91.13
1977–1980	13.65	21.85	17.28	27.88	18.63	99.56
1981–1984	112.75	189.43	21.13	79.53	16.55	419.39
1985–1988	171.13	383.38	135.90	179.33	.10	869.84
1989–1992	75.83	287.68	116.73	150.18	206.80	837.22
Overall mean, 1946–1992	36.48	78.72	32.73	42.06	26.83	216.83

[a]Includes only Costa Rica, El Salvador, Guatemala, Honduras, and Nicaragua.

[b]Millions of U.S. dollars.

[c]The Bush administration cancelled Guatemala's 1990 military assistance of $3.3 million for human rights reasons. That left the aid delivered at less than originally appropriated for the period.

SOURCES: Atkins (1977: Tables D and E; 1989, Tables 10.2 and 10.4); OPB-USAID (1981, 1984, 1986, 1988, 1991, 1993).

TABLE 5 Percent Change in Consumer Prices, 1963–1997

	Costa Rica	*El Salvador*	*Guatemala*	*Honduras*	*Nicaragua*
1963	3.0	0.9	0.1	2.9	0.8
1964	3.3	1.8	–0.2	4.6	9.6
1965	–0.7	1.4[a]	–0.7	3.2	3.9
1966	0.2	–0.9	0.6	0.2	3.9
1967	1.1	1.8	0.5	1.2	1.6
1968	4.0	1.8	1.8	2.6	3.1
1969	2.8	3.2[a]	2.2	1.8	2.0[b]
1970	4.6	2.6	2.4	2.9	5.9
1971	3.1	0.3	–0.5	3.1	5.6
1972	4.6	1.7	0.5	3.4	3.3[b]
1973	15.2	6.4	14.4	4.7	16.8[b]
1974	30.1	16.9	15.9	12.9	20.5[b]
1975	17.4	19.1	13.1	8.1	1.8
1976	3.5	7.0	10.7	5.0	2.9
1978	6.0	13.3	7.9	5.7	4.6
1979	9.2	15.0	11.5	8.8	48.5
1980	18.1	17.3	10.7	18.1	35.9
1981	37.1	14.7	11.4	9.4	23.9
1982	90.1	11.7	5.0	9.4	24.8
1983	32.6	13.1	6.4	8.9	39.9
1984	12.0	13.0	5.0	4.8	48.1
1985	14.6	27.4	28.2	3.7	250.9
1986	11.8	32.0	37.0	4.4	681.5
1987	16.8	24.9	12.3	2.4	911.8
1988	20.8	19.8	10.8	4.6	14,295.3
1989	16.6	17.6	11.4	9.8	4,770.1
1990	19.0	24.1	41.2	23.3	7,485.2
1991	28.7	14.4	33.2	34.0	2,742.3
1992	21.8	11.2	10.0	8.7	20.3
1993	9.8	18.6	11.9	10.8	20.4
1994	13.5	10.6	10.9	21.7	7.8
1995	23.2	10.0	8.4	29.5	11.0
1996	17.5	9.8	11.1	23.8	11.6
1997	13.2	4.5	9.2	20.2	10.0

[a]Assigned mean value of other four nations as estimate.

[b]Estimates based on Nicaraguan Central Bank and other data; see Booth (1982: Table 5).

SOURCES: Data through 1979 from Wilkie and Haber (1981: Tables 2505, 2508, 2511, 2513); 1980–1985 data from Inter-American Development Bank (IADB) (1983: country profile tables); U.S. Department of State (1985); CEPAL (1985: Table 5); 1986–1989 data from IADB (1990: country profile tables); 1990–1996 data from IADB (1997: country profile tables; 1998).

TABLE 6 Real Working-Class Wage Indices, Central American Countries, 1963–1996 (1973=100)

	Costa Rica	*El Salvador*[a]	*Guatemala*[b]	*Honduras*[c]	*Nicaragua*[d]
1963	80	90	–	–	92
1965	–	92	109	–	125
1967	94	93	115	–	137
1970	96	92	109	–	121
1971	107	93	109	–	119
1972	103	94	107	96	114
1973	100	100	100	100	100
1974	108	98	96	94	100
1975	91	90	95	91	106
1976	103	95	97	102	106
1977	113	85	81	95	97
1978	123	87	84	101	88
1979	128	84	84	103	77
1980	129	82	84	97	64
1981	114	76	86	93	64
1982	92	68	92	101	56
1983	102	60	85	92	49
1984	110	57	84	89	46
1985	120	49	72	86	35
1986	126	45	59	83	14
1987	125	49	63	81	15
1988	124	44	66	77	1[e]
1989	131	42	70	70	1[e]
1990	130	40	57	86	2[e]
1991	122	37	53	86	2[e]
1992	123	37	62	72	2[e]
1993	134	35	69	49	2[e]
1994	137	35	74	44	2[e]
1995	134	35	83	43	2[e]
1996	138	32	82	43	2[e]

NOTE: Value of the indices represents an unweighted average of wages in manufacturing, construction, transport, storage and communication, and in agriculture, corrected for consumer prices changes except for items under note e above, which are wages only for persons included in national social security systems. Data for 1985–1996 are drawn from the country profile tables of the Inter-American Development Bank (1990; 1997).

[a]Excludes construction (after 1974); for 1980s, data are for private sector only.

[b]Unweighted average of all sectors.

[c]Unweighted average wages in manufacturing, construction, and agriculture (agricultural wages not included in 1972 and 1973 figures).

[d]Includes wages in manufacturing, transportation (only), and construction.

[e]Hyperinflation and collapse of Nicaraguan exchange rate in the late 1980s render the wage index functionally meaningless. Many Nicaraguans relied upon nonwage resources (food distribution at work places) and informal sector activities to cope with the collapse of effective real wages).

SOURCES: Booth and Walker (1989: Table 4; 1993: Table 5); Wilkie and Haber (1981: Tables 1400, 1401, 1402, 1403); Wilkie and Perkal (1984: Table 1405); and consumer price data in Table 5 above; Wilkie and Lorey (1987: Table 1413); Gallardo and López (1986: 168). The 1978 and 1979 data for Nicaragua are from Mayorga (1985: 65).

TABLE 7 Compensation of Employees as Percent of National Income (1962 = 100)

	Costa Rica		*Honduras*		*Nicaragua*	
	%	*Index*	*%*	*Index*	*%*	*Index*
1962	45.0	100	46.2	100	57.5	100
1965	51.0	113	42.4	92	65.0	113
1967	52.2	116	41.8	90	65.3	114
1968	51.6	115	42.5	92	65.3	114
1969	51.3	114	42.0	91	65.6	114
1970	50.8	113	42.1	91	65.3	114
1971	52.0	116	43.7	95	65.5	114
1972	52.5	117	44.6	97	65.6	114
1973	49.4	110	45.0	97	69.7	121
1974	48.6	108	42.8	93	58.9	102
1975	49.8	111	–	–	59.1	103

SOURCE: Wilkie and Haber (1981: Table 1404).

TABLE 8 Unemployment Trends, 1970–1989 (percentages)

	Costa Rica	*El Salvador*[a]	*Guatemala*[b]		*Honduras*[c]	*Nicaragua*
1970	3.5[d]	16.0	4.8	–	–	3.7
1971	–	–	–	–	8.8	3.6
1972	–	17.0	4.9	24.5	7.7	6.0
1973	7.6[e]	–	–	–	7.4	9.1
1974	–	–	–	–	6.9	7.3
1975	–	18.0	5.1	26.5	9.7	–
1976	4.9[e]	–	–	–	9.4	–
1977	4.4[e]	–	–	–	8.9	13.1[f]
1978	4.6	21.0	5.3	28.6	9.2	14.5
1979	4.7	–	–	–	–	22.9
1980	5.9	24.0	5.5	31.2	8.8	17.8
1981	8.1	25.0	6.0	32.6	9.0	16.6
1982	15.0	30.0	7.0	36.7	9.2	19.9[g]
1983	8.6[g]	33.0	8.0	40.1	9.5	15.2[g]
1984	6.6[g]	30.0	10.0	43.4	10.7	16.3[g]
1985	6.7	–	12.0	–	11.7	–
1986	6.7	–	14.2	–	12.1	–
1987	5.9	–	12.1	–	11.4	–
1988	6.3	–	9.6	–	11.5	–
1989	3.7	–	7.2	–	9.4	–

[a]Salvadoran figures for 1970, 1972, 1975, and 1978 are estimates based on Central American mean unemployment trends (IICA 1982: 256); data for 1981–1984 from U.S. Department of State (1985).

[b]First column of Guatemalan data refers to unemployment; second column refers to combined unemployment and underemployment. These figures are data reported by the Guatemalan Ministry of Labor, cited in *La Nación Internacional* (1982: 12), and by the Guatemalan Secretariat of Economic Planning, reported by Inforpress Centroamericana (1985a: 18). Also used were data for 1981–1984 from the U.S. Department of State (1985). Figures for 1972, 1975, and 1978 are estimates based on earlier and later reported data.

[c]Figures for 1971–1978 are estimates based on projections of economically active population from base years 1974 and 1977 (Wilkie and Haber 1981: Table 1301). Values represent number of unemployed as percent of economically active population. Figures for 1980–1984 are from IADB (1990: Table 10).

[d]Gallardo and López (1986: 189).

[e]DGEC-Costa Rica (1980: Cuadro 196).

[f]From Booth (1982: Table 5.1). Data for 1978 on drawn from CIERA (1983: Cuadro 18).

[g]CEPAL (1985: Table 4).

SOURCES: Unless otherwise noted, data for 1984 and before drawn from Wilkie and Perkal (1984); all data for 1985 through 1989 from IADB (1990: Table 10).

TABLE 9 International Assistance (approximate) to Nicaragua, by Major Origins, 1979–1987 (millions of U.S.$)

	Multilateral	*Western Countries*	*Socialist Countries*	*Total Assistance*
1979	220	140	10	370
1980	190	500	160	850
1981	90	520	180	790
1982	110	320	280	710
1983	80	270	330	680
1984	20	180	600	800
1985	20	160	1,030	1,210
1986	40	120	390	550
1987	30	110	280	420

SOURCE: Figures are estimates based on Conroy (1988: Figure 5).

TABLE 10 Central American Rebel Groups, 1959–1989

	Costa Rica	*El Salvador*	*Guatemala*	*Honduras*	*Nicaragua*
1959					various groups[b] (1959–1961)
1960				FMLH[a]	
1961					FSLN
1962			MR-13 FAR, FGEI[c]		
1963					
1964					
1965					
1966					
1967					
1968					
1969					
1970		FPL			
1971			ORPA		
1972		ERP	EGP		
1973					
1974					
1975		FARN			
1976		PRTCS			
1977				PRTCH	FSLN splits[d]
1978			PGT-DN	MPL	
1979	La Familia	FAL			reunification of FSLN, MPU-FPN[e]
1980	PRTC	FMLN[f] FMLN-FDR[g]	 MRP-Ixim		
1981			URNG[h]	FPR	
1982					
1983				DNU[i]	
1984					
1985					
1986					
1987					
1988					
1989				ERP-27	

[a]Only sporadically active through late 1979, when it resumed armed struggle.

[b]Of some twenty groups formed, only the FSLN survived beyond 1963.

[c]MR-13 disappeared after late 1960s counterinsurgency campaign; core of FAR survived to renew guerrilla activity in 1978; core of FGEI survived counterinsurgency and helped form EGP.

[d]Under heavy counterinsurgency pressure, FSLN split into three factions with tactical differences.

[e]MPU-FPN coalitions linked broad-front political opposition with FSLN.

[f]FMLN included all five Salvadoran guerrilla organizations.

[g]FMLN-FDR linked FMLN guerrillas with broad-front political opposition coalition.

[h]URNG linked the guerrilla groups EGP, FAR, ORPA, and the PGT-DN; MRP-Ixim not a member.

[i]DNU linked the MPL, FPR, and FMLH guerrilla organizations.

TABLE 11 Selected Data on Deaths, Disappearances, and Refugees, El Salvador, 1980–1984

	Annual Number of Deaths and Disappearances					
	1980	*1981*	*1982*	*1983*	*1984*	*1980–1984*
Deaths	13,194	16,376	12,617	5,826	2,206	50,219
Detained/ disappeared	979	927	1,177	526	196	3,805
TOTAL	14,173	17,303	13,794	6,352	2,402	54,024

	Deaths and Disappearances, by Occupation (%)	
Occupation	*Deaths*	*Disappearances*
Workers	14.6	15.3
Students	7.2	17.3
Peasants	67.9	10.6
Merchants	2.6	3.2
Employees	4.5	6.6
Teachers	1.2	1.6
Professionals	1.3	1.0
Housewives	0.3	2.2

Salvadoran Refugees Abroad, by Country (est.)			
Country	*Number*	*Country*	*Number*
United States	500,000	Costa Rica	10,000
Mexico	250,000	Panama	1,500
Guatemala	70,000	Nicaragua	20,000
Belize	7,000	Honduras	32,000
		TOTAL	890,500

SOURCE: CDHES (1984: 87–89).

TABLE 12 Comparative Data on Central Government Expenditures (percent of budget)

	Costa Rica		*El Salvador*	*Guatemala*		*Honduras*	*Nicaragua*
	1978	*1983*	*1984*	*1978*	*1984*[a]	*1976*	*1976*
1. Defense	2.7	3.0	24.6	11.0	13.7	10.5	12.8
2. Education	24.5	19.4	15.5	13.0	12.7	20.7	16.9
3. Health	3.6	22.5	8.1	7.1	7.5	14.7	4.1
4. Social security/ welfare	28.3	14.5	3.7	4.1	3.9	4.7	19.9
5. Total percent on education, health and social security/ welfare (2 + 3 + 4)	56.3	56.3	27.3	24.2	24.1	40.1	40.9
6. Ratio of human services to defense (5:1)	21:1	19:1	1:1	2:1	2:1	4:1	3:1

[a]Slightly different budget breakdowns are used between Wilkie and Perkal and Wilkie and Lorey on the one hand and Inforpress Centroamericana on the other. The 1984 Guatemala data for the social security and welfare category on this measure are assumed to be the same as Inforpress's "labor" and "government" lines combined.

SOURCES: Wilkie and Haber (1981: Table 2323); Wilkie and Lorey (1987: Table 3010); Inforpress Centroamericana (1985a: 5).

ACRONYMS

AID — Agency for International Development
AL — Liberal Alliance (Alianza Liberal) (N)
AMNLAE — Luisa Amanda Espinosa Nicaraguan Women's Association (Asociación de Mujeres Nicaragüenses Luisa Amanda Espinosa)
AMPRONAC — Association of Women Confronting the National Problem (Asociación de Mujeres Frente a la Problemática Nacional) (N)
ANEP — National Association of Private Enterprises (Asociación Nacional de Empresas Privadas) (ES)
ARDE — Revolutionary Democratic Alliance (Alianza Revolucionaria Democrática) (CR-based contra forces)
ARENA — Nationalist Republican Alliance party (Alianza Republicana Nacionalista) (ES)
ASC — Assembly of Civil Society (Asamblea de la Sociedad Civil) (G)
ATC — Rural Workers' Association (Asociación de Trabajadores del Campo) (N)
BPR — Revolutionary Popular Bloc (Bloque Popular Revolucionario) (ES)
CACM — Central American Common Market
CDC — Civil Defense Committee (Comité de Defensa Civil) (N & H)
CDS — Sandinista Defense Committee (Comité de Defensa Sandinista) (N)
CEB — Christian base communities (*comunidades eclesiales de base*)
CGUP — Guatemalan Committee of Patriotic Unity (Comité Guatemalteco de Unidad Patriótica)
CIA — Central Intelligence Agency
CODEH — Human Rights Committee of Honduras (Comité de Derechos Humanos de Honduras)
COSEP — Superior Council of Private Enterprise (Consejo Superior de la Empresa Privada) (N)

Abbreviations of countries: CR = Costa Rica; ES = El Salvador; G = Guatemala; H = Honduras; N = Nicaragua

COSIP	Superior Council of Private Initiative (Consejo Superior de la Iniciativa Privada) (N)
CPI	consumer price index
CRIES	Regional Coordinating Body for Economic and Social Research (N)
CRM	Revolutionary Coordinator of the Masses (Coordinadora Revolucionaria de Masas) (ES)
CSE	Supreme Electoral Council (Consejo Superior Electoral) (N)
CST	Sandinista Workers' Federation (Central Sandinista de Trabajadores) (N)
CUC	Peasant Unity Committee (Comité de Unidad Campesina) (G)
DC	Christian Democratic party (Partido Demócrata Cristiano) (G)
DINADECO	National Community Development Directorate (Dirección Nacional de Desarrollo de la Comunidad) (CR)
DNC	Joint National Directorate (Dirección Nacional Conjunta) (N)
DNU	National Directorate of Unity (Dirección Nacional de Unidad) (H)
EGP	Guerrilla Army of the Poor (Ejército Guerrillero de los Pobres) (G)
EPS	Sandinista People's Army (N)
ERP	Revolutionary Army of the People (Ejército Revolucionario del Pueblo) (ES)
ERP-27	Army of Patriotic Resistance (Ejército de Resistencia Patriótica) (H)
EXA	export agriculture
FAL	Armed Forces of Liberation (Fuerzas Armadas de Liberación) (ES)
FAO	Broad Opposition Front (Frente Amplio Opositor) (N)
FAPU	United Popular Action Front (Frente de Acción Popular Unida) (ES)
FAR	Revolutionary Armed Forces (Fuerzas Armadas Revolucionarias) (G)
FARN	Armed Forces of National Resistance (Fuerzas Armadas de Resistencia Nacional) (ES)
FDCR	Democratic Front Against Repression (Frente Democrático Contra la Represión) (G)
FDN	Nicaraguan Democratic Force (Fuerzas Democráticas Nicaragüenses)
FDNG	New Guatemala Democratic Front (Frente Democrático Nueva Guatemala)
FDR	Revolutionary Democratic Front (Frente Democrático Revolucionario) (ES)
FGEI	Edgar Ibarra Guerrilla Front (Frente Guerrillera Edgar Ibarra) (G)
FMLH	Morazán Front for the Liberation of Honduras (Frente Morazanista para la Liberación de Honduras)

FMLN Farabundo Martí National Liberation Front (Frente Farabundo Martí de Liberación Nacional) (ES)
FNT National Workers' Front (Frente Nacional de Trabajadores) (N)
FP-13 January 13th Popular Front (Frente Popular 13 de Enero) (G)
FPL Popular Forces of Liberation (Fuerzas Populares de Liberación) (ES)
FPN National Patriotic Front (Frente Patriótico Nacional) (N)
FPR Lorenzo Zelaya Popular Revolutionary Forces (Fuerzas Populares Revolucionarias "Lorenzo Zelaya") (H)
FRG Republican Front of Guatemala (Frente Republicano de Guatemala)
FSLN Sandinista National Liberation Front (Frente Sandinista de Liberación Nacional) (N)
FUR United Front of the Revolution (Frente Unido de la Revolución) (G)
FUSEP Public Security Forces (Fuerzas de Seguridad Pública) (H)
GDP gross domestic product
LP-28 28th of February Popular Leagues (Ligas Populares 28 de Febrero) (ES)
MAS Solidarity Action Movement (Movimiento de Acción Solidaria) (G)
MLN National Liberation Movement (Movimiento de Liberación Nacional) (G)
MLP Popular Liberation Movement (Movimiento de Liberación Popular) (ES)
MNR National Revolutionary Movement (Movimiento Nacional Revolucionario) (ES)
MPL Popular Movement for Liberation (Movimiento Popular de Liberación) (H)
MPU United People's Movement (Movimiento Pueblo Unido) (N)
MR-13 13th of November Revolutionary Movement (Movimiento Revolucionario del 13 de Noviembre) (G)
MRP-Ixim People's Revolutionary Movement-Ixim (Movimiento Revolucionario del Pueblo-Ixim) (G)
MRS Sandinista Renovation Movement (Movimiento de Renovación Sandinista) (N)
OAS Organization of American States
OPEC Organization of Petroleum Exporting Countries
ORDEN Nationalist Democratic Organization (Organización Democrática Nacionalista) (ES)
ORPA Organization of the People in Arms (Organización del Pueblo en Armas) (G)
PAN National Advancement party (Partido de Avance Nacional) (G)

PCH	Honduran Communist party (Partido Comunista de Honduras)
PCN	National Conciliation party (Partido de Conciliación Nacional) (ES)
PCS	Communist Party of El Salvador (Partido Comunista de El Salvador)
PDC	Christian Democratic party (Partido Demócrata Cristiano) (ES)
PDCG	Christian Democratic party of Guatemala (Partido Demócrata Cristiano de Guatemala)
PDCH	Christian Democratic Party of Honduras (Partido Demócrata Cristiano de Honduras)
PGT	Guatemalan Labor party (Partido Guatemalteco del Trabajo)
PID	Institutional Democratic party (Partido Institucional Democrático) (G)
PINU	Innovation and Unity party (Partido de Inovación y Unidad) (H)
PLH	Honduran Liberal party (Partido Liberal de Honduras)
PLN	Liberal Nationalist party (Partido Liberal Nacionalista) (N)
PLN	National Liberation party (Partido de Liberación Nacional) (CR)
PNC	National Civil Police (Policía Nacional Civil) (ES)
PR	Revolutionary party (Partido Revolucionario) (G)
PRTC	Revolutionary Party of Central American Workers (Partido Revolucionario de Trabajadores Centroamericanos-Costa Rica)
PRTCH	Revolutionary Party of Central American Workers of Honduras (Partido Revolucionario de Trabajadores Centroamericanos de Honduras)
PRTCS	Revolutionary Party of Central American Workers (Partido Revolucionario de Trabajadores Centroamericanos-El Salvador)
PRUD	Revolutionary Party of Democratic Unification (Partido Revolucionario de Unificación Democrática) (ES)
PSD	Democratic Socialist party (Partido Socialista Demócrata) (G)
PUSC	Social Christian Unity party (Partido de Unidad Social Cristiana) (CR)
RN	Nicaraguan Resistance (Resistencia Nicaragüense)
UDEL	Democratic Liberation Union (Unión Democrática de Liberación) (N)
UDN	Democratic National Union (Unión Democrática Nacionalista) (ES)
UFCO	United Fruit Company
UN	United Nations
UNAG	National Union of Farmers and Ranchers (Unión Nacional de Agricultores y Ganaderos) (N)
UNO	National Opposition Union (Unión Nacional Opositora) (N & ES)
URNG	Guatemalan National Revolutionary Union (Unión Revolucionaria Nacional Guatemalteca)
USAID	U.S. Agency for International Development

NOTES

Notes to Chapter 1

1. John A. Booth and Thomas W. Walker, *Understanding Central America* (Boulder: Westview Press, 1989 ed. and 1993 ed.).

2. The Committee of Santa Fe, Lewis Tambs, ed., *A New Inter-American Policy for the Eighties* (Washington, D.C.: Council for Inter-American Security, 1980). All page citations are from the version published in Bruce D. Larkin, ed., *Vital Interests: The Soviet Issue in U.S. Central American Policy* (Boulder, Colo.: Lynne-Rienner, 1988). Quote from p. 11.

3. Ibid. p. 15.

4. Ibid., p. 27.

5. Ibid. pp. 21–44.

6. National Bipartisan Commission on Central America, *Report of the National Bipartisan Commission on Central America* (Washington, D.C.: January 1984), pp. 88–91.

7. Coauthor John Booth informally surveyed Central America scholars, reviewed lists of the commission's consultants, and discussed at length the commission's operation with one of its members.

8. See for instance, Policy Alternatives for the Caribbean and Central America, *Changing Course: Blueprint for Peace in Central America and the Caribbean* (Washington, D.C.: Institute for Policy Studies, 1984); Inter-American Dialogue, *The Americas in 1984: A Year for Decisions, Report of the Inter-American Dialogue* (Washington, D.C.: Aspen Institute for Humanistic Studies, 1984); William M. LeoGrande, "Through the Looking Glass: The Kissinger Report on Central America," World Policy Journal (Winter 1984), pp. 251–284.

9. Here, and in certain other parts of this volume, much of the wording is from Thomas W. Walker's unsigned contribution to: Presbyterian Church (USA), *Adventure and Hope: Christians and the Crisis in Central America: Report to the 195th General Assembly of the Presbyterian Church* (Atlanta, 1983), pp. 57–91, 97–101. The authors wish to thank the Presbyterian church for its kind permission to publish this material (which Walker wrote in 1982 while he was part of the UPCUSA [United Presbyterian Church (USA)] Task Force on Central America) here in this form.

10. Population estimates for Central America for 1998 based on Inter-American Development Bank, *Economic and Social Progress in Latin America, 1997 Report: Latin America After a Decade of Reforms* (Washington, D.C, 1997), Table A–1. U.S. 1998 population projections from the U.S. Census Bureau, *State Populations Ranking Summary: 1995 and 2025* «http://www.census.gov/population/projections/state/9525 rank».

Notes to Chapter 2

1. Inter-American Development Bank (IADB), *Economic and Social Progress in Latin America: 1997 Report* (Baltimore: Johns Hopkins University Press, 1997), Table B-2. U.S. data from U.S. Bureau of Economic Analysis, "National Accounts Data," Table 3, «www.bea.doc.gov/bea/dn/niptbl-d/hti#Table 1.Part B», April 8, 1998. Estimate of U.S. GDP per capita based on population estimate of 270 million.

2. United Nations Educational, Scientific, and Cultural Organization (UNESCO), *UNESCO Statistical Yearbook, 1997* (Paris and Lanham, Maryland: UNESCO Publishing and Bernam Press, 1997), Table 1.2.

3. Inter-American Development Bank (IADB), *Economic and Social Progress in Latin America: 1994 Report* (Washington, D.C.: Inter-American Development Bank–Johns Hopkins University Press, 1994), country statistical profiles.

4. IADB, 1997 Report, Table A-1; and Inter-American Development Bank, Economic and Social Progress in Latin America: Labor Force and Employment: 1987 Report, (Washington, D.C.: 1987), Table A-1.

5. Urban and rural populations and growth rates for 1996 from IADB, *1997 Report,* Table A-2.

6. Projected growth rates estimated from IADB, *1997 Report,* Table A-1.

7. Wallace W. Atwood and Helen Goss Thomas, *The Americas* (Boston: Ginn and Co., 1929), p. 45.

8. For an overview, see, for instance, Ronald H. Chilcote and Joel C. Edelstein, *Latin America: Capitalist and Socialist Perspectives of Development and Underdevelopment* (Boulder, Colo.; Westview Press, 1986).

Notes to Chapter 3

1. Good histories are Ralph Lee Woodward, Jr., *Central America: A Nation Divided,* 2nd ed. (New York: Oxford University Press, 1985), and Mario Rodríguez, *Central America* (Englewood Cliffs, N.J.: Prentice-Hall, 1965). The best short history is that of Hector Pérez Brignoli, *A Brief History of Central America* (Berkeley: University of California Press, 1989). For a longer treatment, see James Dunkerley, *Power in the Isthmus: A Political History of Modern Central America* (London: Verso, 1988). See also Chapter 3 of John A. Booth, *Costa Rica: Ouest for Democracy* (Boulder: Westview Press 1998).

2. See David Richard Radell, "An Historical Geography of Western Nicaragua: The Spheres of Leon, Granada, and Managua, 1519–1965," Ph.D. dissertation, University of California, Berkeley, 1969, pp. 66–80.

3. For excellent coverage of the Walker period and its aftermath, see Karl Bermann, *Under the Big Stick: Nicaragua and the United States Since 1848* (Boston: South End Press, 1986).

4. Honduras never really developed a landowning aristocracy; economic and political power remained in the hands of regional *hacendados* and newer urban industrial-commercial-financial entrepreneurs.

5. Enrique A. Baloyra, "Reactionary Despotism in Central America," *Journal of Latin American Studies* 15 (November 1983), pp. 295–319.

6. Ibid., pp. 309–310.

7. In Honduras, agrarian colonization and expanding employment in the modern capitalist sector of agriculture continued to absorb much of the growth of the rural labor force.

8. Victor Bulmer-Thomas, *The Political Economy of Central America Since 1920* (Cambridge: Cambridge University Press, 1987), pp. 177–180.

9. John Weeks, "The Industrial Sector," in Thomas W. Walker, ed., *Nicaragua: The First Five Years* (New York: Praeger, 1985), pp. 281–296; and John Weeks, *The Economies of Central America* (New York: Holmes and Meier, 1985), pp. 101–151.

10. Weeks, *The Economies of Central America,* p. 284.

Notes to Chapter 4

1. John A. Booth, "Representative Constitutional Democracy in Costa Rica: Adaptation to Crisis in the Turbulent 1980s," in Steve Ropp and James Morris, eds., *Central America: Crisis and Adaptation* (Albuquerque: University of New Mexico Press, 1984), Table 5.1. Other material on the evolution of Costa Rica drawn from Mitchell A. Seligson and Miguel Gómez, "Ordinary Elections in Extraordinary Times: The Political Economy of Voting in Costa Rica," in John A. Booth and Mitchell A. Seligson, eds., *Elections and Democracy in Central America* (Chapel Hill: University of North Carolina Press, 1989); John A. Booth, "Costa Rica: The Roots of Democratic Stability," in Larry Diamond, Juan J. Linz, and Seymour Martin Lipset, eds., *Democracy in Developing Countries, Volume 4: Latin America* (Boulder, Colo.: Lynne Rienner, 1989), pp. 387–422; Lowell Gudmundson, *Costa Rica Before Coffee* (Baton Rouge: Louisiana State University. Press, 1986); and from interviews by Booth with Costa Rican scholars and political experts during author's visits there in August 1987, January 1988, and December 1990. See also John A. Booth, *Costa Rica: Quest for Democracy* (Boulder, Colo.: Westview Press, 1998), Chapter 3.

2. See Booth, *Costa Rica: Quest for Democracy, pp. 40–42; and Astrid Fischel, Consenso y represión: Una interpretación sociopolítica de la educación costarricense* (San José: Editorial Costa Rica, 1987).

3. Booth, *Costa Rica: Quest for Democracy,* p. 42.

4. Ibid., pp. 75–76 and Table 3.4.

5. Paul Levy, as quoted in Jaime Wheelock Román, *Imperialismo y dictadurat Crisis de una formación social* (México: Siglo Veintiuno Editores, 1975), p. 29.

6. On revolutionary economic policy see Phil Ryan, *The Fall and Rise of the Market in Sandinista Nicaragua* (Montreal: McGill-Queens University Press, 1995); Max Spoor, *The State and Domestic Agricultural Markets in Nicaragua: From Interventions to Neo-Liberalism* (New York and London: St. Martin's Press and Macmillan Press, 1995). On U.S. hostility see, for instance, Thomas W. Walker, ed., *Reagan Versus the Sandinistas: The Undeclared War on Nicaragua* (Boulder, Colo.: Westview Press 1987); and William I. Robinson, *A Faustian Bargain: U.S. Involvement in the Nicaraguan Elections and American Foreign Policy in the Post–Cold War Era* (Boulder, Colo.: Westview Press 1992); and Gary Prevost and Harry Vanden, eds., *The Undermining of the Sandinista Revolution* (New York: St. Martin's Press, 1997).

7. See Tommie Sue Montgomery, *Revolution in El Salvador: Origins and Evolution* (Boulder, Colo.: Westview Press, 1982); and Enrique Baloyra, *El Salvador in Transition* (Chapel Hill: University of North Carolina Press, 1982).

8. As quoted in Montgomery, *Revolution in El Salvador,* p. 46.

9. Baloyra, *El Salvador in Transition,* p. 35.

10. Tommie Sue Montgomery, "El Salvador: The Roots of Revolution," in Steve C. Ropp and James A. Morris, eds., *Central America: Crisis and Adaptation* (Albuquerque: University of New Mexico Press, 1984), p. 78.

11. See Stephen Webre, *José Napoleón Duarte and the Christian Democratic Party in Salvadorean Politics: 1960–1972* (Baton Rouge: Louisiana State University Press, 1979).

12. See Montgomery, *Revolution in El Salvador,* pp. 97–117.

13. George Black et al., *Garrison Guatemala* (New York: Monthly Review Press, 1984), p. 13.

14. Jerry L. Weaver, "Guatemala: The Politics of a Frustrated Revolution," in Howard J. Wiarda and Harvey F. Kline, eds., *Latin American Politics and Development* (Boston: Houghton Mifflin, 1979), p. 337.

15. Richard H. Immerman, *The CIA in Guatemala: The Foreign Policy of Intervention* (Austin: University of Texas Press, 1982), Chapters 2–7.

16. Richard Newbold Adams, *Crucifixion by Power: Essays on Guatemalan National Social Structure, 1944–1966* (Austin: University of Texas Press, 1970), p. 195.

17. See John Sloan, "The Electoral Game in Guatemala," Ph.D. dissertation, University of Texas at Austin, 1968.

18. Black, *Garrison Guatemala,* p. 43.

19. Ibid.

20. Lars Schoultz, "Guatemala: Social Change and Political Conflict," in Martin Diskin, ed., *Trouble in Our Backyard: Central America and the United States in the Eighties* (New York: Pantheon, 1983), pp. 188–189.

21. Americas Watch, *Little Hope: Human Rights in Guatemala, January 1984–1985* (New York, February 1985); British Parliamentary Human Rights Group, *"Bitter and Cruel . . . ": Report of a Mission to Guatemala by the British Parliamentary Human Rights Group* (London: House of Commons, 1985).

22. See John A. Booth et al., *The 1985 Guatemalan National Elections: Will the Military Relinquish Power?* (Washington, D.C.: International Human Rights Law Group-Washington Office on Latin America, 1985); David Carliner et al., *Political Transition and the Rule of Law in Guatemala* (Washington, D.C. International Human Rights Law Group-Washington Office on Latin America, January 1988).

23. Interviews by Booth in Guatemala during visits in April 1987, January 1988, and September 1988. See also the Latin American Studies Association, *Extraordinary Opportunities . . . and New Risks: Final Report of the LASA Commission on Compliance with the Central American Peace Accord* (Pittsburgh: LASA, March 15, 1988), pp. 15–20; and Susanne Jonas, *The Battle for Guatemala: Rebels, Death Squads, and U.S. Power* (Boulder, Colo.: Westview Press, 1991).

24. The so-called Serranazo, had it succeeded, would have resembled Peruvian president Alberto Fujimori's *autogolpe* (literally "self-coup"), in which the constitutionally elected president acted unconstitutionally by closing down Congress and parties and ruling by decree.

25. World Bank Group, *Country Overview: Guatemala,* «http://www.worldbank.org/html/extdr/offrep/lac/guatemal.htm//», (June 17, 1998).

26. Thanks to José García of New Mexico State University for his insight on these matters. See James A. Morris, "Honduras: The Burden of Survival in Central America," in Ropp and Morris, *Central America,* pp. 189–223.

27. James A. Morris, "Honduras: A Unique Case," in Wiarda and Kline, eds. *Latin American Politics and Development,* p. 349.

28. As quoted in "Commentary: The Region," *Mesoamérica,* September 1982, p. 1.

29. See Eva Gold, "Military Encirclement," in Thomas W. Walker, ed., *Reagan Versus the Sandinistas: The Undeclared War on Nicaragua* (Boulder, Colo.: Westview Press, 1987), pp. 39–56.

30. The 1985 election followed the Uruguayan model, which combined a primary and general election. Several candidates ran for president under each major party banner. The Liberals gained the most votes; therefore, their leading vote-winner (Azcona) won the presidency, even though one National party candidate had more votes than he.

31. Mark Rosenberg, "Honduras: The Reluctant Democracy," *Current History* 85 (December 1986), pp. 417–420, 438, 448; and "Can Democracy Survive the Democrats? From Transition to Consolidation in Honduras," in Booth and Seligson, eds., *Elections and Democracy in Central America,* pp. 40–57.

Notes to Chapter 5

1. See John A. Booth and Thomas W. Walker, *Understanding Central America* (Boulder: Westview Press, 1989), Chapter 5.

2. This concept of political regimes draws upon that of Charles W. Anderson, "The Latin American Political System," in Charles W. Anderson, *Politics and Economic Change in Latin America: The Governing of Restless Nations* (New York: Van Nostrand Reinhold, 1967), and also owes something to the conceptualization of John Higley and Michael Burton, "The Elite Variable in Democratic Transitions and Breakdowns," *American Sociological Review* 54, No. 1 (1989), pp. 17–32; and to Gary Wynia's use of the term "political game," in his *Politics of Latin American Development* (Cambridge: Cambridge University Press, 1990), pp. 24–45.

3. Barrington Moore, *Social Origins of Dictatorship and Democracy* (Boston: Beacon, 1966).

4. Guillermo O'Donnell, *Modernization and Bureaucratic Authoritarianism: Studies in South American Politics* (Berkeley and Los Angeles: University of California Press, 1973).

5. Juan J. Linz and Alfred Stepan, eds., *The Breakdown of Democratic Regimes* (Baltimore: Johns Hopkins University Press, 1978); Guillermo O'Donnell, Philippe C. Schmitter, and Lawrence Whitehead, eds., *Transitions from Authoritarian Rule* (Baltimore: Johns Hopkins University Press, 1986).

6. Mark J. Gasiorowski, "Economic Crisis and Regime Change: An Event History Analysis," *American Political Science Review* 89 (1995), pp. 882–897; Mark J. Gasiorowski, "An Overview of the Political Regime Dataset," *Comparative Political Studies* 21 (1996), pp. 469–483.

7. Charles W. Anderson, "Toward a Theory of Latin American Politics," in Howard J. Wiarda, ed., *Politics and Social Change in Latin America: Still a Distinct Tradition?* (Boulder, Colo.: Westview Press, 1992), pp. 239–254.

8. See John Peeler, *Latin American Democracies* (Chapel Hill: University of North Carolina Press, 1985); Deborah J. Yashar, *Demanding Democracy: Reform and Reaction in Costa Rica and Guatemala, 1870s–1950s* (Stanford: Stanford University Press, 1997); and John A. Booth, *Costa Rica: Quest for Democracy* (Boulder, Colo.: Westview Press, 1998).

9. John A. Booth and Thomas W. Walker, *Understanding Central America*, 2nd ed. (Boulder, Colo.: Westview Press, 1993), Chapter 5.

10. Louis Kriesberg, *Social Conflicts*, 2nd ed. (Englewood Cliffs, N.J.: Prentice-Hall, 1982), p. 29.

11. John Walton, *Reluctant Rebels: Comparative Studies in Revolution and Underdevelopment* (New York: Columbia University Press, 1984), p. 13.

12. Walton, *Reluctant Rebels;* Theda Skocpol, *States and Social Revolutions* (Cambridge: Cambridge University Press, 1979); Mancur Olson, "Rapid Growth as a Destabilizing Force," *Journal of Economic History* 23, No. 4 (1963), pp. 529–552; and Jeffrey M. Paige, *Agrarian Revolution: Social Movements and Export Agriculture in the Underdeveloped World* (New York: Free Press, 1975). For specific applications to Central America, see Charles Brockett, *Land, Power, and Poverty: Agrarian Transformation and Political Conflict in Central America* (Boston: Unwin Hyman, 1988); Timothy Wickham-Crowley, *Guerrillas and Revolution in Latin America* (Princeton: Princeton University Press, 1992); Robert Williams, *Export Agriculture and the Crisis in Central America* (Chapel Hill: University of North Carolina Press, 1986); John A. Booth, "Socioeconomic and Political Roots of National Revolts in Central America," *Latin American Research Review* 26, No. 1 (1991), pp. 33–73; Edelberto Torres Rivas, *Crisis del poder in Centroamérica* (San José, Costa Rica: Editorial Universitaria Centroaméricana, 1981).

13. Kriesberg, *Social Conflicts*, pp. 66–106; Charles Tilly, *From Mobilization to Revolution* (Reading, Mass.: Addison-Wesley, 1978); Rod Aya, "Theories of Revolution Reconsidered: Contrasting Models of Collective Violence," *Theory and Society* 8 (June-December 1979), pp. 39–100.

14. Jack A. Goldtone, "An Analytical Framework," in Jack A. Goldstone, Ted Robert Gurr, and Farrokh Moshiri, eds., *Revolutions of the Late Twentieth Century* (Boulder, Colo.: Westview, 1991), pp. 37–51; Ted Robert Gurr, *Why Men Rebel* (Princeton: Princeton University Press, 1970); Walton, *Reluctant Rebels;* Skocpol, *States and Social Revolutions.*

15. Goldstone, "An Analytical Framework"; and James DeFronzo, *Revolutions and Revolutionary Movements* (Boulder, Colo.: Westview, 1991), pp. 7–25.

16. Timothy P. Wickham-Crowley, *Guerrillas and Revolution in Latin America: A Comparative Study of Insurgents and Regimes Since 1956* (Princeton: Princeton University Press, 1992).

17. Ronald Inglehart, "The Renaissance of Political Culture," *American Political Science Review* 82 (November 1988), pp. 1203–1230; Mitchell A. Seligson and John A. Booth, "Political Culture and Regime Type: Evidence from Nicaragua and Costa Rica," *Journal of Politics* 55 (August 1993), pp. 777–792; Edward N. Muller and Mitchell A. Seligson, "Civic Culture and Democracy: The Question of Causal Relationships," *American Political Science Review* 88 (September 1994), pp. 645–652; Larry Diamond, "Introduction: Political Culture and Democracy," and "Causes and Effects," both in Larry Diamond, ed., *Political Culture and Democracy in Developing Countries* (Boulder, Colo.: Lynne Rienner, 1994).

18. Dankwart Rustow, "Transitions to Democracy: Toward a Dynamic Model," *Comparative Politics* 2 (April 1970), pp. 337–363; Adam Przeworski, "Some Problems in the Study of the Transition to Democracy," in O'Donnell, Schmitter, and Whitehead, eds., *Transitions from Authoritarian Rule* (Baltimore: Johns Hopkins University Press, 1986). Samuel P. Huntington, *The Third Wave: Democratization in the Late Twentieth Century* (Norman: University of Oklahoma Press, 1991); Mitchell A. Seligson and John A. Booth,

eds., *Elections and Democracy in Central America, Revisited* (Chapel Hill: University of North Carolina Press, 1995).

19. Seymour Martin Lipset, "Social Requisites of Democracy: Economic Development and Political Legitimacy," *American Political Science Review* 53 (March 1959), pp. 69–105; Tatu Vanhanen, *The Process of Democratization* (New York: Crane Russak, 1990); Dietrich Rueschemeyer, Evelyne Huber Stephens, and John D. Stephens, *Capitalist Development and Democracy* (Chicago: University of Chicago Press, 1992); Robert D. Putnam, "Bowling Alone: America's Declining Social Capital," *Journal of Democracy* 7 (Summer 1996), pp. 38–52; and Robert D. Putnam, *Making Democracy Work: Civic Traditions in Modern Italy* (Princeton: Princeton University Press, 1993).

20. Lawrence Whitehead, "The Imposition of Democracy," in Abraham F. Lowenthal, ed., *Exporting Democracy: The United States and Latin America* (Baltimore: Johns Hopkins University Press, 1991).

21. Peeler, *Latin American Democracies;* Larry Diamond, "Introduction: Politics, Society, and Democracy in Latin America," in Larry Diamond, Juan Linz, and Seymour Martin Lipset, *Democracy in Developing Countries,* Volume 4, *Latin America* (Boulder, Colo.: Lynne Rienner, 1989); John Higley and Richard Gunther, eds., *Elites and Democratic Consolidation in Latin America and Southern Europe* (Cambridge: Cambridge University Press, 1992); and Huntington, *The Third Wave.*

22. For example, Lowenthal, ed., *Exporting Democracy;* Thomas Carothers, *In the Name of Democracy: U.S. Policy Toward Latin America in the Reagan Years* (Berkeley: University of California Press, 1991); Huntington, *The Third Wave;* Dario Moreno, "Respectable Intervention: The United States and Central American Elections," in Mitchell A. Seligson and John A. Booth, eds., *Elections and Democracy in Central America, Revisited* (Chapel Hill: University of North Carolina Press, 1995); Thomas W. Walker, "Introduction: Historical Setting and Important Issues," in Thomas W. Walker, ed., *Nicaragua Without Illusions: Regime Transition and Structural Adjustment in the 1990s* (Wilmington, Del.: Scholarly Resources, 1997); Gary Prevost and Harry E. Vanden, eds., *The Undermining of the Sandinista Revolution* (New York: St. Martin's, 1997); Wickham-Crowley, *Guerrillas and Revolution;* and DeFronzo, *Revolutions and Revolutionary Movements.*

23. Seven such training manuals used between 1982 and 1991 were disclosed by the Department of Defense in September 1996. See U.S. Department of Defense, "Fact Sheet Concerning Training Manuals Containing Materials Inconsistent with U.S. Policy" (Washington, D.C.: September 1996). See also Dana Priest, "U.S. Instructed Latins on Execution, Torture—Manuals Used 1982–1991, Pentagon Reveals," *Washington Post,* September 21, 1996, pp. A1, A9; Lisa Haugaard, "How the US Trained Latin America's Military: The Smoking Gun," *Envio* 16, No. 165 (October 1997), pp. 33–38.

24. The words of a State Department official who appeared with coauthor Thomas Walker on a panel on Central America at California State University, Los Angeles, on April 20, 1979.

Notes to Chapter 6

1. The values are an index indicating relative change for each country, set arbitrarily to equal 100 in 1973. Particular values for Nicaragua should be compared only to other values for Nicaragua, not to other nations' values.

2. Centro de Investigaciones y Estudios de la Reforma Agraria (CIERA), *Informe de Nicaragua a la FAO* (Managua: Ministerio de Desarrollo Agropecuario y Reforma Agraria, 1983), pp. 40–41.

3. Mario A. DeFranco and Carlos F. Chamorro, "Nicaragua: Crecimiento industrial y empleo," in Daniel Camacho et al., *El fracaso social de la integración centroamericana* (San José, Costa Rica: Editorial Universitaria Centroamericana, 1979), Cuadro 2.

4. John A. Booth, *The End and the Beginning: The Nicaraguan Revolution*, 2nd ed. (Boulder, Colo.: Westview Press, 1985), Chapter 5.

5. Note that computational methods vary from nation to nation, so that cross-national comparisons of raw data should not be made. Trends within nations, however, are usefully disclosed.

6. Jaime Wheelock Román, *Imperialismo y dictadura: Crisis de una formación social* (México: Siglo Veintiuno Editores, 1975), pp. 141–198; Amaru Barahona Portocarrero, *Estudio sobre la historia contemporánea de Nicaragua* (San José, Costa Rica: Instituto de Investigaciones Sociales, Universidad de Costa Rica, 1977), pp. 33–44.

7. Donaldo Castillo Rivas, "Modelos de acumulación, agricultura, y agroindustria en Centroamérica," in D. Castillo Rivas, ed., *Centroamérica: Más allá de la crisis* (México: Ediciones SIAP, 1983), pp. 202–205; Consejo Superior Universitaria Centroamericana (CSUCA), *Estructura Agraria, dinámica de población, y desarrollo capitalista en Centroamérica* (San José, Costa Rica: Editorial Universitaria Centroamericana, 1978), pp. 204–254.

8. CIERA, *Informe de Nicaragua*, p. 41.

9. One hectare equals roughly 2.5 acres.

10. Castillo Rivas, "Modelos," p. 203.

11. Material from Ricardo E. Chavarría, "The Nicaraguan Insurrection," in Thomas W. Walker, ed., *Nicaragua in Revolution* (New York: Praeger, 1982), pp. 28–29; Booth, *The End and the Beginning*, Chapter 6.

12. George Black, *Triumph of the People: The Sandinista Revolution in Nicaragua* (London: Zed Press, 1981), pp. 70–72; Centro de Información, Documentación y Análisis del Movimiento Obrero Latinoamericano (CIDAMO), "El movimiento obrero," in G. García Márquez et al., *Los Sandinistas* (Bogotá: Editorial Oveja Negra, 1979), pp. 171–176.

13. Michael Dodson and Tommie Sue Montgomery, "The Churches in the Nicaraguan Revolution," in Walker, ed., *Nicaragua in Revolution*, pp. 163–174; Laura Nuzzi O'Shaughnessy and Luis H. Serra, *The Church and Revolution in Nicaragua* (Athens: Monographs in International Studies, Latin American Series No. 11, Ohio University, 1986).

14. See also T. Walker, "Introduction," in Walker, ed., *Nicaragua: The First Five Years* (New York: Praeger Publishers, 1985), p. 20; Julio López C. et al., *La caída del somocismo y la lucha sandinista en Nicaragua* (San José, Costa Rica: Editorial Universitaria Centroamericano, 1979), pp. 98–112.

15. Thomas W. Walker, *The Christian Democratic Movement in Nicaragua* (Tucson: University of Arizona Press, 1970).

16. Omar Cabezas, *Fire from the Mountain*, trans. Kathleen Weaver (New York: New American Library, 1986).

17. Booth, *The End and the Beginning*, Chapter 8.

18. See ibid., pp. 97–104; López C. et al., *La caída del somocismo*, pp. 71–98.

19. Peter Kornbluh, "The Covert War," in Thomas W. Walker, ed., *Reagan Versus the Sandinistas: The Undeclared War on Nicaragua* (Boulder, Colo.: Westview Press, 1987), p. 21.

20. "A Secret War for Nicaragua," *Newsweek*, November 8, 1982, p. 44.

21. Ariel C. Armony, *Argentina, the United States, and the Anticommunist Crusade in Central America, 1977–1984* (Athens Ohio: University Press, 1997).

22. Tayacán [the CIA], *Psychological Operations in Guerrilla Warfare: The CIA's Nicaragua Manual* (New York: Vintage Books, 1985).

23. Michael Isikoff, "Drug Cartel Gave Contras $10 Million, Court Told," *Washington Post*, November 26, 1991, pp. A1, A8. For a detailed discussion of other ways in which drug money was used to finance the contra effort, see Peter Dale Scott and Jonathan Marshall, *Cocaine Politics: Drugs, Armies and the CIA in Central America* (Berkeley: University of California Press, 1991).

24. COSEP is the successor to COSIP following a name change made around 1979. See also Rose Spalding's *Capitalists and Revolution in Nicaragua: Opposition and Accommodation, 1979–1993*, (Chapel Hill: University of North Carolina Press, 1994).

25. E.g., a detailed report by Latin Americanists, *The Electoral Process in Nicaragua: Domestic and International Influences* (Austin, Tex.: Latin American Studies Association, November 19, 1984); or Booth, *The End and the Beginning*, pp. 215–223.

26. For a balanced treatment of the building of governmental institutions in Sandinista Nicaragua and, in particular, the 1987 constitution, see Andrew A. Reding, "The Evolution of Governmental Institutions," in Thomas W. Walker, ed., *Revolution and Counterrevolution in Nicaragua* (Boulder, Colo.: Westview Press, 1991), pp. 15–47. For more discussion of the constitution—pro and con—as well as a complete English translation, see Kenneth J. Mijeski, ed., *The Nicaraguan Constitution of 1987: English Translation and Commentary* (Athens: Ohio University Press, 1991).

27. For details, see Walker, ed., *Nicaragua in Revolution*, and *Nicaragua: The First Five Years*.

28. For a balanced discussion of Sandinista performance in the field of human rights, see Michael Linfield, "Human Rights," in Walker, ed., *Revolution and Counterrevolution in Nicaragua*, pp. 275–294.

29. Lawyers Committee for International Human Rights, *Nicaragua: Revolutionary Justice* (New York: April 1985), pp. 33–40.

30. John Spicer Nichols, "*La Prensa:* The CIA Connection," *Columbia Journalism Review* 28, No. 2 (July–August 1988), pp. 34, 35.

31. *Los Angeles Times*, June 27, 1986, p. 15.

32. Martin Diskin et al., "Peace and Autonomy on the Atlantic Coast of Nicaragua: A Report of the LASA Task Force on Human Rights and Academic Freedom," Part 2, *LASA Forum* 17 (Summer 1986), p. 15.

33. Americas Watch, *On Human Rights in Nicaragua* (New York, May 1982), pp. 58–80.

34. See Martin Diskin et al., "Peace and Autonomy on the Atlantic Coast of Nicaragua: A Report of the LASA Task Force on Human Rights and Academic Freedom," Part 1, *LASA Forum* 17 (Spring 1986), pp. 1–16; and Part 2, pp. 1–16.

35. Americas Watch, *On Human Rights in Nicaragua*, pp. 58–80.

36. See O'Shaughnessy and Serra, *The Church and Revolution in Nicaragua.*

37. *Los Angeles Times*, June 27, 1986, p. 15; June 30, 1986, p. 7; *New York Times*, July 5, 1986, p. 2.

38. "Latin Presidents Announce Accord on Contra Bases," *New York Times,* February 15, 1989, pp. 1, 4; *New York Times,* February 16, pp. 1, 6; "Nicaragua Pins Hopes on Turning Bureaucrats into Farmers," *Dallas Morning News,* February 22, 1989, p. 12A; and Booth's conversations with Mauricio Díaz of the Popular Social Christian party and Pedro Joaquín Chamorro Barrios; former director of the Nicaraguan Resistance, Montezuma, New Mexico, February 1989.

39. Joseph R. Thome and David Kaimowitz, "Agrarian Reform," in Walker, ed., *Nicaragua: The First Five Years;* and Forrest D. Colburn, *Post-Revolutionary Nicaragua: State, Class, and the Dilemmas of Agrarian Policy* (Berkeley: University of California Press, 1986).

40. John Weeks, "The Industrial Sector," and Michael E. Conroy, "Economic Legacy and Policies: Performance and Critique," in Walker, ed., *Nicaragua: The First Five Years;* and interviews by Booth with COSEP members in León, August 1985.

41. Latin American Studies Association (LASA) Commission to Observe the 1990 Nicaraguan Elections, *Electoral Democracy Under International Pressure* (Pittsburgh: LASA, March 15, 1990), p. 19.

42. The inflation statistics for both 1988 and 1989 are from [United Nations] Comisión Económica para América Latina y el Caribe, "Balance Preliminar de la Economía de América Latina y el Caribe, 1990," *Notas Sobre la Economía y el Desarrollo,* Nos. 500–501 (December 1990), p. 27.

43. This figure is part of eight pages of statistics on the human cost of the war provided to Walker by the Nicaraguan Ministry of the Presidency in January 1990.

44. LASA Commission, *Electoral Democracy,* pp. 24–26.

45. For a useful discussion of the character, role, and evolution of opposition parties during the revolution, see Eric Weaver and William Barnes, "Opposition Parties and Coalitions," in Walker, ed., *Revolution and Counterrevolution in Nicaragua,* pp. 117–142.

46. An unidentified State Department official as quoted in "Chamorro Takes a Chance," *Time Magazine,* May 7, 1990, p. 43. For details and documentation about the massive U.S. intervention in Nicaragua's 1990 election, see William I. Robinson, *A Faustian Bargain: U.S. Involvement in the Nicaraguan Elections and American Foreign Policy in the Post-Cold War Era* (Boulder, Colo.: Westview Press, 1992).

47. Coauthor Thomas Walker is in a particularly good position to attest to this upsurge in contra activity. A member of the LASA Commission to Observe the 1990 Nicaraguan Elections, he was specifically assigned to observe and investigate the campaign and election in the war zone of northern Nicaragua in late 1989 and early 1990.

48. As quoted in "Ortega Livens up San José Summit," *Central America Report* 16, No. 43 (November 3, 1989), p. 340.

49. Philip J. Williams, "Dual Transitions from Authoritarian Rule: Popular and Electoral Democracy in Nicaragua," *Comparative Politics* (January, 1994), pp. 169–185; quote from p. 172.

50. For a systematic and comprehensive examination of this period see Thomas W. Walker, ed. *Nicaragua Without Illusions: Regime Transition and Structural Adjustment in the 1990s,* (Wilmington, Del. Scholarly Resources, 1997).

51. As cited in Nitlapan-*Envío* Team, "President Alemán: First Moves, First Signals," *Envío,* Vol. 16, No. 187–188 (February–March 1997), pp. 3–4.

52. Lic. Juan Alamo, advisor to the minister of education, interviewed in Managua on June 25, 1991, by members of the Latin American Studies Association Research Seminar on Nicaragua (of which Thomas Walker was the coordinator).

53. The term *recontra* comes from the Spanish *contra* as a contraction of "counterrevolutionary" with *re* added to suggest remobilization. Similarly, *recompa* comes from the word *compañero* (roughly "comrade in arms"), which was often used for Sandinista soldiers. *Revueltos,* a term meaning "mixed together" or "scrambled," is the term ordinarily used for scrambled eggs.

54. See, for instance, "Nicaragua: Atlantic Coast Groups Rearm," *Central America Report,* 25, No. 22 (June 11, 1998), p. 3.

55. Shelly A. McConnell, "Institutional Development," pp. 45–64 in Walker, ed., *Nicaragua Without Illusions.*

56. For information concerning the election see "Epilogue: The 1996 National Elections," in Walker, *Nicaragua Without Illusions,* pp. 305–311.

57. The official figure for voter turnout did not include voters in voting places where the tallies were annulled.

58. On the election, see John A. Booth and Patricia Bayer Richard, "The Nicaraguan Elections of October 1996," *Electoral Studies* 16, No. 3 (1997), pp. 386–393; John A. Booth, "Election Observation and Democratic Transition in Nicaragua," in Kevin J. Middlebrook, ed., *Electoral Observation and Democratic Transitions in Latin America* (La Jolla, Calif. Center for U.S.-Mexican Studies of the University of California, San Diego, 1998, forthcoming); *Envío* 15 (December–January, 1996–1997); and Walker, "Epilogue."

59. The authors interviewed various Nicaraguan political leaders during June and July of 1998, including Victor Hugo Tinoco, FSLN representative in the National Assembly; Dora María Téllez, professor, former minister of health, and leader of the MRS; René Núñez, a top official of the FSLN; Mariano Fiallos, professor and former head of the CSE; Alejandro Bendaña, author, former foreign ministry official in the Ortega administration; Antonio Lacayo, businessman, farmer, and former minister of the presidency in the UNO government; Dr. Rigoberto Sampson, mayor of León. There was striking uniformity in their assessment of the FSLN's status.

60. Nitlapan-*Envío* Team, "An Accord Beseiged by Discord," *Envío* 16, No. 196 (November 1997), pp. 3–4.

61. On Alemán's scandal, see Oliver Bodán, "Guasch huyó hacia Miami vía Nica," *Confidencial,* 2 (May 17–23, 1998), pp. 1, 14–15; and Roberto Fonseca L., "¿Era agenta encubierto de la DEA?" *Confidencial,* 2 (May 17–23, 1998), pp. 1, 9. On the scandal involving Ortega, see Juan Ramón Huerta, *El silencio del patriarca* (Managua: Litografía El Renacimiento, 1998); and "Extractos del testimonio desgarrador de Zoliamérica," *Confidencial* 2 (May 24–30, 1998), pp. 1, 9–11.

62. "Población y viviendas afectadas por el huracán Mitch: 20 de noviembre de 1998, 16:30 hrs," «http://www.ops.org.ni/desastre/dcivil/historia/1998/mitch/region20.htm», December 6, 1998; Humberto Meza, "Políticos comentan decisión de Chamorro," *La Prensa,* (Managua: November 23, 1998), «http://www.tmx.com.ni/~˜teleda/23/n3.html»; Mario José Moncada and Gustavo Alvarez, "'Mitch' cambió geografía del Norte," *La Prensa,* (Managua: November 7, 1998), «http://www.tmx.com.ni/~˜teleda/9/n7.html»; Roberto Fonseca L., "¿Qué falló frente al huracán Mitch?," *Confidencial* 118 (November 8–14, 1998), «http://www.confidencial.com.ni/1998-118/confidencial/tema_central.html»; and

Roberto Fonseca L., "Mitch: huracán político del presidente," *Confidencial* 118 (November 8–14, 1998), «http://www.confidencial.com.ni/1998-118/confidencial/analisis.html».

Notes to Chapter 7

1. Hugo Molina, "Las bases económicas del desarrollo industrial *y* la absorción de fuerza de trabajo en El Salvador," in Daniel Camacho et al., *El fracaso social de la integración centroamericana* (San José, Costa Rica: Editorial Universitaria Centroamericana, 1979), pp. 245–254; Phillip L. Russell, *El Salvador in Crisis* (Austin, Tex.: Colorado River Press, 1984), pp. 76–78; Victor Antonio Orellana, *El Salvador: Crisis and Structural Change* (Miami: Latin American and Caribbean Center Occasional Paper Series No. 13, Florida International University, 1985), pp. 5–9; Victor Bulmer-Thomas, *The Political Economy of Central America Since 1920* (Cambridge: Cambridge University Press, 1987), pp. 175–229.

2. See especially Tommie Sue Montgomery, *Revolution in El Salvador: Origins and Evolution* (Boulder, Colo.: Westview Press, 1982); Donaldo Castillo Rivas, "Modelos de acumulación, agricultura, y agroindustria en Centroamérica," in D. Castillo Rivas, ed., *Centroamérica: Más allá de la crisis* (México: Ediciones SIAP, 1983), pp. 204–207; James Dunkerley, *The Long War: Dictatorship and Revolution in El Salvador* (London: Junction Books, 1982), pp. 87–118.

3. Dirección General de Estadística y Censos (DGEC-El Salvador), *Anuario Estadístico, 1981,* Tomos III-V (San Salvador: Ministerio de Economía, 1983), Cuadros 311-01, 311-02; Bulmer-Thomas, *Political Economy of Central America,* pp. 201–207.

4. Orellana, *El Salvador: Crisis,* pp. 5–10; Molina, "Las bases económicas," pp. 245–254.

5. Orellana, *El Salvador: Crisis,* pp. 5–7.

6. Montgomery, *Revolution in El Salvador,* pp. 94–95.

7. Orellana, *El Salvador: Crisis,* pp. 6–7.

8. Material based on Montgomery, *Revolution in El Salvador;* Dunkerley, *The Long War,* pp. 90–102; Jorge Cáceres Prendes, "Radicalización política y pastoral en El Salvador: 1969–1979," *Estudios Sociales Centroamericanos* 33 (September–December 1982), pp. 97–111.

9. Russell, *El Salvador in Crisis,* pp. 71–78; Tomás Guerra, *El Salvador en la hora de su liberación* (San José, Costa Rica: n.p., 1980), pp. 103–108; Enrique Baloyra, *El Salvador in Transition* (Chapel Hill: University of North Carolina Press, 1982), pp. 43–52.

10. DGEC-El Salvador, *Anuario Estadístico, 1981,* Tomos III–V.

11. Rafael Menjívar, *Formación y lucha del proletariado industrial salvadoreño* (San José, Costa Rica: Editorial Universitaria Centroamericano, 1982), pp. 115–162; Russell, *El Salvador in Crisis,* p. 71.

12. See Michael McClintock, *The American Connection,* Vol. 1: *State Terror and Popular Resistance in El Salvador* (London: Zed Books, 1985), pp. 156–209, for details on the rise of repression in El Salvador; see also Inforpress Centroamericano, *Central America Report,* January 20, 1984, p. 23.

13. McClintock, *The American Connection,* pp. 174–177.

14. Tommie Sue Montgomery, "El Salvador: The Roots of Revolution," in S. Ropp and J. Morris, eds., *Central America: Crisis and Adaptation* (Albuquerque: University of New Mexico Press, 1984), pp. 86–90.

15. Taken from DGEC-El Salvador, *Anuario Estadístico* for years 1965, 1966, 1968, 1969, 1971, 1977, 1980, and 1981; the figure reported in the table is the total number of "homicides" plus other, unexplained violent deaths.

16. Based on data reported in Baloyra, *El Salvador in Transition*, p. 190; and Richard Alan White, *The Morass: United States Intervention in Central America* (New York: Harper and Row, 1984), p. 44; and Inforpress Centroamericano, *Central America Report;* January 20, 1984, p. 23.

17. Comisión de Derechos Humanos de El Salvador (CDHES), *Primer Congreso de Derechos Humanos en El Salvador* (San Salvador, El Salvador: CDHES, November 1984), pp. 30–31, authors' translation.

18. Philip J. Williams and Knut Walter, *Militarization and Demilitarization in El Salvador's Transition to Democracy* (Pittsburgh: University of Pittsburgh Press, 1997), pp. 190–113.

19. Ibid. p. 113.

20. Montgomery, *Revolution in El Salvador,* pp. 140–157.

21. Dunkerley, *The Long War,* p. 175.

22. Benjamin C. Schwarz, *American Counterinsurgency Doctrine and El Salvador: The Frustration of Reform and the Illusion of Nation Building* (Santa Monica, Cal.: Rand Corporation, 1991), p. v.

23. Baloyra, *El Salvador in Transition;* José Z. García, "El Salvador: Recent Elections in Historical Perspective," in John A. Booth and Mitchell A. Seligson, eds., *Elections and Democracy in Central America* (Chapel Hill, University of North Carolina Press, 1989), pp. 60–89.

24. Dunkerley, *The Long War,* p. 163.

25. For discussions of problems with the U.S.-backed elections in El Salvador in 1982, 1984, and 1985, see Terry Karl, "Imposing Consent: Electoralism vs. Democratization in El Salvador," in P. Drake and E. Silva, eds., *Elections and Democratization in Latin America* (La Jolla: Center for Iberian and Latin American Studies-Center for U.S.-Mexican Studies, University of California, San Diego, 1986), p. 21; Edward S. Herman and Frank Brodhead, *Demonstration Elections* (Boston: South End Press, 1984), pp. 93–152; and García, "El Salvador: Recent Elections," pp. 60–89.

26. See, for instance, Karl, "Imposing Consent," pp. 18–34; and Clifford Krauss, "El Salvador Army Gains on the Guerrillas," *Wall Street Journal,* July 30, 1986, p. 20.

27. On elections see Enrique A. Baloyra, "Elections, Civil War, and Transition in El Salvador, 1982–1994: A Preliminary Evaluation," in Mitchell A. Seligson and John A. Booth, eds., *Elections and Democracy in Central America, Revisited* (Chapel Hill: University of North Carolina Press, 1995). On the military and peace negotiations, see Williams and Walter, *Militarization and Demilitarization in El Salvador,* Chapters 6 and 7; and Ricardo Córdova Macías, "El proceso de diálogo-negociación y las perspectivas de paz," in *El Salvador: Guerra, política, y paz, 1979–1989* (San Salvador: CINAS-CRIES, 1988), pp. 195–219. Ricardo Córdova Macías, *El Salvador: Las negociaciones de paz y los retos de la postguerra* (San Salvador: Instituto de Estudios Latinoamericanos, 1989).

28. Karl, "Imposing Consent."

29. Comisión de la Verdad, *De la locura a la esperanza: La guerra de doce años en El Salvador. Informe de la Comisión,* published in *Estudios Centroamericanos* 158 (March 1993), San Salvador.

30.

31. Inter-American Development Bank (IABD), *Economic and Social Progress in Latin America: Science and Technology: 1988 Report* (Washington, D.C., 1988), Table B.1.

32. Points made in two lengthy interviews with three official FMLN spokespersons conducted by members of the Central American Task Force of the United Presbyterian Church's Council on Church and Society in Managua in November 1992. Coauthor Thomas Walker, a member of that task force, was present for the interviews.

33. Schwarz, *American Counterinsurgency Doctrine,* pp. v, vi.

34. Written Statement of Representative Joe Moakley, chairman of the Speaker's Task Force on El Salvador, November 18, 1991; see also the account in Comisión de la Verdad, *De la locura a la esperanza.*

35. See, for instance, Freedom House, *Freedom in the World: The Annual Survey of Political Rights and Civil Liberties, 1993–1994* (New York: 1994), pp. 242–243; Comisión de la Verdad, *De la locura a la esperanza; La Prensa Gráfica,* (July 31, 1994, pp. 4A–5A; August 1, 1994, pp. 4A–5A; August 2, 1994, pp. 4A–5A; August 4, 1994, pp. 4A–5A); Williams and Walter, *Militarization and Demilitarization,* Chapters 7 and 8; and "Penal Laws Cause Controversy," *Central America Report,* May 7, 1998, p. 4.

Notes to Chapter 8

1. Inforpress Centroamericana, *Guatemala: Elections 1985* (Guatemala City, 1985), p. 19.

2. Guatemala was judged to be one of the countries most affected by rising unemployment in the early 1980s. See Eugenio Rivera Urrutia, Ana Sojo, and José Roberto López, *Centroamérica: Política económica y crisis* (San José, Costa Rica: Editorial Departamento Ecuménico de Investigaciones-Universidad Nacional Autónoma, 1986), pp. 138–141.

3. Ibid.; Thomas P. Anderson, *Politics in Central America: Guatemala, El Salvador, Honduras, and Nicaragua* (New York: Praeger, 1982), pp. 19–62; "Guatemala," *Mesoamérica,* May 1982; Consejo Superior Universitaria Centroamericana (CSUCA), *Estructura agrária, dinámica de poplación, y desarrollo capitalista en Centroamérica* (San José, Costa Rica: Editorial Universitaria Centroamericana, 1978), pp. 77–132; Technical Commission of the Great National Dialogue, *Economic and Social Policy Recommendations to the Head of State* (Guatemala City, 1985); Lars Schoultz, "Guatemala: Social Change and Political Conflict," in Martin Diskin, ed., *Trouble in Our Backyard* (New York: Pantheon, 1983), pp. 178–183; Brockett, *Land, Power, and Poverty,* pp. 99–123; and Jonas, *The Battle for Guatemala,* Chapter 5.

4. Julio Castellano Cambranes, "Origins of the Crisis of the Established Order in Guatemala," in Ropp and Morris, eds., *Central America: Crisis,* Table 4.2.

5. Mitchell A. Seligson et al., *Land and Labor in Guatemala: An Assessment* (Washington, D.C.: Agency for International Development-Development Associates, 1982), pp. 1–18.

6. George Black et al., *Garrison Guatemala* (New York: Monthly Review Press, 1984), pp. 34–37; Schoultz, "Guatemala," p. 181; Seligson et al., *Land and Labor.*

7. Gustavo A. Noyola, "Integración centroamericana y absorción de mano de obra: Guatemala," in Camacho et al., *El fracaso.*

8. Richard Newbold Adams, *Crucifixion by Power: Essays on Guatemalan National Social Structure, 1944–1966* (Austin: University of Texas Press, 1970); Black et al., *Garrison Guatemala,* pp. 48–51.

9. John A. Booth, "A Guatemalan Nightmare: Levels of Political Violence, 1966–1972," *Journal of Interamerican Studies and World Affairs* 22 (May 1980), pp. 195–225.

10. Material here drawn mainly from Oscar Rolando Sierra Pop, "Iglesia y conflicto social en Guatemala," *Estudios Sociales Centroamericanos* 33 (September-December 1982), pp. 66–86; Black et al., *Garrison Guatemala,* pp. 61–107; Anderson, *Politics,* pp. 19–60; Inforpress Centroamericana, *Guatemala: Elections 1985,* pp. 8–11; Jonathan Fried et al., *Guatemala in Rebellion: Unfinished History* (New York: Grove, 1983), pp. 151–316; Jonas, *The Battle for Guatemala,* Chapters 5–7.

11. Héctor Rosado Granados, *Guatemala 1984: Elecciones para Asamblea Nacional Constituyente* (San José, Costa Rica: Instituto Centroamericano de Derechos Humanos-Centro de Asesoría y Promoción Electoral, 1985), p. 41; "Guatemala," *Mesoamérica,* March 1982, pp. 2–4; Margaret E. Roggensack and John A. Booth, *Report of the International Human Rights Law Group and the Washington Office on Latin America Advance Election Observer Mission to Guatemala* (Washington, D.C., 1985), Appendix B; Robert Trudeau, "Guatemalan Elections: The Illusion of Democracy," paper presented to the National Conference on Guatemala, Washington, D.C., June 15, 1984.

12. Gabriel Aguilera Peralta, Romero Imery, et al., *Dialéctica del terror en Guatemala* (San José, Costa Rica: Editorial Universitaria Centroamericana, 1981); Americas Watch, *Human Rights in Guatemala: No Neutrals Allowed* (New York, 1982), and *Little Hope: Human Rights in Guatemala, January 1984–1985* (New York, 1985); John A. Booth et al., *The 1985 Guatemalan Elections: Will the Military Relinquish Power?* (Washington, D.C.: International Human Rights Law Group-Washington Office on Latin America, 1985); see also Gordon L. Bowen, "The Origins and Development of State Terrorism," in Donald E. Schulz and Douglas H. Graham, eds., *Revolution and Counterrevolution in Central America and the Caribbean* (Boulder, Colo.: Westview Press, 1984); and "Guatemala," *Mesoamérica,* July-August 1982, pp. 2–4; Jonas, *The Battle for Guatemala,* pp. 145–177; Brockett, *Land, Power, and Poverty,* pp. 112–119.

13. Data for selected periods drawn from U.S. Embassy—Guatemala reports from 1966 through 1984, reported in Booth, "A Guatemalan Nightmare," and U.S. Department of State, *Country Report on Human Rights Practices* (Washington, D.C.: U.S. Government Printing Office, February 2, 1981), p. 441; later data came from Inforpress Centroamericana, *Central America Report,* February 1, 1985, p. 31; November 22, 1985, p. 357; January 21, 1988, p. 12.

14. For 1982 and after see U.S. Embassy—Guatemala, "A Statistical Comparison of Violence (1982–1985)," Guatemala City, xerox, 1985. Recent investigations have confirmed the extent of the violence; see for instance, Francisco Mauricio Martínez, "Guatemala, Never More: 55,000 Human Rights Violations," and "URNG Committed 44 Massacres," both from *La Prensa Libre* (Guatemala City), April 14, 1998, translated into English in Human Rights News Clips, Foundation for Human Rights in Guatemala, «http:www.fhrg.org/042098.htm//G», July 13, 1998, pp. 1–3.

15. Quoted by Allan Nairn in "Guatemala Can't Take 2 Roads," *New York Times,* July 20, 1982, p. 23A. Material on the reformist military regime drawn in part from U.S. Department of State, *Background Notes: Guatemala,* Bureau of Inter-American Affairs, March

1998, «http://www.state.gov/www/background_notes/guatemala_0398_bgn.html», pp. 3–4.

16. Booth's conversation with U.S. Embassy personnel, Guatemala City, September 1985; see also Roggensack and Booth, *Report.*

17. Material based on Booth's field observations in Guatemala in 1985, plus Americas Watch, *Human Rights in Guatemala* and *Little Hope;* Booth et al., *The 1985 Guatemalan Elections;* Inforpress Centroamericana, *Guatemala: Elections 1985;* British Parliamentary Human Rights Group, *"Bitter and Cruel . . . ": Report of a Mission to Guatemala by the British Parliamentary Human Rights Group* (London: House of Commons, 1985); and Black et al., *Garrison Guatemala,* pp. 61–113. Much of the volume (55,000 deaths) and responsibility (80 percent military, 20 percent URNG) for human rights abuses in this period alleged in early reports has been confirmed and fleshed out in a preliminary report to a national truth commission compiled by the human rights office of the Archdiocese of Guatemala; see Martínez, "Guatemala, Never More," and "URNG Committed."

18. Black et al., *Garrison Guatemala,* pp. 107–109.

19. Interviews with Guatemalan labor sources, September-October 1985 and April-May 1987, Guatemala City; see Booth et al., *The 1985 Guatemalan Elections,* pp. 39–40, and David Carliner et al., *Political Transition and the Rule of Law in Guatemala* (Washington, D.C.: International Human Rights Law Group—Washington Office on Latin America, January 1988), pp. 7–8. For confirmation see also Jonas, *The Battle for Guatemala.*

20. Booth et al., *The 1985 Guatemalan Elections.*

21. Interviews with spokesmen for various parties, September–October 1985, Guatemala.

22. See Latin American Studies Association (LASA), *Extraordinary Opportunities . . . and New Risks: Final Report of the LASA Commission on Compliance with the Central America Peace Accord* (Pittsburgh: LASA, 1988), pp. 15–20; Booth's interviews with various Guatemalan political figures and expert observers, September 1988; "Año de tumulto en Guatemala," *Excelsior* (Mexico City), December 30, 1988, p. 4A; *Christian Science Monitor,* February 14, 1989, p. 3.

23. U.S. Department of State, *Background Notes: Guatemala,* Bureau of Inter-American Affairs, March 1998. áhhp://www.state.gov/www/backqround_notes/guatemala_0398_bgn.htmlñ, *Amparo* and *habeas corpus* are court orders for the government to cease violating constitutional rights, helpful in protecting citizens from wrongful detention and other abuses of power.

24. On the impact of counterinsurgency on the indigenous, see Washington Office on Latin America, *Who Pays the Price? The Cost of War in the Guatemalan Highlands* (Washington, D.C., April 1988). See also Carliner et al., *Political Transition;* LASA, *Extraordinary Opportunities . . . and New Risks,* pp. 15–20; "Guatemala," *Mesoamérica,* April 1990, pp. 4–5; "Guatemala," *Mesoamérica,* May 1990, p. 6; "Guatemala," *Mesoamérica,* June 1990, pp. 4–5; "Guatemala," *Mesoamérica,* July 1990, p. 2; "Guatemala," *Mesoamérica,* August 1990, pp. 5–6; "Guatemala," *Mesoamérica,* October 1990, pp. 2–3; "Guatemala," *Mesoamérica,* November 1990, pp. 2–3; "Guatemala," *Mesoamérica,* January 1991, pp. 1–2; "Four Guatemalan Troops Charged in Killings," *Boston Globe,* September 30, 1990, pp. 1–2; "Amnesty International Reports Guatemalan Police and Private Sector Forces Torture and Murder Street Children," *Excelsior* (Mexico City), November 10, 1990, p. 2A.

25. "Guatemala," *Mesoamérica,* April 1991, pp. 3–4; "Guatemala," *Mesoamérica,* May 1991, pp. 10–11; "Guatemala," *Mesoamérica,* June 1991, pp. 4–5; "Guatemala," *Meso-*

américa, August 1991, pp. 11–12; "Guatemala," *Mesoamérica,* September 1991, pp. 1–2; Katherine Ellison, "Celebrity of Guatemalan Rights Activists Could Save His Life," *Miami Herald,* November 22, 1990, p. 20B; "Guatemalan Troops Said to Kill 11 Protesting Raid," *New York Times,* December 3, 1990, p. 8A; "Government Accuses Death Squads of Wave of Killings, Denies Connections to Armed Forces," *Excelsior,* August 5, 1991, p. 2A; Haroldo Shetemul, "National Blackout in Guatemala: Police Chief Assassinated," *Excelsior,* August 6, 1991, p. 2A; "Attacks on Journalists Condemned by President Serrano Elias," *Excelsior,* September 1, 1991, p. 2A.

26. Susanne Jonas, "Electoral Problems and the Democratic Prospect in Guatemala," and John A. Booth, "Introduction: Elections and Democracy in Central America: A Framework for Analysis," both in Mitchell A. Seligson and John A. Booth, eds., *Elections and Democracy in Central America, Revisited* (Chapel Hill: University of North Carolina Press, 1995), pp. 35–36, p. 1.

27. Susanne Jonas, "The Democratization of Guatemala Through the Peace Process," paper presented to the Seminar on Guatemalan Development and Democratization: Proactive Responses to Globalization, Universidad del Valle de Guatemala, Guatemala City, March 27, 1998, pp. 3–4; and U.S. Department of State, *Background Notes: Guatemala,* pp. 4–5.

28. This section drawn mainly from Jonas's "The Democratization of Guatemala," pp. 3–6.

29. The indigenous rights accord, a landmark in this country profoundly marked by anti-Indian racism, stated that Guatemala is a multiethnic, multicultural, and multilingual society and provided for education reform and indigenous representation in governmental structures; see Kay B. Warren, "Pan-Mayanism and Multiculturalism in Guatemala," a paper presented at the Symposium on Development and Democratization in Guatemala: Proactive Responses to Globalization, Universidad del Valle, Guatemala City, March 18, 1998, pp. 1–5.

30. Ibid., pp. 4–5; and U.S. Department of State, *Guatemala: Background Notes,* p. 5; "Mayans Win Local Representation," *Cerigua* (Peace Net) (Guatemala City), Weekly Briefs, No. 3, January 18, 1996; Guatemala City; Tim Johnson, "Maya Mayor Triumphs over Entrenched Racism," *Miami Herald,* January 15, 1996, p. 1A.

31. "FDNG Activists Assassinated," *Cerigua* (Peace Net), Weekly Briefs, No. 2, January 11, 1996; "Human Rights Violations Continue to Rise," *Cerigua* (Peace Net), Weekly Briefs, No. 5, February 1, 1996; Michael Riley, "Refugees Outside Looking In," *Christian Science Monitor,* January 10, 1996, p. 5; Larry Rohter, "Specter in Guatemala: Iron-Fisted General Looms Large Again," *New York Times,* January 10, 1996, p. 4A; "Arzú Greeted by Strikes and Protests," *Central America Report* (Guatemala City), January 19, 1996, p. 3.

32. Jonas, "The Democratization of Guatemala," pp. 6–10; U.S. Department of State, *Background Notes: Guatemala,* pp. 10–11.

33. See Appendix, Table 1. See also U.S. Department of State, *Background Notes: Guatemala,* pp. 5–8; Jonas, "The Democratization of Guatemala," pp. 10–20; "Uncertain Future: Social Watch Evaluates Guatemala," *Cerigua,* Weekly Briefs, June 4, 1998; "President Accused of 'Killing the Media,'" *Central America Report,* March 26, 1998, p. 1; Celina Zubieta, "Victims of Death Squads or Gang Warfare?" *InterPress Service* (Peace Net) March 31, 1998; Mike Lanchin, "Death Squad Claims Responsibility for Bishop's Death," *National Catholic Reporter,* May 22, 1998, p. 2; Francisco Mauricio Martínez, "Progress Towards

Peace Evaluated," *La Prensa Libre,* «www.prensalibre.com», December 28, 1998; and Michael Riley, "Stealing Guatemala's Peace Dividend."

34. *Jaguar Justiciero* translates, albeit quite awkwardly into English, as "justice-dealing" or "justice-dispensing jaguar."

35. "CEH Pressured to Denounce Genocide," *Central America Report,* May 21, 1998, p. 5; Lanchin, "Death Squad Claims", p. 12.

Notes to Chapter 9

1. John A. Booth and Thomas W. Walker, *Understanding Central America* (Boulder Colo.: Westview Press, 1993), Appendix, Table 2, p. 176.

2. This theory is explained in detail in ibid., Chapter 5.

3. See also Victor Bulmer-Thomas, *The Political Economy of Central America Since 1920* (New York: Cambridge University Press, 1987), Table 10.7, p. 219; Víctor Hugo Cèspedes, Alberto di Mare, and Ronulfo Jiménez, *Costa Rica: La economía en 1985* (San José, Costa Rica: Academia de Centroamèrica, 1986), Cuadro 19, p. 71.

4. Víctor Hugo Cèspedes, *Evolución de la distribución del ingreso en Costa Rica* (San Josè, Costa Rica: Instituto de Investigación en Ciencias Económicas, Universidad de Costa Rica, 1979), Cuadro 6; and Cèspedes et al., *Costa Rica: La economía en 1985,* Cuadro 20, p. 73.

5. See also David Felix, "Income Distribution and the Quality of Life in Latin America: Patterns, Trends, and Policy Implications," *Latin American Research Review* 18, No. 2 (1983), pp. 3–34.

6. For further data, see John A. Booth, "Representative Constitutional Democracy in Costa Rica: Adaptation to Crisis in the Turbulent 1980s," in S. Ropp and J. Morris, eds., *Central America: Crisis and Adaptation* (Albuquerque: University of New Mexico Press, 1984), p. 171. On the operation and impact of the Costa Rican development model, see John A. Booth, *Costa Rica: Quest for Democracy* (Boulder Colo.: Westview Press, 1998), Chapters 3 and 8.

7. Mitchell A. Seligson, *Peasants of Costa Rica and the Development of Agrarian Capitalism* (Madison, University of Wisconsin Press, 1980), pp. 122–170; see also Francisco Barahona Riera, *Reforma agraria y poder político* (San José: Editorial Universidad de Costa Rica, 1980), pp. 221–422; Donaldo Castillo Rivas, "Modelos de acumulación, agricultura, y agroindustria en Centroamérica," in D. Castillo Rivas, ed., *Centroamérica: Más allá de la crisis* (Mèxico: Ediciones SIAP, 1983), pp. 210–213.

8. Thomas P. Anderson, *Politics in Central America: Guatemala, El Salvador, Honduras, and Nicaragua* (New York: Praeger, 1982), pp. 109–147.

9. Victor Meza, *Honduras: La evolución de la crisis* (Tegucigalpa: Editorial Universitaria, 1982), pp. 19–29; J. Mark Ruhl, "Agrarian Structure and Political Stability in Honduras," *Journal of Inter-American Studies and World Affairs* 26 (February 1984), pp. 33–68. Booth's conversation with Lucas Aguilera, member of the executive committee of the Union Nacional Campesina, Tegucigalpa, and members of the Unión Maraíta cooperative farm, Departamento Francisco Morazán, August 21, 1985. On recent unrest, see "Guatemala," *Mesoamérica,* June 1991, pp. 1–2; "Guatemala," *Mesoamérica,* August 1991, p. 16.

10. "Guatemala," *Mesosamérica,* July–August 1982: 7; Castillo Rivas, "Modelos," pp. 199–201; Mario Posas, *El movimiento campesino hondureño* (Tegucigalpa: Editorial Guaymuras, 1981), pp. 34–42.

11. Booth's conversation with Lucas Aguilera, member of the executive committee of the Union Nacional Campesina, Tegucigalpa, and members of the Unión Maraíta cooperative farm, Departamento Francisco Morazán, August 21, 1985. On recent unrest, see "Guatemala," *Mesoamérica,* June 1991, pp. 1–2; "Guatemala," *Mesoamérica,* August 1991, p. 16.

12. This material from John A. Booth, "Costa Rica: The Roots of Democratic Stability," in Larry Diamond, Juan J. Linz, and Seymour Martin Lipset, eds. *Democracy in Developing Countries, Volume 4: Latin America.* Boulder, Colo.: Lynne Rienner; and Booth, "Representative Constitutional Democracy."

13. E. Lederman et al., "Trabajo y empleo," in Chester Zelaya, ed., *Costa Rica contemporánea,* Tomo II (San José: Editorial Costa Rica, 1979; James Backer, *La Iglesia y el sindicalismo en Costa Rica,* (San José: Editorial Costa Rica, 1978), pp. 135–207; Gustavo Blanco and Orlando Navarro, *El solidarismo: Pensamiento y dinámica social de un movimiento obrero patronal* (San José: Editorial Costa Rica, 1984).

14. Rodrigo Fernández Vásquez, "Costa Rica: Interpretación histórica sobre reforma social y acción eclesiástica: 1940–1982," *Estudios Sociales Centroamericanos* 33 (September–December 1982), pp. 221–248.

15. "Costa Rica," *Mesoamérica,* April 1990, pp. 11–12; "Costa Rica," *Mesoamérica,* July 1990, pp. 7–8; "Costa Rica," *Mesoamérica,* October 1990, p. 9; "Costa Rica," *Mesoamérica,* November 1990, pp. 9–10; "Costa Rica," *Mesoamérica,* December 1990, p. 11; "Costa Rica," *Mesoamérica,* January 1991, pp. 4–7; "Costa Rica," *Mesoamérica,* February 1991, pp. 4–5; "Costa Rica," *Mesoamérica,* April 1991, pp. 1–2.

16. Lowell Gudmundson, "Costa Rica," in Jack W. Hopkins, ed., *Latin American and Caribbean Contemporary Record,* Vol. 3: *1983–1984* (New York: Holmes and Meier, 1985), pp. 499–508.

17. Mitchell A. Seligson and Edward Muller, "Democracy, Stability, and Economic Crisis: Costa Rica, 1978–1983," *International Studies Quarterly* 31 (September 1987), pp. 301–326; and Booth "Costa Rican Democracy."

18. Discussion of Honduras based on Victor Meza, *Historia del movimiento obrero hondureño* (Tegucigalpa: Editorial Guaymuras, 1980), pp. 123–167, and Meza, *Honduras: La evolución,* pp. 14–41; Anderson, *Politics,* pp. 109–121; Posas, *El movimiento campesino.*

19. James A. Morris, "Government and Politics," in James D. Rudolph, ed., *Honduras: A Country Study* (Washington, D.C.: American University Foreign Area Studies series, U.S. Government Printing Office, 1984), pp. 168–193; Rosa María Pochet Coronado, "El reformismo estatal y la Iglesia en Honduras 1949–1982," *Estudios Sociales Centroamericanos* 33 (September–December 1982), pp. 155–188.

20. Steve C. Ropp, "National Security," in Rudolph, ed., *Honduras: A Country Study,* pp. 391–396.

21. "Honduras," *Mesoamérica,* April 1990, p. 9; "Honduras," *Mesoamérica,* February 1991, pp. 10–11; "Honduras," *Mesoamérica,* May 1991, p. 12; "Honduras," *Mesoamérica,* June 1991, p. 2; *Excelsior,* January 13, 1991, p. 2A.

22. Booth, "Representative Constitutional Democracy," pp. 173–176; Booth, "Costa Rican Democracy," pp. 39–40; Seligson, *Peasants,* pp. 105–114; U.S. Department of State, *Country Reports on Human Rights Practices* (Washington, D.C.: U.S. Government Printing Office, February 2, 1981), pp. 241–244. See also Booth, *Costa Rica: Quest for Democracy,* pp. 114–121.

23. Booth, *Costa Rica: Quest for Democracy,* Chapter 8.

24. Ibid., pp. 166–172 and Table 8.5; election data from Tables 3.4 and 4.1.

25. Ibid., Chapter 7.

26. Richard L. Millett, "Historical Setting," in Rudolph, ed., *Honduras: A Country Study,* p. 47.

27. Ramón Custodio, "The Human Rights Crisis in Honduras," in Mark Rosenberg and Phillip Shepherd, eds., *Honduras Confronts its Future* (Boulder, Colo.: Lynne Reinner Publishers, 1986), pp. 69–71.

28. U.S. Department of State, *Country Reports on Human Rights,* p. 46; Morris, "Government and Politics," pp. 192–193; and James A. Morris, "Honduras: The Burden of Survival in Central America," in Ropp and Morris, eds., *Central America,* pp. 217–219; Charles W. Anderson, *Politics and Economic Change in Latin America: The Governing of Restless Nations* (New York: Van Nostrand Reinhold, 1967), pp. 116–132.

29. Americas Watch, *Review of the Department of State's Country Reports on Human Rights Practices for 1982: An Assessment* (New York, February 1983), p. 55. The discrepancy between this figure and the number of 40 cited earlier probably stems from a combination of two factors: different reporting agencies are involved, and they are reporting on somewhat different phenomena. The two figures may not, in fact, be incongruent.

30. *Washington Report on the Hemisphere,* October 28, 1987, pp. 1, 60.

31. James A. Morris, "Honduras: The Burden of Survival in Central America" in Ropp and Morris, *Central America,* pp. 201–204.

32. Mark Rosenberg, "Can Democracy Survive the Democrats? From Transition to Consolidation in Honduras," in John A. Booth and Mitchell A. Seligson, eds., *Elections and Democracy in Central America* (Chapel Hill, University of North Carolina Press, 1989); Latin American Studies Association (LASA), *Extraordinary Opportunities . . . and New Risks: Final Report of the LASA Commission on Compliance with the Central American Peace Accord* (Pittsburgh: LASA, 1988), pp. 20–26.

33. "Honduras," *Mesoamérica,* April 1990, pp. 8–9; "Honduras," *Mesoamérica,* January 1991, pp. 9–10; "Honduras," *Mesoamérica,* February 1991, p. 10; "Honduras," *Mesoamérica,* May 1991, p. 12; "Honduras," *Mesoamérica,* June 1991, p. 2; "Honduras," *Mesoamérica,* September 1991, pp. 8–9; *Excelsior,* December 12, 1990, p. 2A; *Miami Herald,* December 15, 1990, p. 24A; and *Miami Herald,* December 2, 1990, p. 22A.

34. J. Mark Ruhl, "Honduras: Militarism and Democratization in Troubled Waters," a paper presented at the 21st Congress of the Latin American Studies Association, Chicago, Illinois, September 25, 1998.

35. Edward Orlebar, "Honduran President Faces Battle with His Own Military," *Los Angeles Times,* December 18, 1993, p. 2A; "Demilitarization Runs into Problems," *Central America Report,* November 21, 1996, p. 1; "Transfer of Police from Military to Civil Power Ratified," *Central America Report,* January 10, 1997, p. 6; "Honduras," *Mesoamérica,* June 6, 1997, p. 4; Thelma Mejía, "Vice President Implicated in Disappearances," *Interpress Service*/Spanish (Peacenet), January 23, 1998; "Military Files Confiscated," *Central American Report,* February 12, 1998, p. 3; "New Government Seeks to Broaden Support," *Central America Report,* January 29, 1998, p. 7; Thelma Mejía, "Extra-Judicial Executions on the Rise," *Interpress Service*/Spanish (PeaceNet), February 4, 1998; "Death Squads Assassinate Human Rights Leader," *Interpress Service*/Spanish (PeaceNet), February 11, 1998; Thelma Mejía, "The Army Wants You!" *InterPress Service*/Spanish (PeaceNet), January 21, 1997; "Honduran Death Squads Active Again, Report Says," *Houston Chronicle,* January 15, 1998, p. 19A.

Notes to Chapter 10

1. Paper presented by Thomas W. Walker to the U.S. Department of State conference on Central America: U.S. Policy Interests and Concerns, Washington, D.C., March 19, 1979. This paper was subsequently published as "The U.S. and Central America," *Caribbean Review* 8, No. 3 (Summer 1979), pp. 18–23.

2. The only modification we would now make to the 1979 statement is that surprisingly, even in the late 1980s, flawed U.S. policy still had not produced high levels of anti-Americanism. Even in Nicaragua, most citizens, including most Sandinistas, were able to distinguish between the American people, on the one hand, and the U.S. government, on the other. Rightly or wrongly, the former were not held responsible for the behavior of the latter.

3. Charles W. Anderson, "The Latin American Political System," in his *Politics and Economic Change in Latin America: The Governing of Restless Nations* (New York: Van Nostrand Reinhold Co., 1967), pp. 87–114.

4. For a sophisticated analysis of democratic theories, see Robert A. Dahl, A *Preface to Democratic Theory* (Chicago: University of Chicago Press, 1956). For a critical analysis of the significance of participation as a basis for democratic process, see E. E. Schatt-Schneider, *The Semisovereign People: A Realist's View of Democracy in America* (New York: Holt, Rinehart, and Winston, 1960).

5. See, for instance, John A. Booth and Mitchell A. Seligson, eds., *Elections and Democracy in Central America* (Chapel Hill: University of North Carolina Press, 1989), passim.

6. National Bipartisan Commission on Central America, *Report of the National Bipartisan Commission on Central America* (Washington, D.C., 1984), p. 30.

7. Paulo Freire, *The Pedagogy of the Oppressed* (New York: Herder and Herder, 1968).

8. Coauthor Thomas W. Walker served as a U.S. Peace Corps volunteer in Mompós, Colombia, from 1963 to 1965.

9. Second General Conference of Latin American Bishops, *The Church and the Present-Day Transformation of Latin America in the Light of the Council* (Washington, D.C.: United States Catholic Conference, 1973).

10. For more information about the changing Catholic church in the past three decades, see Edward L. Cleary, O.P., *Crisis and Change: The Church in Latin America Today* (Maryknoll, N.Y.: Orbis Books, 1985).

11. After the victory, the women's organization changed its name to the Luisa Amanda Espinosa Nicaraguan Woman's Association (Asociación de Mujeres Nicaragüenses Luisa Amanda Espinosa—AMNLAE) and the CDCs became the Sandinista Defense Committees (Comités de Defensa Sandinista—CDS), but other than that, all five movements remained essentially the same.

12. This information was revealed on June 25, 1985, by an official in the U.S. Embassy to a group of which coauthor Thomas Walker was part.

13. For more information about mobilization in Nicaragua, see Luis Serra, "The Grass-Roots Organizations," in Thomas W. Walker, ed., *Nicaragua: The First Five Years* (New York: Praeger, 1985), pp. 65–89, or Gary Ruchwarger, *People in Power: Forging a Grassroots Democracy in Nicaragua* (Granby, Mass.: Bergin and Garvey Publishers, 1987).

14. See Deborah Barndt, "Popular Education," in Walker, ed., *Nicaragua: The First Five Years,* pp. 317–345.

15. The only Central American country in which some popular mobilization and socioeconomic reform has succeeded with U.S. support is Costa Rica, where the social-democratic reformers of the National Liberation party were associated with a political movement that ousted Communists from power in 1948.

16. For an illuminating discussion of the nature of the U.S. policymaker's perception of a Communist threat in Latin America, see Lars Schoultz, "Communism," in his *National Security and United States Policy Toward Latin America* (Princeton: Princeton University Press, 1987), pp. 106–139.

17. See Tayacán, *Psychological Operations in Guerrilla Warfare: The CIA's Nicaragua Manual,* prepared by the Central Intelligence Agency (New York: Vintage Books, 1985). See also U.S. Department of Defense, "Fact Sheet Concerning Training Manuals Containing Materials Inconsistent with U.S. Policy" (Washington, D.C.: September 1996), and this volume, Chapter 5, note 23, for sources on other similar manuals.

18. Michael McClintock, *The American Connection,* Volume 1, *State Terror and Popular Resistance in El Salvador* (London: Zed Books, 1985), p. 47.

19. See Michael Klare, *War Without End* (New York: Alfred A. Knopf, 1972), Chapter 9.

20. Americas Watch, *Review of the Department of State's Country Reports on Human Rights Practices for 1982: An Assessment* (New York: February 1983), pp. 1–9, 37–46, 55–61, 63–70. The report stated, for instance, that "a special effort appears to have been made to exculpate current leaders considered friends of the United States—such as . . . President Ríos Montt of Guatemala" (p. 5).

21. Latin American Studies Association, *The Electoral Process in Nicaragua: Domestic and International Influences* (Austin, Tex.: LASA, 1984), p. 17.

22. For detailed discussion and documentation, see Thomas W. Walker, "The Armed Forces," in Walker, ed., *Revolution and Counterrevolution in Nicaragua,* (Boulder, Colo.: Westview Press, 1991).

23. Ortega, as interviewed by Pierre Hurel, "Ortega ne rend pas les armes," *Paris Match,* March 22, 1990, pp. 78–81.

24. Mary B. Vanderlaan, *Revolution and Foreign Policy in Nicaragua* (Boulder, Colo.: Westview Press, 1986), p. 322.

25. Excerpts from State Department and Pentagon, *Congressional Presentation Document,* Security Assistance Programs, FY 1981, as reproduced in Robert Matthews, "The Limits of Friendship: Nicaragua and the West," *NACLA Report on the Americas* 19, No. 3 (May–June 1985), p. 24.

26. Michael McClintock, *The American Connection,* Volume 2, *State Terror and Popular Resistance in Guatemala* (London: Zed Books, 1985), pp. 32–33. This volume is also a source of documentation for the general observations in the next two paragraphs. For additional information about demobilization in Guatemala see Tom Barry and Deb Preusch, *The Soft War: The Uses and Abuses of U.S. Economic Aid in Central America* (New York: Grove Press, 1988).

27. According to one detailed study, "Israel had already been the Guatemalan military's largest supplier of arms since 1977" (Andrew and Leslie Cockburn, *Dangerous Liaisons: The Inside Story of the U.S. Israeli Covert Relationship* [New York: Harper Collins 1991], p. 218). Even so, in 1981, early in the Reagan administration, Secretary of State Alexander Haig, Jr., reportedly "prompted Israel to do more in Guatemala" (Leslie H. Gelb, "Israelis Said to Step Up Role as Arms Suppliers to Latins," *New York Times,* December 17, 1982, p. A.11). This request appears to have fallen on receptive ears because in that same year, Is-

raeli Economic Coordination Minister Ya'acov Meridor reportedly informed a group of Israeli businessmen that "Israel coveted the job of top Washington proxy in Central America" (quoted in George Black, "Israeli Connection: Not Just Guns for Guatemala," *NACLA Report on the Americas* 17, No. 3 [May–June 1983], pp. 43–44). Later, Israeli Knesset member General Matityahu Peled commented that "in Central America, Israel is the 'dirty work' contractor for the U.S. administration. Israel is acting as an accomplice and arm of the United States" (quoted in Benjamin Beit-Hallahmi, *The Israeli Connection: Who Israel Arms and Why* [New York: Pantheon Books, 1987], p. 78). In addition to direct revenues from sales, the payoff for Israel was obvious: By mid-1983 unnamed U.S. officials reportedly had commented that this cooperation "was a factor in the improvement in Israeli-United States relations, which had been cooling during the first half of the Reagan Administration" (Philip Taubman, "Israel Said to Aid Latin Aims of U.S.," *New York Times,* July 21, 1983, p. A4). The authors wish to thank Richard E. Clinton, Jr., a Ph.D. candidate in contemporary history at Ohio University, for his research in this matter.

28. Lindsey Gruson, "Terror's Toll Builds Again in El Salvador," *New York Times,* December 20, 1988, p. 1.

29. Just prior to the Sandinista victory in Nicaragua, coauthor Thomas Walker and two other U.S. academicians were invited to speak at a dinner seminar for high-level U.S. government officials from various foreign policymaking departments. Though the seminar was designed explicitly to "focus on the prospects for political and economic stability in . . . [Central America], paying particular attention to the impact of a radical, pro-Cuban regime in Managua," Walker accepted the invitation on the condition that he be allowed to deliver a sharply critical evaluation of U.S. policy. The condition was accepted in writing on July 18, and the event took place on August 2, 1988. After the short academic presentations, the government officials in attendance, including CIA Director Admiral Stansfield Turner, broke into a remarkably frank strategy discussion in which the ideas contained in the three sentences in the text preceding this endnote number emerged as part of an apparent consensus among the policymakers.

30. See McClintock, *The American Connection,* Vol. 1.

31. For a good description and documentation of the role of James Cheek, see Tommie Sue Montgomery, *Revolution in El Salvador: Origins and Evolution,* 2nd ed. (Boulder, Colo.: Westview Press 1995, Chapter 7.

32. For material on U.S. officials' efforts to persuade El Salvador to improve its human rights performance, see "El Salvador," *Mesoamérica,* November 1982, p. 6; "El Salvador," *Mesoamérica,* October 1983, p. 6; "El Salvador," *Mesoamérica,* November 1983, p. 6; and "El Salvador," *Mesoamérica,* December 1983, pp. 5–6; and the *Miami Herald,* December 19, 1983, p. 1.

33. One can get a sense of this barbarity by reading, for instance, Organization of American States, *Report on the Situation of Human Rights in Nicaragua: Findings of the "On-site" Observation in the Republic of Nicaragua, October 3–12, 1978* (Washington, D.C.: General Secretariat of the OAS, 1978).

34. Richard L. Millett, *Guardians of the Dynasty: A History of the U.S.-Created Guardia Nacional de Nicaragua and the Somoza Family* (Maryknoll, N.Y.: Orbis Press, 1977), p. 252.

35. A 1985 U.S. Congressional investigation revealed that forty-six of the forty-eight officers in the main contra army were former Somoza officers (Arms Control and Foreign Policy Caucus, the U.S. House of Representatives, "Who Are the Contras?" *Congressional Record* 131, 48 [Daily Edition, April 23, 1985], H2335). Though this embarrassing revela-

tion led the Reagan administration to expand and reshuffle the officers' corps, the real control of the contras in the field remained firmly in the hands of ex-guardsmen. Indeed, the head of the contras was a former guard officer, Enrique Bermúdez.

36. Booth's interview with Dora María Tellez, former FSLN guerrilla and former minister of health in the revolutionary government, Managua, June 30, 1998.

37. Tayacán [the CIA], *Operaciones sicológicas en guerra de guerrillas,* [1983]. This was later translated and published commercially as *Psychological Operations in Guerrilla Warfare: The CIA's Nicaragua Manual* (New York: Vintage Books, 1985).

38. The documentation of contra brutality is massive. The numerous reports of Americas Watch are good sources. Others are Reed Brody, *Contra Terror in Nicaragua, Report of a Fact-Finding Mission: September 1984-January 1985* (Boston: South End Press, 1985); and Christopher Dickey, *With the Contras: A Reporter in the Wilds of Nicaragua* (New York: Simon and Schuster, 1985).

39. These statistics are from eight pages of charts provided by the Nicaraguan Ministry of the Presidency in January 1990.

40. From an argument overheard by members of the Latin American Studies Association Commission to Observe the 1990 Election on February 26, 1990, in Managua.

41. As quoted in Thomas W. Walker, "The 1994 Research Seminar in Nicaragua," *LASA Forum* 25, No. 3 (Fall 1994), p. 14.

Notes to Chapter 11

1. National Bipartisan Commission on Central America, *Report of the National Bipartisan Commission on Central America* (Washington, D.C.: 1984).

2. Rubén Zamora in an interview with the Presbyterian Task Force on Central America (UPCUSA) in Managua, in November, 1982. Official spokespersons for the FMLN whom the Task Force also interviewed in Managua at that time agreed and went into detail about their intent to fight only until a negotiated settlement could be achieved. Thomas Walker, a member of the Task Force was present at those meetings.

3. For more detail see, "Epilogue: The 1996 National Elections," *Nicaragua Without Illusions: Regime Transition and Structural Adjustment in the 1990s,* Thomas W. Walker, ed. (Wilmington, DE: Scholarly Resources, 1997), pp. 306–7.

4. For an interesting attempt to interpret U.S. policy making in regard to the first Somoza in this way, see: Paul Coe Clarke, Jr. *The United States and Somoza, 1933–1956: A Revisionist Look* (Westport, CT: Praeger Publishers, 1992.)

5. The most articulate defense of the "practical" approach to regime types was made by Jeane J. Kirkpatrick in her article "Dictatorships and Double Standards," *Commentary,* 68 (November, 1979), pp. 34–45. In it Kirkpatrick, who soon became President Reagan's first Ambassador to the United Nations and major advisor on Latin American affairs, argued that it was better to support "traditional autocracies" than run the risk of Communist totalitarian regimes.

6. The literature on democratization in Central America includes John A. Booth and Mitchell A. Seligson, eds., *Elections and Democracy in Central America* (Chapel Hill: University of North Carolina Press, 1989); Mitchell A. Seligson and John A. Booth, eds., *Elections and Democracy in Central America, Revisited* (Chapel Hill: University of North Carolina Press, 1995); Deborah J. Yashar, *Demanding Democracy: Reform and Reaction in Costa*

Rica and Guatemala, 1870s–1950s (Stanford: Stanford University Press, 1997); John A. Booth, *Costa Rica: Quest for Democracy* (Boulder, Colo: Westview Press, 1998); and Philip J. Williams and Knut Walter, *Militarization and Demilitarization in El Salvador's Transition to Democracy* (Pittsburgh: University of Pittsburgh Press, 1997). Among the major sources on democratization in Latin America that also include studies or discussion of Central America are John Peeler, *Latin American Democracies* (Chapel Hill: University of North Carolina Press, 1985); Larry Diamond, Juan Linz, and Seymour Martin Lipset, eds., *Democracy in Developing Countries, Volume 4: Latin America* (Boulder: Lynne Rienner Publishers, 1989); Guillermo O'Donnell, Philippe C. Schmitter, and Laurence Whitehead, eds. *Transitions from Authoritarian Rule: Latin America* (Baltimore: Johns Hopkins University Press, 1986); James M. Malloy and Mitchell A. Seligson, eds., *Authoritarians and Democrats: Regime Transition in Latin America* (Pittsburgh: University of Pittsburgh Press, 1987); Paul Drake and Eduardo Silva, eds., *Elections and Democratization in Latin America* (La Jolla, CA: Center for Iberian and Latin American Studies-Center for U.S.-Mexican Studies, University of California San Diego, 1986); and Dietrich Reuschemeyer, Evelyne Huber Stephens, and John D. Stephens, *Capitalist Development and Democracy* (Chicago: University of Chicago Press, 1992.)

7. Michael Burton, Richard Gunther, and John Higley, "Introduction: Elite Transformations and Democratic Regimes," in John Higley and Richard Gunther, eds. *Elites and Democratic Consolidation in Latin America and Southern Europe,* Cambridge: Cambridge University Press, 1992, pp. 3–4) treat democratic consolidation somewhat differently than this—that is as equivalent to, rather than merely including, an elite settlement: "A *consolidated democracy* is a regime that meets all the procedural criteria of democracy and also in which all politically significant groups accept established political institutions and adhere to democratic rules of the game" (p. 3).

8. See, Peeler, *Latin American Democracies;* Burton, et al., "Introduction: Elite Transformations . . ."; John A. Booth, "Elections and Democracy in Central America: A Framework for Analysis," in Booth and Seligson, *Elections and Democracy,* pp. 19–21; and Mitchell A. Seligson and John A. Booth, "Political Culture and Regime Type: Evidence from Nicaragua and Costa Rica," *Journal of Politics* 55 (August 1993): 777–792.

9. Larry Diamond and Juan J. Linz, "Introduction: Politics, Society and Democracy in Latin America," in Larry Diamond, Juan J. Linz, and Seymour Martin Lipset, eds., *Democracy in Developing Countries, Volume 4: Latin America* (Boulder, Colo.: Lynne Rienner, 1989), p. 15.

10. John A. Booth, "Toward Reconciliation and Democracy in Central America: Possible Roles for External Assistance," in Joaquín Roy, ed., *The Reconstruction of Central America: The Role of the European Community* (Coral Gables, FL: Iberian Studies Institute, University of Miami-European Community Research Institute, 1992), pp. 331–352; Diamond and Linz, "Introduction," pp. 10–17.

11. Diamond and Linz, "Introduction . . ."; Samuel Huntington, *The Third Wave: Democratization in the Late Twentieth Century* (Norman: University of Oklahoma Press, 1991), p. 208–316; Booth, "Elections and Democracy in Central America . . .", pp. 16–21.

12. Peeler, *Latin American Democracies;* John Peeler, "Elites and Democracy in Central America," in John A. Booth and Mitchell A. Seligson, eds., *Elections and Democracy in Central America* (Chapel Hill: University of North Carolina Press, 1989); and John Peeler, "Autumn of the Oligarchs?" in Mitchell A. Seligson and John A. Booth, eds., *Elections and Democracy in Central America* (Chapel Hill: University of North Carolina Press, 1995).

13. John A. Booth and Patricia Bayer Richard, "Repression, Participation, and Democratic Norms in Urban Central America," *American Journal of Political Science* 40 (1996), pp. 1205–1232; and John A. Booth and Patricia Bayer Richard, "Civil Society, Political Capital, and Democratization in Central America," *Journal of Politics* 60 (August 1998), pp. 780–800.

BIBLIOGRAPHY

Adams, Richard Newbold. 1970. *Crucifixion by Power: Essays on Guatemalan National Social Structure, 1944–1966.* Austin: University of Texas Press.

Aguilera Peralta, Gabriel. 1983. "Guatemala: Estado, militarismo, y lucha política." In Castillo Rivas, ed. 1983a.

Aguilera Peralta, Gabriel, Romero Imery, et al. 1981. *Dialéctica del terror en Guatemala.* San José, Costa Rica: Editorial Universitaria Centroamericana.

Americas Watch. 1982a. *Human Rights in Guatemala: No Neutrals Allowed.* New York.

______. 1982b. *On Human Rights in Nicaragua.* New York. May.

______. 1983. *Review of the Department of State's Country Reports on Human Rights Practices for 1982: An Assessment.* New York. February.

______. 1985. *Little Hope: Human Rights in Guatemala, January 1984–1985.* New York. February.

______. 1991. *El Salvador's Decade of Terror: Human Rights Since the Assassination of Archbishop Romero.* New Haven: Yale University Press.

"Amnesty International Reports Guatemalan Police and Private Sector Forces Torture and Murder Street Children." 1990. Excelsior (Mexico City). November 10, 2A.

Anderson, Charles W. 1967a. "The Latin American Political System." In Charles W. Anderson, *Politics and Economic Change in Latin America: The Governing of Restless Nations.* New York: Van Nostrand Reinhold, 1967.

Anderson, Charles W. 1967b. *Politics and Economic Change in Latin America: The Governing of Restless Nations.* New York: Van Nostrand Reinhold.

______. 1992. "Toward a Theory of Latin American Politics." In Howard J. Wiarda, ed., *Politics and Social Change in Latin America: Still a Distinct Tradition?* Boulder, Colo.: Westview Press.

Anderson, Thomas P. 1982. *Politics in Central America: Guatemala, El Salvador, Honduras, and Nicaragua.* New York: Praeger.

"Año de tumulto en Guatemala." 1988. *Excelsior* (Mexico City). December 30: 4A.

Armony, Ariel C. 1997. *Argentina, the United States, and the Anticommunist Crusade in Central America, 1977–1984.* Athens: Ohio University Press.

Arms Control and Foreign Policy Caucus, U.S. House of Representatives. 1985. "Who Are the Contras?" *Congressional Record* 131, 48 (Daily Edition, April 23), H2335.

Atkins, G. Pope. 1977. *Latin America in the International Political System.* New York: The Free Press.

______. 1989. *Latin America in the International Political System.* Boulder, Colo.: Westview Press.

"Attacks on Journalists Condemned by President Serrano Elias." 1991. *Excelsior.* September 1: 2A.

Atwood, Wallace W., and Helen Goss Thomas. 1929. *The Americas.* Boston: Ginn and Co.

Aya, Rod. 1979. "Theories of Revolution Reconsidered: Contrasting Models of Collective Violence." *Theory and Society* 8 (June–December): 39–100.

Backer, James. 1978. *La Iglesia y el sindicalismo en Costa Rica.* San José, Costa Rica: Editorial Costa Rica.

Baloyra, Enrique A. 1982. *El Salvador in Transition.* Chapel Hill: University of North Carolina Press.

______. 1983. "Reactionary Despotism in Central America." *Journal of Latin American Studies* 15 (November): 295–319.

Baloyra, Enrique A. 1995. "Elections, Civil War, and Transition in El Salvador, 1982–1994: A Preliminary Evaluation." In Mitchell A. Seligson and John A. Booth, eds., *Elections and Democracy in Central America, Revisited.* Chapel Hill: University of North Carolina Press.

Barahona Portocarrero, Amaru. 1977. *Estudio sobre la historia contemporánea de Nicaragua,* San José, Costa Rica: Instituto de Investigaciones Sociales, Universidad de Costa Rica.

Barahona Riera, Francisco. 1980. *Reforma agraria y poder político.* San José, Costa Rica: Editorial Universidad de Costa Rica.

Barndt, Deborah. 1985. "Popular Education." In Walker, ed. 1985b.

Barry, Tom, and Deb Preusch. 1988. *The Soft War: The Uses and Abuses of U.S. Economic Aid in Central America.* New York: Grove Press.

Beit-Hallahmi, Benjamin. 1987. *The Israeli Connection: Who Israel Arms and Why.* New York: Pantheon Books.

Bermann, Karl. 1986. *Under the Big Stick: Nicaragua and the United States since 1948.* Boston: South End Press.

Berryman, Phillip. 1984. *The Religious Roots of Rebellion: Christians in the Central American Revolutions.* Maryknoll, N.Y.: Orbis Books.

______. 1985. *Inside Central America,* New York: Pantheon Books.

Black, George. 1981. *Triumph of the People: The Sandinista Revolution in Nicaragua.* London: Zed Press.

______. 1983. "Israeli Connection Not Just Guns for Guatemala." *NACLA Report on the Americas* 17, No. 3 (May–June): 43–44.

Black, George, with Milton Jamail and Norma Stoltz Chinchilla. 1984. *Garrison Guatemala.* New York: Monthly Review Press.

Blanco, Gustavo, and Orlando Navarro. 1984. *El solidarismo: Pensamiento y dinámica social de un movimiento obrero patronal.* San José: Editorial Costa Rica.

Bodán, Oliver. 1998. "Guasch huyó hacia Miami vía Nica." *Confidencial* (Managua) 2, May 17–23, 1, 14–15.

Booth, John A. 1980. "A Guatemalan Nightmare: Levels of Political Violence, 1966–1972." *Journal of Interamerican Studies and World Affairs* 22 (May): 195–225.

______. 1982. *The End and the Beginning: The Nicaraguan Revolution.* Boulder, Colo.: Westview Press.

______. 1984. "Representative Constitutional Democracy in Costa Rica: Adaptation to Crisis in the Turbulent 1980s." In Ropp and Morris, eds. 1984.

______. 1985. *The End and the Beginning: The Nicaraguan Revolution.* 2nd ed. Boulder, Colo.: Westview Press.

______. 1989a. "Costa Rica: The Roots of Democratic Stability." In Diamond, Linz, and Lipset, eds. 1989.

______. 1989b. "Nicaragua." In Malloy and Gamarra, eds. 1989.

Booth, John A. 1989c. "Elections and Democracy in Central America: A Framework for Analysis." In John A. Booth and Mitchell A. Seligson, eds., *Elections and Democracy in Central America.* Chapel Hill: University of North Carolina Press.

______. 1991a. "Socioeconomic and Political Roots of National Revolts in Central America." *Latin American Research Review* 26 (No. 1): 33–74.

______. 1991b. "Theories of Religion and Rebellion: The Central American Experience." *Journal of Third World Studies* 8 (No. 2).

Booth, John A. 1992. "Toward Reconciliation and Democracy in Central America: Possible Roles for External Assistance." In Joaquín Roy, ed., *The Reconstruction of Central America: The Role of the European Community.* Coral Gables, Fla.: Iberian Studies Institute, University of Miami–European Community Research Institute.

Booth, John A. 1995. "Introduction: Elections and Democracy in Central America: A Framework for Analysis." In Mitchell A. Seligson and John A. Booth, eds., *Elections and Democracy in Central America, Revisited.* Chapel Hill: University of North Carolina Press.

Booth, John A. 1998a. *Costa Rica: Quest for Democracy.* Boulder, Colo.: Westview Press.

Booth, John A. 1998b. "Election Observation and Democratic Transition in Nicaragua." In Kevin J. Middlebrook, ed., *Electoral Observation and Democratic Transitions in Latin America.* La Jolla, Calif.: Center for U.S.-Mexican Studies of the University of California, San Diego.

Booth, John A., and Patricia Bayer Richard. 1996. "Repression, Participation, and Democratic Norms in Urban Central America." *American Journal of Political Science* 40: 1205–1232.

Booth, John A., and Patricia Bayer Richard. 1997. "The Nicaraguan Elections of October 1996." *Electoral Studies* 16 (No. 3): 386–393.

Booth, John A., and Patricia Bayer Richard. 1998. "Civil Society, Political Capital, and Democratization in Central America." *Journal of Politics* 60 (August): 780–800.

Booth, John A., and Mitchell A. Seligson, eds. 1989. *Elections and Democracy in Central America.* Chapel Hill: University of North Carolina Press.

Booth, John A., et al. 1985. *The 1985 Guatemalan National Elections: Will the Military Relinquish Power?* Washington, D.C.: International Human Rights Law Group-Washington Office on Latin America. February.

Booth, John A., and Thomas W. Walker. 1989. *Understanding Central America.* Boulder, Colo.: Westview Press.

Booth, John A., and Thomas W. Walker. 1993. *Understanding Central America.* Boulder, Colo.: Westview Press.

Bowen, Gordon L. 1984. "The Origins and Development of State Terrorism." In Schulz and Graham, eds. 1984.

British Parliamentary Human Rights Group. 1985. *"Bitter and Cruel . . . ": Report of a Mission to Guatemala by the British Parliamentary Human Rights Group.* London: House of Commons.

Brockett, Charles D. 1988. *Land, Power, and Poverty: Agrarian Transformation and Political Conflict in Central America.* Boston: Unwin Hyman.

Brody, Reed. 1985. *Contra Terror in Nicaragua, Report of a Fact-finding Mission: September 1984–January 1985.* Boston: South End Press.

Bulmer-Thomas, Victor. 1983. "Economic Development Over the Long Run—Central America Since 1920." *Journal of Latin American Studies* 15 (November): 269–294.

______. 1987. *The Political Economy of Central America Since 1920.* Cambridge: Cambridge University Press.

Burns, E. Bradford. 1991. *Patriarch and Folk: The Emergence of Nicaragua, 1798–1858.* Cambridge: Harvard University Press.

Burton, Michael, Richard Gunther, and John Higley. 1992. "Introduction: Elite Transformations and Democratic Regimes." In John Higley and Richard Gunther, eds. *Elites and Democratic Consolidation in Latin America and Southern Europe.* Cambridge: Cambridge University Press.

Cabezas, Omar. 1986. *Fire From the Mountain.* Kathleen Weaver, trans. New York: New American Library.

Cáceres Prendes, Jorge. 1982. "Radicalización política y pastoral en El Salvador: 1969–1979." *Estudios Sociales Centroamericanos* 33 (September–December): 97–111.

Camacho, Daniel, et al. 1979. *El fracaso social de la integración centroamericana,* San José, Costa Rica: Editorial Universitaria Centroamericana.

Carliner, David, et al. 1988. *Political Transition and the Rule of Law in Guatemala,* Washington, D.C.: International Human Rights Law Group-Washington Office on Latin America. January.

Carothers, Thomas. 1991. *In the Name of Democracy: U. S. Policy Toward Latin America in the Reagan Years.* Berkeley: University of California Press.

Castellano Cambranes, Julio. 1984. "Origins of the Crisis of the Established Order in Guatemala." In Ropp and Morris, eds. 1984.

Castillo Rivas, Donaldo, ed. 1983a. *Centroamérica: Más allá de la crisis.* México: Ediciones SIAP.

______. 1983b. "Modelos de acumulación, agricultura, y agroindustria en Centroamérica." In Castillo Rivas, ed. 1983a.

CDHES (Comisión de Derechos Humanos de El Salvador). 1984. *Primer Congreso de Derechos Humanos en El Salvador.* San Salvador, El Salvador. November.

Central America Report. 1989. "Ortega Livens up San José Summit." November 3, 340.

Central America Report. 1996a. "Arzú Greeted by Strikes and Protests." January 19, 3.

Central America Report. 1996b. "Demilitarization Runs into Problems." November 21, 1.

Central America Report. 1997. "Transfer of Police from Military to Civil Power Ratified." January 10, 6.

Central America Report. 1998a. "New Government Seeks to Broaden Support." January 29, 7.

Central America Report. 1998b. "Military Files Confiscated." February 12, 3.

Central America Report. 1998c. "President Accused of 'Killing the Media.'" March 26, 1.

Central America Report. 1998d. "Penal Laws Cause Controversy." May 7, 4.

Central America Report. 1998e. "CEH Pressured to Denounce Genocide." May 21, 5.

Central America Report. 1998f. "Nicaragua: Atlantic Coast Groups Rearm." June 11, 3.

Central Intelligence Agency. 1993. *The World Factbook, 1993.* Washington, D.C.

CEPAL (Comisión Económica para América Latina y el Caribe). 1985. *Preliminary Overview of the Latin American Economy: 1985.* Santiago, Chile: United Nations. December.

______. 1986. *Preliminary Overview of the Latin American Economy: 1986.* Santiago, Chile: United Nations. December.

Cerigua/Peace Net (Guatemala City). 1996a. "FDNG Activists Assassinated." Weekly Briefs, No. 2, January 11.

Cerigua/Peace Net. 1996b. "Human Rights Violations Continue to Rise," Weekly Briefs, No. 5, February 1.

Cerigua/Peace Net. 1996c. "Mayans Win Local Representation." January 18.

Cerigua/Peace Net. 1998. "Uncertain Future: Social Watch Evaluates Guatemala," Weekly Briefs, June 4.

Céspedes, Víctor Hugo. 1979. *Evolución de la distribución del ingreso en Costa Rica.* San José, Costa Rica: Instituto de Investigación en Ciencias Económicas, Universidad de Costa Rica.

Céspedes, Víctor Hugo, Alberto di Mare, and Ronulfo Jiménez. 1986. *Costa Rica: La economía en 1985.* San José, Costa Rica: Academia de Centroamérica.

"Chamorro Takes a Chance." 1990. *Time Magazine.* May 7, p. 43.

Chavarría, Ricardo E. 1982. "The Nicaraguan Insurrection." In Walker, ed. 1982.

Chilcote, Ronald H., and Joel C. Edelstein. 1986. *Latin America: Capitalist and Socialist Perspectives of Development and Underdevelopment.* Boulder, Colo.: Westview Press.

Christian Science Monitor 1989. February 14, 3.

CIDAMO (Centro de Información, Documentación y Análisis del Movimiento Obrero Latinoamericano). 1979. "El movimiento obrero," in García Márquez et al., 1979.

CIERA (Centro de Investigaciones y Estudios de la Reforma Agraria). 1983. *Informe de Nicaragua a la FAO.* Managua: Ministerio de Desarrollo Agropecuario y Reforma Agraria.

Clarke, Paul Coe, Jr. 1992. *The United States and Somoza, 1933–1956: A Revisionist Look.* Westport, Conn. Praeger.

Cleary, Edward L., O.P. 1985. *Crisis and Change: The Church in Latin America Today.* Maryknoll, N.Y.: Orbis Books.

Cockburn, Andrew, and Leslie Cockburn. 1991. *Dangerous Liaisons: The Inside Story of the U.S.-Israeli Covert Relationship.* New York: Harper Collins Publishers.

Cohan, A. S. 1975. *Theories of Revolution: An Introduction.* New York: Wiley-Halstead Press.

Colburn, Forrest D. 1986. *Post-Revolutionary Nicaragua: State, Class, and the Dilemmas of Agrarian Policy.* Berkeley: University of California Press.

Comisión de la Verdad. 1993. *De la locura a la esperanza: La guerra de doce años en El Salvador. Informe de la Comisión.* Published in *Estudios Centroamericanos* (San Salvador) 158: March.

Comisión Económica para América Latina y el Caribe. 1990. "Balance Preliminar de la Economía de América Latina y el Caribe, 1990." *Notas Sobre la Economía y el Desarrollo* Nos. 500–501 (December): 27.

"Commentary: The Region." 1982. *Mesoamérica* (San José, Costa Rica). September: 1.

Committee of Santa Fe. 1980. *A New Inter-American Policy for the Eighties.* Washington, D.C.: Council for Inter-American Security, as cited in Bruce D. Larkin, ed., *Vital Interests: The Soviet Issue in U.S. Central American Policy.* Boulder: Colo.: Lynne Rienner, 1988.

Conroy, Michael E. 1985. "Economic Legacy and Policies: Performance and Critique." In Walker, ed. 1985b.

______. 1987. "Economic Aggression as an Instrument of Low-Intensity Warfare." In Walker, ed. 1987.

______. 1988. "Nicaragua: Structure, Dynamics, and Conditions of the Economy in 1988: The Economic Dilemmas of Peace and Democracy." Paper presented at the VII Congreso Centroamericano de Sociología. October 10–15, Guatemala City.

Córdova Macías, Ricardo. 1988. "El proceso de diálogo-negociación y las perspectivas de paz." In *El Salvador: Guerra, política, y paz, 1979–1989.* San Salvador: CINAS-CRIES.

Córdova Macías, Ricardo. 1989. *El Salvador: Las negociaciones de paz y los retos de la postguerra.* San Salvador: Instituto de Estudios Latinoamericanos.

"Costa Rica." 1990a. *Mesoamérica.* April: 11–12.

"Costa Rica." 1990b. *Mesoamérica.* July: 7–8.

"Costa Rica." 1990c. *Mesoamérica.* October: 9.

"Costa Rica." 1990d. *Mesoamérica.* November: 9–10.

"Costa Rica." 1990e. *Mesoamérica.* December: 11.

"Costa Rica." 1991a. *Mesoamérica.* January: 4–7.

"Costa Rica." 1991b. *Mesoamérica.* February: 4–5.

"Costa Rica." 1991c. *Mesoamérica.* April: 1–2.

CSUCA (Consejo Superior Universitaria Centroamericana). 1978. *Estructura agrária, dinámica de población, desarrollo capitalista en Centroamérica,* San José, Costa Rica: Editorial Universitaria Centroamericana.

Custodio, Román. 1986. "The Human Rights Crisis in Honduras." In Rosenberg and Shepherd, eds., 1986.

Dahl, Robert A. 1956. *A Preface to Democratic Theory.* Chicago: University of Chicago Press.

Davies, James C. 1962. "Towards a Theory of Revolution." *American Sociological Review* 27: 5–18.

DeFranco, Mario A., and Carlos F. Chamorro. 1979. "Nicaragua: Crecimiento industrial y empleo." In Camacho et al. 1979.

DeFronzo, James. 1991. *Revolutions and Revolutionary Movements.* Boulder, Colo.: Westview Press.

DGEC-Costa Rica (Dirección General de Estadística y Censos). 1980. *Anuario estadístico de Costa Rica, 1977.* San José, Costa Rica.

DGEC-El Salvador (Dirección General de Estadística y Censos). 1967. *Anuario Estadístico, 1965.* San Salvador: Ministerio de Economía.

______. 1968. *Anuario Estadístico, 1966.* San Salvador: Ministerio de Economía.

______. 1970. *Anuario Estadístico, 1968.* San Salvador: Ministerio de Economía.

______. 1971. *Anuario Estadístico, 1969.* San Salvador: Ministerio de Economía.

______. 1973. *Anuario Estadístico, 1971.* San Salvador: Ministerio de Economía.

______. 1979. *Anuario Estadístico, 1977.* San Salvador: Ministerio de Economía.

______. 1982. *Anuario Estadístico, 1980.* San Salvador: Ministerio de Economía.

______. 1983. *Anuario Estadístico, 1981.* Tomos III-V. San Salvador: Ministerio de Economía.

"Death Squads Assassinate Human Rights Leader." 1998. *InterPress Service/Spanish (Peacenet),* February 11.

Diamond, Larry, and Juan Linz. 1989. "Introduction: Politics, Society, and Democracy in Latin America." In Larry Diamond, Juan Linz, and Seymour Martin Lipset, eds. *Democracy in Developing Countries,* Volume 4, *Latin America.* Boulder, Colo.: Lynne Rienner.

Diamond, Larry. 1994a. "Causes and Effects." In Larry Diamond, ed., *Political Culture and Democracy in Developing Countries.* Boulder, Colo.: Lynne Rienner.

Diamond, Larry. 1994b. "Introduction: Political Culture and Democracy." In Larry Diamond, ed., *Political Culture and Democracy in Developing Countries.* Boulder, Colo.: Lynne Rienner.

Diamond, Larry, Juan J. Linz, and Seymour Martin Lipset, eds. 1989. *Democracy in Developing Countries, Volume 4: Latin America.* Boulder, Colo.: Lynne Rienner.

Dickey, Christopher. 1985. *With the Contras: A Reporter in the Wilds of Nicaragua.* New York: Simon and Schuster.

Diskin, Martin, ed. 1983. *Trouble in Our Backyard: Central America and the United States in the Eighties.* New York: Pantheon Books.

Diskin, Martin, Thomas Bossert, Salomon Nahmad, and Stefano Varese. 1986a. "Peace and Autonomy on the Atlantic Coast of Nicaragua: A Report of the LASA Task Force on Human Rights and Academic Freedom," Part 1, *LASA* [Latin American Studies Association] *Forum* 17 (Spring): 1–16.

______. 1986b. "Peace and Autonomy on the Atlantic Coast of Nicaragua: A Report of the LASA Task Force on Human Rights and Academic Freedom," Part 2. *LASA* [Latin American Studies Association] *Forum* 17 (Summer): 1–16.

Dodson, Michael, and Tommie Sue Montgomery. 1982. "The Churches in the Nicaraguan Revolution." In Walker, ed. 1982.

Dodson, Michael, and Laura Nuzzi O'Shaughnessy. 1990. *Nicaragua's Other Revolution: Religious Faith and Political Struggle.* Chapel Hill: University of North Carolina Press.

Drake, Paul, and Eduardo Silva, eds. 1986. *Elections and Democratization in Latin America.* La Jolla: Center for Iberian and Latin American Studies-Center for U.S.-Mexican Studies, University of California, San Diego.

Dunkerley, James. 1982. *The Long War: Dictatorship and Revolution in El Salvador.* London: Junction Books.

______. 1988. *Power in the Isthmus: A Political History of Modern Central America.* London: Verso.

Ellison, Katherine. 1990. "Celebrity of Guatemalan Rights Activists Could Save His Life." *Miami Herald.* November 22: 20B.

"El Salvador." 1982. *Mesoamérica.* November: 5–6.

"El Salvador." 1983a. *Mesoamérica.* October: 5–6.

"El Salvador." 1983b. *Mesoamérica.* November: 4–7.

"El Salvador." 1983c. *Mesoamérica.* December: 5–6.

Enders, Thomas O. 1982. "The Central American Challenge." *AEI Foreign Policy and Defense Review* 4 (No. 2): 8–12.

Enriquez, Laura J. 1991. *Harvesting Change: Labor and Agrarian Reform in Nicaragua, 1979–1990.* Chapel Hill: University of North Carolina Press.

Envío. 1996–1997. Volume 15 (December–January).

Excelsior (Mexico City). 1990. December 12, 2A.

Excelsior. 1991. January 13, 2A.

"Extractos del testimonio desgarrador de Zoliamérica." 1998. *Confidencial* (Managua) 2, May 24–30, pp. 1, 9–11.

Falcoff, Mark, and Robert Royal, eds. 1984. *Crisis and Opportunity: U.S. Policy in Central America and the Caribbean.* Washington, D.C.: Ethics and Public Policy Center.

Feinberg, Richard, ed. 1982. *Central America: International Dimensions of the Crisis.* New York: Holmes and Meier.

Felix, David. 1983. "Income Distribution and the Quality of Life in Latin America: Patterns, Trends, and Policy Implications." *Latin American Research Review* 18 (No. 2): 3–34.

Fernández Vásquez, Rodrigo. 1982. "Costa Rica: Interpretación histórica sobre reforma social y acción eclesiástica: 1940–1982." *Estudios Sociales Centroamericanos* 33 (September–December): 221–248.

Fischel, Astrid. 1987. *Consenso y represión: Una interpretación socio-política de la educación costarricense.* San José: Editorial Costa Rica.

Foltz, William J. 1990. "External Causes." In Schutz and Slater, eds. 1990.

Fonseca L., Roberto. 1998a. "¿Era agenta encubierto de la DEA?" *Confidencial* (Managua) 2, May 17–23, pp. 1, 9.

______. 1998b. "Mitch: Huracán político del presidente." *Confidencial* (Managua) 118, November 8–14. «http://www.confidencial.com.ni/1998–118/confidencial/analisis.html».

______. 1998c. "¿Qué falló frente al huracán Mitch?" *Confidencial* (Managua), 118, November 8–14. «http://www.confidencial.com.ni/1998–118/confidencial/analisis.html».

"Four Guatemalan Troops Charged in Killings." 1990. *Boston Globe.* September 30, 1–2.

Freedom House. 1994. *Freedom in the World: The Annual Survey of Political Rights and Civil Liberties, 1992–1994.* New York: Freedom House.

Freire, Paulo. 1968. *The Pedagogy of the Oppressed.* New York: Herder and Herder.

Fried, Jonathan, et al. 1983. *Guatemala in Rebellion: Unfinished History.* New York: Grove.

Gallardo, María Eugenia, and José Roberto López. 1986. *Centroamérica: La crisis en cifras.* San José, Costa Rica: Instituto Interamericano de Cooperación para la Agricultura (IICA)-Facultad Latinoamericano de Ciencias Sociales (FLACSO).

García, José Z. 1989. "El Salvador: Recent Elections in Historical Perspective." In Booth and Seligson, eds. 1989.

García Márquez, Gabriel, et al. 1979. *Los Sandinistas.* Bogotá: Editorial Oveja Negra.

Gasiorowski, Mark J. 1995. "Economic Crisis and Regime Change: An Event History Analysis." *American Political Science Review* 89: 882–897.

Gasiorowski, Mark J. 1996. "An Overview of the Political Regime Dataset." *Comparative Political Studies* 21: 469–483.

Gelb, Leslie H. 1982. "Israelis Said to Step Up Role as Arms Suppliers to Latins." *New York Times.* December 17, p. A–11.

Gilbert, Dennis, and David Block. 1990. *Sandinistas: Key Documents/Documentos Claves.* Ithaca, N.Y.: Cornell University.

Gleijeses, Piero. 1991. *Shattered Hope: The Guatemalan Revolution and the United States, 1944–1954.* Princeton, N.J.: Princeton University Press.

Gold, Eva. 1987. "Military Encirclement." In Walker, ed. 1987.

Goldstone, Jack A. 1991. "An Analytical Framework." In Goldstone, Gurr, and Moshiri, eds. 1991.

Goldstone, Jack A., Ted Robert Gurr, and Farrokh Moshiri, eds. 1991. *Revolutions of the Late Twentieth Century.* Boulder, Colo.: Westview Press.

Gorman, Stephen C. 1984. "Social Change and Political Revolution: The Case of Nicaragua." In Ropp and Morris, eds. 1984.

"Government Accuses Death Squads of Wave of Killings, Denies Connections to Armed Forces." 1991. *Excelsior.* August 5: 2A.

Grabendorff, Wolf, et al., eds. 1984. *Political Change in Central America: Internal and External Dimensions.* Boulder, Colo.: Westview Press.

Graham, Douglas H. 1984. "The Economic Dimensions of Instability and Decline in Central America and the Caribbean." In Schulz and Graham, eds. 1984.
Gruson, Lindsey. 1988. "Terror's Toll Builds Again in El Salvador." *New York Times*. December 20: 1.
"Guatemala." 1982a. *Mesoamérica*. March: 2–4.
"Guatemala." 1982b. *Mesoamérica*. May: 2–3.
"Guatemala." 1982c. *Mesoamérica*. July–August: 2–3.
"Guatemala." 1990a. *Mesoamérica*. April: 4-5.
"Guatemela." 1990b. *Mesoamérica*. May: 6.
"Guatemela." 1990c. *Mesoamérica*. June: 4–5.
"Guatemala." 1990d. *Mesoamérica*. July: 2.
"Guatemala." 1990e. *Mesoamérica*. August: 5–6.
"Guatemala." 1990f. *Mesoamérica*. October: 2–3.
"Guatemala." 1990g. *Mesoamérica*. November: 2–3.
"Guatemala." 1991a. *Mesoamérica*. January: 1–2.
"Guatemala." 1991b. *Mesoamérica*. April: 3–4.
"Guatemala." 1991c. *Mesoamérica*. May: 10–11.
"Guatemala." 1991d. *Mesoamérica*. June: 1–2, 4–5.
"Guatemala." 1991e. *Mesoamérica*. August: 11–12, 16.
"Guatemala." 1991f. *Mesoamérica*. September: 1–2.
"Guatemalan Troops Said to Kill 11 Protesting Raid." 1990. *New York Times*. December 3: 8A.
Gudmundson, Lowell. 1985. "Costa Rica." In Hopkins, ed., 1985.
______. 1986. *Costa Rica Before Coffee*. Baton Rouge: Louisiana State University Press.
Guerra, Tomás. 1980. *El Salvador en la hora de su liberación*. San José, Costa Rica: n.p.
Gurr, Ted R. 1971. *Why Men Rebel*. Princeton: Princeton University Press.
Haugaard, Lisa. 1997. "How the U.S. Trained Latin America's Military: The Smoking Gun." *Envío* 16 (No. 165, October): 33–38.
Herman, Edward S., and Frank Brodhead. 1984. *Demonstration Elections*. Boston: South End Press.
Higley, John, and Michael Burton. 1989. "The Elite Variable in Democratic Transitions and Breakdowns." *American Sociological Review* 54 (No. 1): 17–32.
Higley, John, and Richard Gunther, eds. 1992. *Elites and Democratic Consolidation in Latin America and Southern Europe*. Cambridge: Cambridge University Press.
"Honduras." 1990. *Mesoamérica*. April: 8–9.
"Honduras." 1991a. *Mesoamérica*. January: 9–10.
"Honduras." 1991b. *Mesoamérica*. February: 10–11.
"Honduras." 1991c. *Mesoamérica*. May: 12.
"Honduras." 1991d. *Mesoamérica*. June: 2.
"Honduras." 1991e. *Mesoamérica*. September: 8–9.
"Honduras." 1997. *Mesoamérica*. June 6: 4.
Hopkins, Jack W., ed. 1985. *Latin American and Caribbean Contemporary Record*, Vol. 3: *1983–1984*. New York: Holmes and Meier: 499–508.
Houston Chronicle. 1998. "Honduran Death Squads Active Again, Report Says." January 15, 19A.
Huerta, Juan Ramón. 1998. *El silencio del patriarca*. Managua: Litografía del Renacimiento.
Huntington, Samuel P. 1991. *The Third Wave: Democratization in the Late Twentieth Century*. Norman: University of Oklahoma Press.

Hurel, Pierre. 1990. "Ortega ne rend pas les armes." *Paris Match.* March 22: 78–81.

IADB (Inter-American Development Bank). 1983. *Economic and Social Progress in Latin America: Natural Resources. 1983 Report.* Washington, D.C.: Inter-American Development Bank.

______. 1987. *Economic and Social Progress in Latin America: Labor Force and Employment. 1987 Report.* Washington, D.C.: Inter-American Development Bank.

______. 1988. *Economic and Social Progress in Latin America: Science and Technology: 1988 Report.* Washington, D.C.: Inter-American Development Bank.

______. 1990. *Economic and Social Progress in Latin America: The Working Women of Latin America: 1990 Report.* Washington, D.C.: Inter-American Development Bank.

IADB. 1994. *Economic and Social Progress in Latin America: 1994 Report.* Baltimore: Johns Hopkins University Press.

IADB. 1995. *Economic and Social Progress in Latin America: Overcoming Volatility, 1995 Report.* Baltimore: Johns Hopkins University Press.

IADB. 1997. *Economic and Social Progress in Latin America, 1997 Report: Latin America After a Decade of Reforms.* Washington, D.C.

IADB. 1998. *Basic Socioeconomic Data for March 16 1998.* «http://database.iadb.org/INT/-brptpubframe.htm», June 17.

IICA (Instituto Interamericano de Cooperación para la Agricultura). 1982. "América Central frente a la década de los años ochenta." In *América Central frente a la década de los años de los 80.* Heredia, Costa Rica: Escuela de Relaciones Internacionales, Universidad Nacional Autónoma.

Immerman, Richard H. 1982. *The CIA in Guatemala: The Foreign Policy of Intervention.* Austin: University of Texas Press.

Inglehart, Ronald. 1988. "The Renaissance of Political Culture." *American Political Science Review* 82 (November): 1203–1230.

Inforpress Centroamericana. 1984. *Central America Report* (Guatemala). January 20.

______. 1985a. *Central America Report.* January 11.

______. 1985b. *Central America Report.* February 1.

______. 1985c. *Central America Report.* November 22.

______. 1985d. *Guatemala: Elections 1985.* Guatemala City.

______. 1988. *Central America Report.* January 21.

Inter-American Dialogue. 1984. *The Americas in 1984: A Year for Decisions; Report of the Inter-American Dialogue.* Washington, D.C.: Aspen Institute for Humanistic Studies.

Interamerican Research Center. 1988. *Nicaraguan Public Opinion: Preliminary Report of a Random Sample Poll Conducted in Managua by the Newly-Formed Nicaraguan Institute of Public Opinion.* Los Angeles. June 30.

International Verification and Follow-up Commission. 1988. "Comments, Observations and Conclusions of the International Verification and Follow-up Commission." In Kim and Walker, eds. 1992.

Isikoff, Michael. 1991. "Drug Cartel Gave Contras $10 Million, Court Told." *Washington Post.* November 26: A1, A8.

Johnson, Tim. 1996. "Maya Mayor Triumphs Over Racism." *Miami Herald.* January 15, 1A.

Jonas, Susanne. 1991. *The Battle for Guatemala: Rebels, Death Squads, and U.S. Power.* Boulder, Colo.: Westview Press.

Jonas, Susanne. 1995. "Electoral Problems and the Democratic Prospect in Guatemala." In Mitchell A. Seligson and John A. Booth, eds., *Elections and Democracy in Central America, Revisited.* Chapel Hill: University of North Carolina Press.

Jonas, Susanne. 1998. "The Democratization of Guatemala Through the Peace Process." Paper presented to the Seminar on Guatemalan Development and Democratization: Proactive Responses to Globalization, Universidad del Valle de Guatemala, Guatemala City, March 27.

Karl, Terry. 1986. "Imposing Consent: Electoralism vs. Democratization in El Salvador." In Drake and Silva, eds. 1986.

Kirkpatrick, Jeane J. 1979. "Dictatorships and Double Standards," *Commentary* 68 (November): 34–45.

______. 1984. "This Time We Know What's Happening." In Falcoff and Royal, eds. 1984.

Klare, Michael. 1972. *War Without End.* New York: Alfred A. Knopf.

Kornbluh, Peter. 1987. "The Covert War." In Walker, ed., 1987.

Krauss, Clifford. 1986. "El Salvador Army Gains on the Guerrillas." *Wall Street Journal.* July 30:20.

Kriesberg, Louis. 1982. *Social Conflicts.* 2nd ed. Englewood Cliffs, N.J.: Prentice-Hall.

Krumweide, Heinrich-W. 1984. "Regimes and Revolution in Central America." In Grabendorff et al., eds. 1984.

LaFeber, Walter. 1983. *Inevitable Revolutions: The United States in Central America.* New York: W. W. Norton.

Laidi, Zaki. 1990. "East-West Relations." In Schutz and Slater, eds. 1990.

La Nación Internacional (San José, Costa Rica). 1982. 26 August–1 September: 12.

Lanchin, Mike. 1998. "Death Squad Claims Responsibility for Bishop's Death." *National Catholic Reporter,* May 22, p. 2.

Larkin, Bruce D., ed. 1988. *Vital Interests: The Soviet Issue in U.S. Central American Policy.* Boulder, Colo.: Lynne Rienner.

LASA (Latin American Studies Association). 1984. *The Electoral Process in Nicaragua: Domestic and International Influences.* Austin, Tex. November 19.

______. 1988. *Extraordinary Opportunities . . . and New Risks: Final Report of the LASA Commission on Compliance with the Central American Peace Accord.* Pittsburgh. March 15.

______. 1990. *Electoral Democracy Under International Pressure: The Report of the Latin American Studies Association Commission to Observe the 1990 Nicaraguan Elections.* Pittsburgh: LASA.

"Latin Presidents Announce Accord on Contra Bases." 1989. *New York Times.* February 15: 1, 4.

Lawyers Committee for International Human Rights. 1985. *Nicaragua: Revolutionary Justice.* New York. April.

Lederman, E., et al. 1979. "Trabajo y empleo." In Zelaya, ed. 1979.

LeoGrande, William M. 1984. "Through the Looking Glass: The Kissinger Report on Central America." *World Policy Journal.* Winter: 251–284.

Linfield, Michael. 1991. "Human Rights." In Walker, ed. 1991.

Linz, Juan J., and Alfred Stepan, eds. 1978. *The Breakdown of Democratic Regimes.* Baltimore: Johns Hopkins University Press.

Lipset, Seymour Martin. 1959. "Social Requisites of Democracy: Economic Development and Political Legitimacy." *American Political Science Review* 53 (March): 69–105.

López C., Julio, Orlando Núñez S., Carlos Fernando Chamorro Barrios, and Pascual Serres. 1979. *La caída del somocismo y la lucha sandinista en Nicaragua.* San José, Costa Rica: Editorial Universitaria Centroamericano.

Lowenthal, Abraham F., ed. 1991. *Exporting Democracy: The United States and Latin America.* Baltimore: Johns Hopkins University Press.

Malloy, James M., and Mitchell A. Seligson, eds. 1987. *Authoritarians and Democrats: Regime Transition in Latin America.* Pittsburgh: University of Pittsburgh Press.

Malloy, James M., and Eduardo Gamarra, eds. 1989. *Latin American and Caribbean Contemporary Record,* Vol. 7. New York: Holmes and Meier.

Martínez, Francisco Mauricio. 1998a. "Progress Towards Peace Evaluated." *La Prensa Libre* (Guatemala City), «www.prensalibre.com», December 28.

Martínez, Francisco Mauricio. 1998b. "Guatemala, Never More: 55,000 Human Rights Violations." *La Prensa Libre* (Guatemala City), April 14, translated into English in "Human Rights News Clips, Foundation for Human Rights in Guatemala," «http:www.fhrg.org/042098.htm//G», July 13, 1–2.

Martínez, Francisco Mauricio. 1998c. "URNG Committed 44 Massacres." *La Prensa Libre* (Guatemala City), April 14, translated into English in "Human Rights News Clips, Foundation for Human Rights in Guatemala," «http:www.fhrg.org/042098.htm//G», July 13, 2–3.

Mason, T. David. 1990. "Indigenous Factors." In Schutz and Slater, eds. 1990.

Matthews, Robert. 1985. "The Limits of Friendship: Nicaragua and the West." *NACLA Report on the Americas* 19(No. 3, May/June): 22–23.

Mayorga, Francisco J. 1985. *The Economic Trajectory of Nicaragua, 1980–1984: An Overview.* Miami: Latin American and Caribbean Center, Occasional Paper Series No. 14, Florida International University.

McClintock, Michael. 1985a. *The American Connection,* Vol. 1: *State Terror and Popular Resistance in El Salvador.* London: Zed Books.

______. 1985b. *The American Connection,* Vol. 2: *State Terror and Popular Resistance in Guatemala.* London: Zed Books.

McConnell, Shelly A. 1997. "Institutional Development." In Thomas W. Walker, ed., *Nicaragua Without Illusions: Regime Transition and Structural Adjustment in the 1990s.* Wilmington, Del.: Scholarly Resources.

Mejía, Thelma. 1997. "The Army Wants You!" *InterPress Service*/Spanish (PeaceNet), January 21.

Mejía, Thelma. 1998a. "Vice President Implicated in Disappearances." *Interpress Service*/Spanish (Peacenet), January 23.

Mejía, Thelma. 1998b. "Extra-Judicial Executions on the Rise." *Interpress Service*/Spanish (PeaceNet), February 4.

Menjívar, Rafael. 1982. *Formación y lucha del proletariado industrial salvadoreño.* San José, Costa Rica: Editorial Universitaria Centroamericano.

Meza, Humberto. 1998. "Políticos comentan decisión de Chamorro." *La Prensa* (Managua), November 23, «http://www.tmx.com.ni/~˜teleda/23/n3.html.

Meza, Víctor. 1980. *Historia del movimiento obrero hondureño.* Tegucigalpa: Editorial Guaymuras.

______. 1982. *Honduras: La evolución de la crisis.* Tegucigalpa: Editorial Universitaria.

Miami Herald. 1983. December 19, 1.

Miami Herald. 1990a. December 2, 22A.

Miami Herald. 1990b. December 15, 24A.

Mijeski, Kenneth J., ed. 1991. *The Nicaraguan Constitution of 1987: English Translation and Commentary.* Athens: Ohio University Press.

Millett, Richard L. 1977. *Guardians of the Dynasty: A History of the U.S.-Created Guardia Nacional de Nicaragua and the Somoza Family.* Maryknoll, N.Y.: Orbis Books.

______. 1984. "Historical Setting." In Rudolph, ed. 1984.

Ministerio de Educación. 1979. *Situación del sistema educativo después de 45 años de dictadura militar Somocista y perspectivas que planted la revolución Sandinista.* Managua, Nicaragua.

Molina, Hugo. 1979. "Las bases económicas del desarrollo industrial y la absorción de fuerza de trabajo en El Salvador." In Camacho et al. 1979.

Moncada, Mario José, and Gustavo Alvarez. 1998. "'Mitch' Cambió geografía del Norte." *La Prensa* (Managua), November 7, «http://www.tmx.com.ni/˜teleda/9/n7*.html».

Montgomery, Tommie Sue. 1982a. "The Churches in the Nicaraguan Revolution." In Walker, ed. 1982.

______. 1982b. *Revolution in El Salvador: Origins and Evolution.* Boulder, Colo.: Westview Press.

______. 1984. "El Salvador: The Roots of Revolution." in Ropp and Morris, eds. 1984.

______. 1995. *Revolution in El Salvador: Origins and Evolution.* 2nd ed. Boulder, Colo.: Westview Press.

Moore, Barrington. 1966. *Social Origins of Dictatorship and Democracy.* Boston: Beacon Press.

Moreno, Dario. 1995. "Respectable Intervention: The United States and Central American Elections." In Mitchell A. Seligson and John A. Booth, eds., *Elections and Democracy in Central America, Revisited.* Chapel Hill: University of North Carolina Press.

Morris, James A. 1979. "Honduras: A Unique Case." In Wiarda and Kline, eds. 1979.

______. 1984a. "Government and Politics." In Rudolph, ed. 1984.

______. 1984b. "Honduras: The Burden of Survival in Central America." In Ropp and Morris, eds. 1984.

Moshiri, Farrokh. 1991. "Revolutionary Conflict in an Evolutionary Perspective." In Goldstone, Gurr, and Moshiri, eds. 1991.

Muller, Edward N., and Mitchell A. Seligson. 1994. "Civic Culture and Democracy: The Question of Causal Relationships." *American Political Science Review* 88 (September): 645–652.

Nairn, Allan. 1982. "Guatemala Can't Take 2 Roads." *New York Times.* July 20: 23A.

National Bipartisan Commission on Central America. 1984. *Report of the National Bipartisan Commission on Central America.* Washington, D.C.

"Nicaragua Pins Hopes on Turning Bureaucrats into Farmers." 1989. *Dallas Morning News.* February 22: 12A.

Nichols, John Spicer. 1988. "*La Prensa:* The CIA Connection." *Columbia Journalism Review* 28 (No. 2, July-August): 34, 35.

Nitlapan-*Envío* Team. 1997a. "President Alemán: First Moves, First Signals." *Envío* 16 (No. 187–188, February-March): 3–4.

Nitlapan-*Envío* Team, 1997b. "An Accord Beseiged by Discord," *Envío,* 16 (No. 196, November): 3–4.

Norsworthy, Kent. 1990. *Nicaragua: A Country Guide.* Albuquerque, N.M.: The Inter-Hemispheric Education Resource Center.

Noyola, Gustavo A. 1979. "Integración centroamericana y absorción de mano de obra: Guatemala." In Camacho et al. 1979.

OAS (Organization of American States). 1978. *Report on the Situation of Human Rights in Nicaragua: Findings of the "On-site" Observation in the Republic of Nicaragua, October 3–12, 1978.* Washington, D.C.: General Secretariat of the Organization of American States.

O'Donnell, Guillermo. 1973. *Modernization and Bureaucratic-Authoritarianism: Studies in South American Politics.* Berkeley and Los Angeles: University of California Press.

O'Donnell, Guillermo, Philippe C. Schmitter, and Lawrence Whitehead, eds. 1986. *Transitions from Authoritarian Rule.* Baltimore: Johns Hopkins University Press.

Olson, Mancur. 1963. "Rapid Growth as a Destabilizing Force." *Journal of Economic History* 23 (No. 4): 529–552.

OPB-USAID (Office of Planning and Budgeting, U.S. Agency for International Development). 1981. *U.S. Overseas Loans and Grants and Assistance from International Organizations: Obligations and Loan Authorizations, July 1, 1945–September 30, 1980.* Washington, D.C.: Congressional Information Service, Microfiche.

______. 1984. *U.S. Overseas Loans and Grants and Assistance from International Organizations: Obligations and Loan Authorizations, July 1, 1945–September 30, 1983.* Washington, D.C.: Congressional Information Service, Microfiche.

______. 1986. *U.S. Overseas Loans and Grants and Assistance from International Organizations: Obligations and Loan Authorizations, July 1, 1945–September 30, 1985.* Washington, D.C.: Congressional Information Service, Microfiche.

______. 1988. *U.S. Overseas Loans and Grants and Assistance from International Organizations: Obligations and Loan Authorizations, July 1, 1945–September 30, 1987.* Washington, D.C.: Congressional Information Service, Microfiche.

______. 1991. *U.S. Overseas Loans and Grants and Assistance from International Organizations: Obligations and Loan Authorizations, July 1, 1945–September 30, 1990.* Washington, D.C.: Congressional Information Service, Microfiche.

OPB-USAID. 1993. *U.S. Overseas Loans and Grants and Assistance from International Organizations: Obligations and Loan Authorizations, July 1, 1945–September 30, 1992.* Washington, D.C.: Congressional Information Service, Microfiche.

Orellana, Víctor Antonio. 1985. *El Salvador: Crisis and Structural Change.* Miami: Latin American and Caribbean Center Occasional Paper Series No. 13, Florida International University.

Orlebar, Edward. 1993. "Honduran President Faces Battle with His Own Military." *Los Angeles Times,* December 18, p. 2A.

Ortega Saavedra, Daniel. 1984. Letter to the Contadora Foreign Ministers. September 21. Quoted in Goodfellow 1987.

O'Shaughnessy, Laura Nuzzi, and Luis H. Serra. 1986. *The Church and Revolution in Nicaragua.* Athens: Monographs in International Studies, Latin American Series No. 11, Ohio University Press.

Paige, Jeffrey M. 1975. *Agrarian Revolution: Social Movements and Export Agriculture in the Underdeveloped World.* New York: The Free Press.

Pérez Brignoli, Hector. 1989. *A Brief History of Central America.* Berkeley: University of California Press.

Peeler, John. 1985. *Latin American Democracies.* Chapel Hill: University of North Carolina Press.

______. 1989. "Elites and Democracy in Central America." In John A. Booth and Mitchell A. Seligson, eds. *Elections and Democracy in Central America.* Chapel Hill: University of North Carolina Press.

______. 1995. "Autumn of the Oligarchs?" In Mitchell A. Seligson and John A. Booth, eds. *Elections and Democracy in Central America.* Chapel Hill: University of North Carolina Press.

Pérez Brignoli, Héctor, with Yolanda Baíres Martínez. 1983. "Growth and Crisis in the Central American Economies, 1950–1980." *Journal of Latin American Studies* 15 (November): 365–398.

Pochet Coronado, Rosa María. 1982. "El reformismo estatal y la Iglesia en Honduras 1949–1982." *Estudios Sociales Centroamericanos* 33 (September-December): 155–188.

Policy Alternatives for the Caribbean and Central America. 1984. *Changing Course: Blueprint for Peace in Central American and the Caribbean.* Washington, D.C.: Institute for Policy Studies.

"Población y viviendas afectadas por el Huracán Mitch: 20 de noviembre de 1998, 16:30 hrs." 1998. «http://www.ops.org.ni/desastre/d-civil/historia/1998/mitch/region20.htm».

Population Reference Bureau. 1981. *1981 World Population Data Sheet.* Washington, D.C.

Posas, Mario. 1981. *El movimiento campesino hondureño.* Tegucigalpa: Editorial Guaymuras.

Prensa Gráfica (San Salvador). 1994a. July 31, pp. 4A–5A.

______. 1994b. August 1, pp. 4A–5A.

______. 1994c. August 2, pp. 4A–5A.

______. 1994d. August 4, pp. 4A–5A.

Presbyterian Church (USA). 1983. *Adventure and Hope: Christians and the Crisis in Central America: Report to the 195th General Assembly of the Presbyterian Church.* Atlanta.

Prevost, Gary, and Harry E. Vanden, eds. 1997. *The Undermining of the Sandinista Revolution.* New York: St. Martin's.

Priest, Dana. 1996. "U.S. Instructed Latins on Execution, Torture—Manuals Used 1982–1991, Pentagon Reveals." *Washington Post,* September 21, pp. A1, A9.

"Procedure for the Establishment of a Strong and Lasting Peace in Central America" [Central American Peace Accord]. 1987. August 7.

Przeworski, Adam. 1986. "Some Problems in the Study of the Transition to Democracy." In Guillermo O'Donnell, Philippe M. Schmitter, and Lawrence Whitehead, eds. *Transitions from Authoritarian Rule.* Baltimore: Johns Hopkins University Press.

Putnam, Robert D. 1993. *Making Democracy Work: Civic Traditions in Modern Italy.* Princeton: Princeton University Press.

Putnam, Robert D. 1996. "Bowling Alone: America's Declining Social Capital." *Journal of Democracy* 7 (Summer): 38–52.

Radell, David Richard. 1969. "An Historical Geography of Western Nicaragua: The Spheres of León, Granada, and Managua, 1519–1965." Ph.D. dissertation, University of California-Berkeley.

Reagan, Ronald. 1983. "U.S. Responsibility in Central America." Address to Congress (April 28). In Falcoff and Royal, eds. 1984.

Reding, Andrew A. 1991. "The Evolution of Governmental Institutions." In Walker, ed. 1991.

Riley, Michael. 1996. "Refugees Outside Looking In." *Christian Science Monitor,* January 10, p. 5.

______. 1997. "Stealing Guatemala's Peace Dividend." *Dallas Morning News,* December 25, p. 45A.

Rivera Urrutia, Eugenio, Ana Sojo, and José Roberto López. 1986. *Centroamérica: Política económica y crisis.* San José, Costa Rica: Editorial Departamento Ecuménico de Investigaciones-Universidad Nacional Autónoma.

Robinson, William I. 1992. *A Faustian Bargain: U.S. Involvement in the Nicaraguan Elections and American Foreign Policy in the Post-Cold War Era.* Boulder, Colo.: Westview Press.

Rodrígues, Mario. 1965. *Central America.* Englewood Cliffs, N.J.: Prentice Hall.

Roggensack, Margaret E., and John A. Booth. 1985. *Report of the International Human Rights Law Group and the Washington Office on Latin America Advance Election Observer Mission to Guatemala.* Washington, D.C.: International Human Rights Law Group-Washington Office on Latin America.

Rohter, Larry. 1996. "Specter in Guatemala: Iron-Fisted General Looms Large Again." *New York Times,* January 10, p. 4A.

Ropp, Steve C. 1984. "National Security." In Rudolph, ed. 1984.

Ropp, Steve C., and James A. Morris, eds. 1984. *Central America: Crisis and Adaptation.* Albuquerque: University of New Mexico Press.

Rosado Granados, Hector. 1985. *Guatemala 1984: Elecciones para Asamblea Nacional Constituyente.* San José, Costa Rica: Instituto Centroamericano de Derechos Humanos-Centro de Asesoría y Promoción Electoral.

Rosenberg, Mark. 1986. "Honduras: The Reluctant Democracy." *Current History* 85 (December): 417–420, 438, 448.

______. 1989. "Can Democracy Survive the Democrats? From Transition to Consolidation in Honduras." In Booth and Seligson, eds. 1989.

Rosenberg, Mark, and Phillip Shepherd, eds. 1986. *Honduras Confronts its Future.* Boulder, Colo.: Lynne Reinner Publishers.

Ruchwarger, Gary. 1987. *People in Power: Forging a Grassroots Democracy in Nicaragua.* Granby, Mass.: Bergin and Garvey Publishers.

Rudolph, James D., ed. 1984. *Honduras: A Country Study.* Washington D.C.: American University Foreign Area Studies Series, U.S. Government Printing Office.

Rueschemeyer, Dietrich, Evelyne Huber Stephens, and John D. Stephens. 1992. *Capitalist Development and Democracy.* Chicago: University of Chicago Press.

Ruhl, J. Mark. 1984. "Agrarian Structure and Political Stability in Honduras." *Journal of Inter-American Studies and World Affairs* 26 (February): 33–68.

______. 1998. "Honduras: Militarism and Democratization in Troubled Waters." Paper presented at the 21st Congress of the Latin American Studies Association, Chicago, Illinois, September 25.

Russell, Phillip L. 1984. *El Salvador in Crisis.* Austin, Tex.: Colorado River Press.

Rustow, Dankwart. 1970. "Transitions to Democracy: Toward a Dynamic Model." *Comparative Politics* 2 (April): 337–363.

Ryan, Phil. 1995. *The Fall and Rise of the Market in Sandinista Nicaragua.* Montreal: McGill-Queens University Press.

Salert, Barbara. 1976. *Revolutions and Revolutionaries: Four Theories.* New York: Elsevier.

Schattschneider, E. E. 1960. *The Semisovereign People: A Realist's View of Democracy in America.* New York: Holt, Rinehart, and Winston.

Schoultz, Lars. 1983. "Guatemala: Social Change and Political Conflict." In Diskin, ed. 1983.

______. 1987. *National Security and United States Policy Toward Latin America.* Princeton: Princeton University Press.

Schulz, Donald E. 1984. "Ten Theories in Search of Central American Reality." In Schulz and Graham, eds. 1984.

Schulz, Donald E., and Douglas H. Graham, eds. 1984. *Revolution and Counterrevolution in Central America and the Caribbean.* Boulder, Colo.: Westview Press.

Schutz, Barry M., and Robert O. Slater, eds. 1990. *Revolution and Social Change in the Third World.* Boulder, Colo.: Lynne Rienner.

Schwarz, Benjamin C. 1991. *American Counterinsurgency Doctrine and El Salvador: The Frustration of Reform and the Illusion of Nation Building.* Santa Monica, Cal.: Rand Corporation.

Scott, Peter Dale, and Jonathan Marshall. 1991. *Cocaine Politics: Drugs, Armies and the CIA in Central America.* Berkeley: University of California Press.

Second General Conference of Latin American Bishops. 1973. *The Church and the Present-Day Transformation of Latin America in the Light of the Council.* Washington, D.C.: United States Catholic Conference.

"A Secret War for Nicaragua." 1982. *Newsweek.* November 8.

Seligson, Mitchell A. 1980. *Peasants of Costa Rica and the Development of Agrarian Capitalism.* Madison: University of Wisconsin Press.

Seligson, Mitchell A., and John A. Booth. 1993. "Political Culture and Regime Type: Evidence from Nicaragua and Costa Rica." *Journal of Politics* 55 (August): 777–792.

Seligson, Mitchell A., and John A. Booth, eds. 1995. *Elections and Democracy in Central America, Revisited.* Chapel Hill: University of North Carolina Press.

Seligson, Mitchell A., and Edward Muller. 1987. "Democracy, Stability, and Economic Crisis: Costa Rica, 1978–1983." *International Studies Quarterly* 31 (September): 301–326.

Seligson, Mitchell A., and Miguel Gómez. 1989. "Ordinary Elections in Extraordinary Times: The Political Economy of Voting in Costa Rica." In Booth and Seligson, eds. 1989.

Seligson, Mitchell A., et al. 1982. *Land and Labor in Guatemala: An Assessment.* Washington, D.C.: Agency for International Development-Development Associates.

Serra, Luis, 1985. "The Grass-Roots Organizations." In Walker, ed. 1985b.

Shetemul, Haroldo. 1991. "National Blackout in Guatemala: Police Chief Assassinated." *Excelsior.* August 6: 2A.

Sierra Pop, Oscar Rolando. 1982. "Iglesia y conflicto social en Guatemala." *Estudios Sociales Centroamericanos* 33 (September–December): 66–86.

Skocpol, Theda. 1979. *States and Social Revolutions.* Cambridge: Cambridge University Press.

Sloan, John. 1968. "The Electoral Game in Guatemala." Ph.D. dissertation, University of Texas at Austin.

Snarr, Neil (and associates). 1990. *Sandinista Nicaragua: Annotated Bibliography with Analytical Introductions* (two volumes). Ann Arbor, Mich.: The Pierian Press.

Spalding, Rose, 1994. *Capitalists and Revolution in Nicaragua: Opposition and Accommodation.* Chapel Hill: University of North Carolina Press.

Spoor, Max. 1995. *The State and Domestic Agricultural Markets in Nicaragua: From Interventions to Neo-Liberalism.* New York and London: St. Martin's Press and Macmillan Press.

Taubman, Philip. 1983. "Israel Said to Aid Latin Aims of U.S." *New York Times,* July 21, p. A4.

Tayacán. 1985. *Psychological Operations in Guerrilla Warfare: The CIA's Nicaragua Manual.* Prepared by the Central Intelligence Agency. New York: Vintage Books.

Taylor, Stan. 1984. *Social Science and Revolutions.* New York: St. Martin's Press.

Technical Commission of the Great National Dialogue. 1985. *Economic and Social Policy Recommendations to the Head of State.* Guatemala City.

Thome, Joseph R., and David Kaimowitz. 1985. "Agrarian Reform." In Walker, ed. 1985b.

Tilly, Charles. 1978. *From Mobilization to Revolution.* Reading, Mass.: Addison-Wesley.

______. 1981. "Introduction." In Tilly and Tilly, eds. 1981.

Tilly, Louise A., and Charles Tilly, eds. 1981. *Class Conflict and Collective Action.* Beverly Hills: Sage Publications.

Torres Rivas, Edelberto. 1981. *Crisis del poder en Centroamérica.* San José, Costa Rica: Editorial Universitaria Centroaméricana.

______. 1982. "Cambio social y crisis en la década de los añios ochenta." In *Ameérica Central frente a la década de los años de los 80.* Heredia, Costa Rica: Escuela de Relaciones Internacionales, Universidad Nacional Autónoma.

Trudeau, Robert. 1984. "Guatemalan Elections: The Illusion of Democracy." Papet presented to the National Conference on Guatemala, Washington, D.C. June 15.

UNESCO (United Nations Educational, Scientific, and Cultural Organization). 1997. *UNESCO Statistical Yearbook, 1997.* Paris and Lanham, Md.: UNESCO Publishing and Bernam Press.

U.S. Bureau of Economic Analysis. 1998. "National Accounts Data," Table 3. «www.bea.doc.gov/bea/dn/niptbl-d/hti#Table 1.Part B», April 8.

U.S. Census Bureau. 1998. *State Populations Ranking Summary: 1995 and 2025.* «http:/www.census.gov/population/projections/state/9525rank», June 15.

U.S. Department of Defense. 1996. "Fact Sheet Concerning Training Manuals Containing Materials Inconsistent with U.S. Policy." Washington, D.C. (September).

U.S. Department of State. 1981. *Country Reports on Human Rights Practices.* Washington, D.C.: U.S. Government Printing Office. February 2.

______. 1985. Data in xerox ms. Office of Regional Economic Policy, Bureau of Inter-American Affairs. Washington, D.C.

U.S. Department of State. 1998. *Background Notes: Guatemala.* Bureau of Inter-American Affairs, (March). «http://www.state.gov/www/background_notes/guatemala_0398_bgn.html».

U.S. Embassy—Guatemala. 1985. "A Statistical Comparison of Violence (1982–1985)." Guatemala City. Xerox.

Vanden, Harry E., and Thomas W. Walker. 1991. "The Reimposition of U.S. Hegemony over Nicaragua." In Kenneth M. Coleman and George C. Herring, eds., *Understanding the Central American Crisis.* Wilmington, Del.: Scholarly Resources, Inc.

Vanderlaan, Mary B. 1986. *Revolution and Foreign Policy in Nicaragua.* Boulder, Colo.: Westview Press.

Vanhanen, Tatu. 1990. *The Process of Democratization.* New York: Crane Russak.

Villagrán Kramer, Francisco. 1982. "The Background to the Current Political Crisis in Central America." In Feinberg, ed. 1982.

Walker, Thomas W. 1970. *The Christian Democratic Movement in Nicaragua,* Tucson: University of Arizona Press.

______. 1979a. Paper presented to the U.S. Department of State conference on Central America: U.S. Policy Interests and Concerns. Washington, D.C. March 19.

______. 1979b. "The U.S. and Central America." *Caribbean Review* 8 (No. 3, Summer): 18–23.

______, ed. 1982. *Nicaragua in Revolution.* New York: Praeger.

______. 1985a. "Introduction." in Walker, ed. 1985b.

______, ed. 1985b. *Nicaragua: The First Five Years.* New York: Praeger.

______, ed. 1987. *Reagan Versus the Sandinistas: The Undeclared War on Nicaragua.* Boulder, Colo.: Westview Press.

______. 1991. "The Armed Forces." In Walker, ed. 1991.

______. 1991. *Nicaragua: The Land of Sandino.* 2nd ed. Boulder, Colo.: Westview Press.

______, ed. 1991. *Revolution and Counterrevolution in Nicaragua.* Boulder, Colo.: Westview Press.

Walker, Thomas W. 1994. "The 1994 Research Seminar in Nicaragua." *LASA Forum* 25 (No. 3, Fall): 14.

______ 1997a. "Epilogue: The 1996 National Elections." In Thomas W. Walker, ed., *Nicaragua Without Illusions: Regime Transition and Structural Adjustment in the 1990s.* Wilmington, Del.: Scholarly Resources.

______. 1997b. "Introduction: Historical Setting and Important Issues." In Thomas W. Walker, ed., *Nicaragua Without Illusions: Regime Transition and Structural Adjustment in the 1990s.* Wilmington, Del.: Scholarly Resources.

Walker, Thomas W., ed. 1997c. *Nicaragua Without Illusions: Regime Transition and Structural Adjustment in the 1990s.* Wilmington, Del.: Scholarly Resources.

Walton, John. 1984. *Reluctant Rebels: Comparative Studies in Revolution and Underdevelopment.* New York: Columbia University Press.

Warren, Kay B. 1998. "Pan-Mayanism and Multiculturalism in Guatemala." Paper presented at the Symposium on Development and Democratization in Guatemala: Proactive Responses to Globalization, Universidad del Valle, Guatemala City, March 18.

Washington Office on Latin America. 1988. *Who Pays the Price? The Cost of War in The Guatemalan Highlands.* Washington, D.C.: April.

Washington Report on the Hemisphere. 1987. October 28.

Weaver, Eric, and William Barnes. 1991. "Opposition Parties and Coalitions." In Walker, ed. 1991.

Weaver, Jerry L. 1979. "Guatemala: The Politics of a Frustrated Revolution." In Wiarda and Kline, eds. 1979.

Webre, Stephen. 1979. *José Napoleón Duarte and the Christian Democratic Party in Salvadorean Politics: 1960–1972.* Baton Rouge: Louisiana State University Press.

Weeks, John. 1985a. *The Economies of Central America.* New York: Holmes and Meier.

______. 1985b. "The Industrial Sector." In Walker, ed. 1985b.

Wheelock Román, Jaime. 1975. *Imperialismo y dictadura: Crisis de una formación social.* México: Siglo Veintiuno Editores.

White, Richard Alan. 1984. *The Morass: United States Intervention in Central America.* New York: Harper and Row.

Whitehead, Lawrence. 1991. "The Imposition of Democracy." In Abraham F. Lowenthal, ed., *Exporting Democracy: The United States and Latin America.* Baltimore: Johns Hopkins University Press.

Wiarda, Howard J. 1982. "The Central American Crisis: A Framework for Understanding." *AEI Foreign Policy and Defense Review* 4 (No. 2): 2–7.

Wiarda, Howard J., and Harvey F. Kline, eds. 1979. *Latin American Politics and Development.* Boston: Houghton Mifflin.

Wickham-Crowley, Timothy. 1992. *Guerrillas and Revolution in Latin America.* Princeton: Princeton University Press.

Wilkie, James W., and Steven Haber, eds. 1981. *Statistical Abstract of Latin America,* Vol. 21. Los Angeles: University of California Latin America Center Publications.

Wilkie, James W., and David Lorey, eds. 1987. *Statistical Abstract of Latin America,* Vol. 25. Los Angeles: University of California Latin America Center Publications.

Wilkie, James W., and Adam Perkal, eds. 1984. *Statistical Abstract of Latin America,* Vol. 23. Los Angeles: University of California Latin America Center Publications.

Williams, Philip J. 1994. "Dual Transitions from Authoritarian Rule: Popular and Electoral Democracy in Nicaragua." *Comparative Politics* (January): 169–185.

Williams, Philip J., and Knut Walter. 1997. *Militarization and Demilitarization in El Salvador's Transition to Democracy.* Pittsburgh: University of Pittsburgh Press.

Williams, Robert G. 1986. *Export Agriculture and the Crisis in Central America.* Chapel Hill: University of North Carolina Press.

Wolf, Eric. 1969. *Peasant Revolts of the Twentieth Century.* New York: Harper and Row.

Woodward, Ralph Lee, Jr. 1985. *Central America: A Nation Divided.* 2nd ed. New York: Oxford University Press.

World Bank Group. 1998. *Country Overview: Guatemala.* «http://www.worldbank.org/html/extdr/offrep/lac/guatemal.htm//», June 17.

Wynia, Gary. 1990. *Politics of Latin American Development.* Cambridge: Cambridge University Press.

Yashar, Deborah J. 1997. *Demanding Democracy: Reform and Reaction in Costa Rica and Guatemala, 1870s–1950s.* Stanford: Stanford University Press.

Zelaya, Chester, ed. 1979. *Costa Rica Contemporanea, Tomo II.* San José: Editorial Costa Rica.

Zubieta, Celina. 1998. "Victims of Death Squads or Gang Warfare?" *InterPress Service* (Peace Net), March 31.

ABOUT THE BOOK AND AUTHORS

Since the 1960s, political violence and war in Nicaragua, El Salvador, and Guatemala have taken 300,000 lives, displaced millions, and reversed decades of economic gains. Regional and international efforts to promote peace eventually brought negotiated ends to the region's wars. The politico-economic turmoil within the region and evolving policy in Washington also drove a process of regime change that by the late 1990s left all five Central American nations formally democratic. In this new, third edition of a widely praised book, two of the most respected writers on Central American politics examine the origins and development of the region's political conflicts, efforts to resolve them, and regional democratization. Highlights of the new edition include analyses of the peace processes and accords that ended the region's wars, the end of the Nicaraguan revolution and the Sandinistas' exit from power, recent elections, and the politics of the new civilian democratic regimes throughout the region.

The authors trace the roots of underdevelopment and crisis in the region by examining the shared and individual histories of the Central American nations. They offer a theory about regime change in Central America that explains both the rebellions of the 1970s and 1980s and the eventual development of civilian democratic regimes in all five nations. This theory accounts for the striking contrast between war-torn Guatemala, El Salvador, and Nicaragua and the stability of Costa Rica and Honduras. Booth and Walker examine the forces driving popular mobilization—economic change, liberation theology, and Marxism—and evaluate the dramatic changes in U.S. policy toward Central America since the early 1990s, and especially since the end of the cold war, as well as the implications of those changes for the future of the region.

John A. Booth is regents professor of political science at the University of North Texas. He is author of *The End and the Beginning: The Nicaraguan Revolution* and *Costa Rica: Quest for Democracy,* and has written widely on political conflict and democracy in Latin America. **Thomas W. Walker** is professor of political science and director of Latin American Studies Program at Ohio University. He is author of *Nicaragua: The Land of Sandino* and the editor/coauthor of *Reagan Versus the Sandinistas: The Undeclared War on Nicaragua* and *Nicaragua Without Illusions: Regime Transition and Structural Adjustment in the 1990s.*

INDEX